Nearest East

IN THE SERIES *Politics, History, and Social Change,*
EDITED BY JOHN C. TORPEY

ALSO IN THIS SERIES:

Rebecca Jean Emigh, *The Undevelopment of Capitalism: Sectors and Markets in Fifteenth-Century Tuscany*

Aristide R. Zolberg, *How Many Exceptionalisms? Explorations in Comparative Macroanalysis*

Thomas Brudholm, *Resentment's Virtue: Jean Améry and the Refusal to Forgive*

Patricia Hill Collins, *From Black Power to Hip Hop: Racism, Nationalism, and Feminism*

Daniel Levy and Natan Sznaider, translated by Assenka Oksiloff, *The Holocaust and Memory in the Global Age*

Brian A. Weiner, *Sins of the Parents: The Politics of National Apologies in the United States*

Heribert Adam and Kogila Moodley, *Seeking Mandela: Peacemaking between Israelis and Palestinians*

Marc Garcelon, *Revolutionary Passage: From Soviet to Post-Soviet Russia, 1985–2000*

Götz Aly and Karl Heinz Roth, translated by Assenka Oksiloff, *The Nazi Census: Identification and Control in the Third Reich*

Immanuel Wallerstein, *The Uncertainties of Knowledge*

Michael R. Marrus, *The Unwanted: European Refugees from the First World War through the Cold War*

Nearest East

American Millennialism and Mission to the Middle East

Hans-Lukas Kieser

TEMPLE UNIVERSITY PRESS
PHILADELPHIA

TEMPLE UNIVERSITY PRESS
Philadelphia, Pennsylvania 19122
www.temple.edu/tempress

Paperback edition published 2012

Library of Congress Cataloging-in-Publication Data

Kieser, Hans-Lukas.
Nearest East : American millennialism and mission to the Middle East / Hans-Lukas Kieser.
p. cm. — (Politics, history, and social change)
Includes bibliographical references and index.
ISBN 978-1-4399-0222-6 (cloth : alk. paper)
1. United States—Relations—Middle East. 2. Middle East—Relations—United States. 3. Millennialism—Political aspects—United States—History. 4. Christianity and politics—United States—History. 5. Missionaries—United States—History. 6. Missionaries—Middle East—History. 7. Christian Zionism—United States—History. 8. United States—Relations—Israel. 9. Israel—Relations—United States. I. Title.
DS63.2.U5K54 2010
303.48'273056—dc22 2009032146

ISBN 978-1-4399-0223-3 (paperback : alk. paper)
ISBN 978-1-4399-0224-0 (e-book)

Printed in the United States of America

080612P

In memory of Justus Kieser (1921–1973)

Contents

Acknowledgments *ix*

Introduction *1*

1 The United States and the Near East, circa 1800 *15*

2 A Quest for "Zion" and Peace on Earth: Mission to the Bible Lands *34*

3 Dream and Trauma: Missionary America and Young Turkey, 1908–1923 *63*

4 Oil, Palestine-Israel, and Empire of the Good *98*

5 American Steps and Shortcuts to "Zion" after 1967 *137*

Conclusion *153*

Notes *165*

Selected Bibliography *197*

Index *201*

Acknowledgments

I thank Kevork Bardakjian in Ann Arbor, Hamit Bozarslan in Paris, Lucien Palser in Zurich, Elmar Plozza in Bern, and the anonymous reviewer for Temple University Press (TUP) for their valuable feedback on the manuscript. I am grateful for discussions with my students, who heard the main ideas of this book in seminars and lectures at the University of Zurich, the University of Bamberg, the University of Michigan at Ann Arbor, and the University of Freiburg, Germany, from 2005 to 2009. I thank Joanne Glättli (Basel) for patiently reading the manuscript and polishing my English. I also owe thanks to Google, whose digitalization project has permitted me to enlarge by a considerable measure my collection of American religious literature of the nineteenth century without having to make my way, as I did in the 1990s, to the remotest corners of American university libraries. I add special thanks to Joanna L. Mullins, my copy editor; to Joan S. Vidal, TUP production editor; and to John C. Torpey, series editor, who in 2006 in Salzburg invited me to submit a manuscript to Temple University Press. I have much appreciated the reliable and friendly communication with my editors at TUP, as well as their professionalism and promptness.

A few portions of this book have appeared in different forms and languages in the following publications: Hans-Lukas Kieser, *Der verpasste Friede: Mission, Ethnie und Staat in den Ostprovinzen der Türkei 1839–1938* (Zurich: Chronos, 2000); Hans-Lukas Kieser, "Some Remarks on Alevi Responses to the Missionaries in Eastern Anatolia (19th–20th cc.)," in *Altruism and Imperialism: Western Cultural and Religious Missions to the Middle East (19th–20th cc.),* ed. E. Tejirian and R. Spector Simon (New York: Columbia University Press, 2002), 120–142; Hans-Lukas Kieser, *A Quest for Belonging: Anatolia beyond Empire and Nation (19th–21st centuries)* (Istanbul: Isis, 2007), 11–65 ("Missionary America and Ottoman Turkey: The Seminal Break of World War I" chapter); Hans-Lukas Kieser, "Removal of American Indians, Destruction of Ottoman Armenians: American Missionaries and Demographic Engineering," *European Journal of Turkish Studies,* Thematic Issue No. 7 (2008), available at http://www.ejts.org/document2873.html.

Introduction

Background

Departing from Beirut in June 1911, looking back from the ship, an Ottoman Muslim journalist described his thoughts: "The city in front of us is a picture of a passage. My eyes automatically turned to the American Protestant Establishment [the Syrian Protestant College, later the American University of Beirut] and remained fixed on those great, majestic buildings. But they could not penetrate inside the walls. There is the spirit of today's Beirut, in these and similar buildings. There, a young world is nourished. But this nourishment is poison to Ottoman identity." A deep resentment, a distressing feeling of exclusion and inferiority, emerged in this journalist, for whom his Ottoman heritage and the American promise visible in most provinces of the Ottoman Empire seemed incompatible. The Americans, he felt, worked for a Near East that was new indeed but did not belong to him, the Muslim journalist and Ottoman civil servant Ahmed Şerif. American agency fundamentally subverted what he believed to be Ottoman and Muslim, and therefore his own. Şerif visited American hospitals, universities, village schools, and school classes in the Ottoman Balkans, Anatolia, and Syria but always ended up perceiving them as part of an evil outside force that strove for a future he did not want, even if he conceded that the effort rationally spoke well for the Americans. He looked with bitter self-criticism on the Muslim and Ottoman realities. Muslim reactionaries "who cannot penetrate to the sources of Islam, and its highest thoughts, to true humanity and general fraternity, according to today's world, are an obstacle for progress," he wrote. "We must agree with those who rightly state this. Yes, with our blindness and insolence we merit such libels."[1]

Where would the American impact lead? Ottoman Muslims experienced it first of all as a thorough challenge of their cultural self-confidence, both confusing and dangerous. Where it would lead, they did not know. Americans, ultimately, did not know either. In the early nineteenth century, the most committed of them just wanted to give the best they believed they had to the most promising region they knew, the Bible lands, hoping to build up there "Zion" and hasten Jesus' coming or omnipresence and, with this, the near and happy end time of the churches whose role was accomplished once the "millennium" began. For the missionary community, "Zion" meant Jesus made visible: the shining truth of the Gospel together with a restored, reempowered Jerusalem and Israel of which he was the soul and the king, according to promises to be read in the Bible. From Zion in the Near East, the Kingdom of God, the millennium, would spread over the earth. This "millennialism" existed long before oil interests shaped American interaction with the region. The commitment to a Kingdom of God on earth was the most distinctive note of American Christians, American theologian Helmut Richard Niebuhr has stated. The earthly Kingdom of God was part of the American Dream, of the deeper idea of manifest destiny, but also of a rhetorically pervasive "political catechism" in U.S. political culture. In contrast to isolationism in diplomacy, mission had a global orientation from the beginning. It set its globalist goals beyond patriotism, continental expansion, or the pilgrim fathers' identification of America as a new Canaan. It believed in its vocation to global evangelization and the preparation of the Kingdom to come.[2]

American Protestant overseas missions began in 1810, when the American Board of Commissioners for Foreign Missions (ABCFM) was founded in Boston and the United States was thirty-four years old. The ABCFM started with India and Ceylon but soon centered its efforts on the "Nearer East," the Bible lands.[3] Unlike most books on U.S. relations with the Middle East, this book deals with faith, vision, and identity building as these relate to the intimate American–Near Eastern encounter. It studies American identity building through the interactions with a world that was both precarious and promising in American eyes. It addresses worlds of faith and imagination (in French: *imaginaire*) as made visible in projects, encounters, and (self-)representations. It pays attention to conflicting apocalypticisms, or representations of both past and future based on sacred scriptures. It draws attention to the elements of a "symbolic economy," to symbols, assumptions, and beliefs; to paradigms of success and patterns of resentment. Unlike many other books on apocalypticism and millennialism however, it studies not only the symbols and rhetorics but also their concrete long-term impact on the history of relations with the Middle East.

Not only as a heritage of a Eurocentric geographic perspective but also as the "Bible land," for the geotheological and geostrategic place that it holds, the Middle East was and remains near to the United States—even nearer than to Europe, of which the United States was an offshoot. For this reason, this book refers to the Near East instead of using the familiar contemporary term *Middle East.* Globally, but particularly in the Near East, peace on earth, the new order of Jesus, was to be won with the decisive help of American agency. From the Near East, peace had to spread out globally. In the 1990s, I wrote a doctoral dissertation and used many American missionary sources but did not elaborate on the aspects I address here.[4] The general interest in the Middle East and the particular interest in religion and culture led, after 2000, to a prolific academic production on America, religion, and the Middle East. Before this, the American missions had remained for decades at the margins of academic interest, as had the rich missionary archives.[5]

Ahmet Şerif toured the Ottoman Empire in the years between the hopeful Young Turk revolution of 1908 and the World War I. In this time he wrote his pieces for a Young Turk newspaper. His "picture of a passage" portrays an important issue: a dynamic American mission to the Ottoman world, motivated by both biblical millennialist and modern ideas, inspired the Near Easterners' respect, yet a Muslim majority and their leaders felt excluded from the new dynamism because excluded from both the premises and the promises of the underlying millennialism. From the beginning of interactions on the ground in the early nineteenth century, American millennialism considered Muslims and their heritage as being deficient, as did many Europeans of the period with regard to the Jews. Muslims could hardly cope with American millennialism, less so as American missions did not know and appreciate relevant Muslim resources.

As the ruling group of the empire, moreover, Ottoman Sunni Muslims were on the defensive and not ready to revise their self-understanding as rulers. They feared that introducing the political participation of all groups, as postulated by Ottoman non-Muslims and by Westerners, would lead to the fall of their imperial power and low regard for their religion, since both were inseparable (*din ü devlet*). In the late nineteenth century and in particular on the eve of the World War I, mutual tensions and increasingly aggressive Muslim fear led to a dramatic breakdown of confidence both within Ottoman society and between the Ottoman rulers and Americans. The fact that more than a quarter of the students in the Syrian Protestant College were Sunni Muslims—though Arabs, not Turks—contradicted Şerif's feeling of inaccessibility. Moreover, the Young Turk revolution had led to new, more pluralistic terms with regard to religious expression and instruction in the college. World War I, however, interrupted innovative departures. With its high proportion of Muslim students, the Syrian Protestant College had been an exception among the foreign schools in the Ottoman Empire.[6]

Ottomans and the Americans were unable to accomplish a lasting synergy during or before the decisive 1910s. Cultural assumptions, macro-history in the age of imperialism, and the rise of fierce ethnonationalism all played a fatal role. It is fair to say that the respective societies have still not yet (fully) come to terms with this past. The experience of U.S. invasion in Iraq in 2003 aroused undiluted Ottoman nostalgia in Turkey, as, for example, in the Hollywood-like action blockbuster *The Valley of the Wolves—Iraq*. The film includes the fictional scene of an apocalyptical prayer by the U.S. chief agent in northern Iraq, the "bad guy" of the film. In this example, a millennialist core component of American Christianity is perceived and distorted as religiously aberrant. The film was very popular, even among "Islamic Calvinists," as Turkey's religiously inspired capitalists have recently been called (most of whom approve Turkey's accession to the European Union).[7]

From the first overseas missionaries in the early nineteenth century to the political game in the early twenty-first, American millennialism conserved its impact but changed its forms. "America has the infinite privilege of fulfilling her destiny and saving the world," said President Woodrow Wilson at the end of the World War I.[8] He looked then to the Old World, the deeply damaged worlds of Europe and the Ottoman Empire. Peacemaking in the Near East became, and has remained to this day, the crucial but unfulfilled challenge of American presidency. In contrast, the ruling Muslim class of the Ottoman Empire, after the conquests and the imperial Sunnitization of the sixteenth century, did not seek anything essential for itself outside its own imperial realms. It is true that the Red Apple symbolized, until the second attack on Vienna in the late seventeenth century, the Ottomans' expansive integration of desirable foreign Christian areas of high civilization. The Red Apple (*Kızıl Elma*), an important symbol of early Ottoman imperialism and, later, a Turkish nationalist symbol, had an eschatological touch; eschatological voices, however, which took the sultan as a provisional earthly master (*sahip-kıran*)—who soon would have to cede his place to the apocalyptic master (*mahdi*)—became marginal in the sixteenth century.[9] It is also true that the reforming state, since the end of the eighteenth century, called on foreign know-how, but only in order to escape total collapse. Ottoman

Muslim self-understanding, like that of most elites of settled empires, did not have a millennialist touch. Ottoman power definitely did not constitute itself as an ongoing project according to the vision of a Zion to be built up in a process that would culminate with believers gladly sharing or giving away their own power—as did pioneering missionary America.

The first strategy of the American mission to the Near East centered on "the Jews" to be "restored to Palestine and to Jesus." This was believed to be the precondition of the Near East–centered global kingdom of peace. For pragmatic reasons, the missionaries soon reoriented themselves to the Armenians of Asia Minor, that is, Anatolia, with many of whom they quickly developed warm individual relationships. At the same time, they became more church-oriented and less "revolutionary" with regard to both Ottoman society and the end of the churches. In the mid-nineteenth century therefore, a revised missionary strategy of restored Christianity attempted to "revive" Armenians and other Oriental Christians. The establishment of an Ottoman Protestant community (*millet*) was a by-product of this altered emphasis. In an again readjusted strategy after the Young Turk revolution of 1908, missionary America set millennialist hopes on Young Turkey but was traumatically deluded during and after World War I, when the Young Turk regime eradicated Christianity in Anatolia. In American minds, the legacy of an unfulfilled relationship with the Ottoman world endured. Mission was drastically reduced in the interwar period; a new generation of representatives, professional diplomats, turned to a postmissionary realpolitik.

The period of the world wars (1914–1945) marked the passage from a prevailing "postmillennialist," historically optimistic perspective on the Near East to a deeply ambivalent attitude (see also under "Terminology," below). Despite turbulent revolutions in the Old World, in 1918 one could not have hopefully read that "we live in a most interesting period of the world; in a period distinguished above all others for the wonderful magnitude and variety of its revolutions. . . . Everything in the scientific, and political, and moral world indicates that the reign of darkness upon the earth is approaching its catastrophe," as the *Missionary Herald,* a monthly paper produced in the missionary home center of Boston, had written in 1818. "Surely these are the times foretold by the prophets of old, when many shall run to and fro, and knowledge shall be increased; when wars shall cease unto the ends of the earth; when nation shall not lift up sword against nation, neither shall they learn war any more. And the times are at hand, when the knowledge of the Lord shall cover the earth as the water covers the sea."[10]

The period of the world wars, in particular the relevant experience of the Turkey Mission in the 1910s, gave impetus to a culturally more pessimistic "premillennialism," whose rise had paralleled the fundamentalist movement in U.S. evangelicalism in the nineteenth century. Hence the new American attitude toward the Near East, which began to prevail in the interwar period, and its new protagonists combined such disparate elements as humanitarianism, realpolitik, and, with a new kind of mission, premillennialism. This form of millennialism anticipates inevitable global catastrophes, a climax to the "reign of darkness"—not its imminent end, as did the postmillennialism of the early nineteenth century. After World War II, the United States, now a superpower, turned back in a new way to its initial concept of Israel "restored to Palestine"; at the same time, it entered a fascinating and ambivalent interaction of political globalism, evangelical mission, and biblicist ideology.

Nearest East uses American, Near Eastern, and other primary sources. Telling an intimate faith story, including its contexts, the book traces nearly two centuries of history to the eve of today's topical debates. It sketches elements of diplomatic history but studies primarily what went on in the minds of those involved: what motivated, what was believed, prayed for, and dreamed. This includes by-products of the millennialist current, for example, successful literature, and their socioreligious and political impact in the United States. The book's leitmotifs are the Near East–centered millennialist mission and its persistence, changes, traumas, and vital hopes. For missionary insiders, the intimate move toward the Near East was manifest destiny from the beginning, more manifest than was the American move toward the West Coast. Outsiders may be struck by the persistence of this missionary challenge throughout two centuries. This book considers the move to and interaction with the Near East as constitutive of the United States, a country built up by Bible believers from the Old World of whom the most serious never considered America to be the fulfillment of history and biblical prophecy.

"America" is a European project. Europeans in quest for a future beyond the Old World—in particular, persecuted Protestants—drove it, since Europe had become an uncertain, divided, peaceless place of religious wars in the sixteenth and seventeenth centuries. Even after the establishment of the United States in the late eighteenth century, America remained an open, unfinished project whose entrepreneurial spirit, energy, and peculiar sense of urgency, including Protestant mission and secular globalism, have shaped the modern world. For many, this proved to be an empowering encounter; for others, a disconcerting one. This is particularly true of Sunni Islam, which reigned politically and symbolically in the Ottoman world. Because of "Barbary" (North African) piracy against American ships, Muslim and Ottoman Muslim rule had made a bad impression on the young United States.[11]

When two young American missionaries left their country and began, tentatively, to enter the Near East in 1819, soon to die of fever and exhaustion, they followed the idea of a necessary, salutary new order and a mission of peace, both in the Near East and globally, for which the Gospel, including the "restoration of Israel," would be the leaven or mustard seed. Nearly two centuries later, when U.S. troops invaded Iraq in 2003, some of the rhetoric was similar, but the main American agencies in the Near East—military might versus powerless missionaries—differed significantly.

This books attempts to measure this long, twisted historical and mental road. It is a personal book. It takes up questions with which I was confronted, partly at least, as a teenager when my father, a pastor of the Evangelical-Reformed State Church of Zurich, died prematurely at the age I am now. This occurred in the years after the Six-Day War and the 1968 youth revolution, still during the Vietnam War. Unfinished discussions unfolded at the large family table, often with guests, where we listened eagerly to the news of Swiss Radio Beromünster (among them, the daily comparative American body counting). The United States, Israel, the Near East, and World War II were strongly present in our talks, as were the meaning of the Bible, of history, and of the term *Kingdom of God.* As a child of Swiss Protestantism; later, a student of philosophy, literature, history, and theology at universities in Zurich, Basel, and Paris; finally, a historian of the Near East; and by marriage, half a Near Easterner myself for two decades, I have dared to come back to some old questions. It is no accident that, in substance, the book ends with the 1970s, with the (tentative) answers that could not, the youngster strangely felt, be given to him or that he could not understand at that time.

Terminology

"America" and "American" in this book mostly stand for the United States, if the context is clear. "Millennialism" (variants: *millenarism, millenarianism*) or "chiliasm"—from the Latin *mille anni,* "thousand years," and the Greek χιλια ετη—respectively, refers to a vision in the Revelation or Apocalypse. This last book of the Christian Bible is a source of apocalyptic spirituality and forms the grammar of Christian apocalyptic imagery. "They [the slain Jesus-believers] came to life and reigned with Christ a thousand years" (Rev. 20:4). Millennialism, accordingly, is the belief that Jesus Christ and his saints will one day openly reign on earth for a thousand years; *millennium* is the term for this reign. Referring to this vision in the Revelation, *millennialism* is a more specific term than *messianism,* the belief in the saving role of a messiah or a "messianic force" (e.g., communism, Zionism, perhaps "American exceptionalism"—significantly, the term *messianism* was coined in the early nineteenth century).[12] In contrast to the broader and more often treated messianism and American messianism, I decided to research the biblically and historically more specific phenomenon of American millennialism. Millennialism and messianism nevertheless have much in common, as have *millennium* and *messiah.* If separated from the belief in a personal messiah, both concepts may be considered powerful "ideologies," that is, ideas within a politically mobilizing discourse and mythologies of world-saving power.

Discourse about "final things," according to the prophetic scriptures, is called eschatology (from the Greek εσχατον, last). In the Greek Bible, αποκαλυψις, "apocalypse," means primarily the uncovering, revealing, or exposure of contemporary history before a horizon of long-term history and even eternity. The last book of the Bible, written, according to its first lines, by a servant of Jesus called John, is a complex composition that addresses the Jesus-believers while turning toward the earth, its inhabitants, and its Lord. It attempts to strip contemporary history to its "true meaning," that is, to an already achieved victory of life over destruction, of the resurrected Christ over death. The fall of Mosaic Israel was to be not primarily a disaster but instead the key for spreading the faith in Israel's God on the whole earth. Jesus, "King of the Jews," as was written on his cross, heir and king of Israel, would finally be revealed as the true and legitimate king of the whole earth. The Revelation was written and composed in a time of catastrophes, when Jewish Jesus-believers were persecuted by the Roman power and the Jewish establishment, the destruction of Jerusalem in 70 C.E. either was imminent or had taken place, and divisions threatened the young church. Accordingly, an apocalyptic understanding of contemporary first-century history took global history as a field where Jesus would prove his final victory. Using Jewish apocalyptical sources (above all the biblical book of Daniel) and opening up a universal perspective in the Son of Man—true humanity revealed as Jesus, the first of and door to a universal childhood—this understanding opposed the nullity of contemporary experiences and the hubris of imperial power with the unabrogated divine lordship of this earth. This lordship was accessible at that time only in outlines, symbols, allusions, and metaphors but was to be fully revealed in the future.[13]

These are the basics of millennialism, including modern American apocalyptic spirituality. American millennialism refers directly to the Bible, in particular to its last book. In contrast to Europe's enlightened demiurge Napoleon Bonaparte and other modern geniuses of history or "Providence," it claimed the God of the Bible, and in particular the God of the Revelation, for the modern remaking of the world.[14] Jesus, his saints, and the "restored"

Jews would finally prevail, not autocratic power, zealotry, or those who adored power. American experiences were part of this apocalyptic spirituality: the Puritans' persecution in and exodus from the Old World; the building up of an American democracy when the Old World, Europe and the Near East, were mostly autocratic; a reconciling mission of blessed America to the world; and a mission in particular to the Bible lands, where crucial millennial events had to take place and be hastened by evangelical agents, the missionaries. *Kingdom of God* and *Kingdom of Jesus*—or simply, *Kingdom*—were broader terms than *millennium,* since they included the "virtual millennium" believed to reign already among Christians and, individually, in their hearts; and the Kingdom would not finish when the millennium was expected to end.

Specific, but not exclusive, to American millennialism is the distinction between premillennialism and postmillennialism. Literally, these terms refer to the distinction between Jesus' coming before or after the millennium. Postmillennialism was millennialism plus modern Enlightenment; it entrusted missionary America with the task of preparing the Kingdom, in inter- and transnational cooperation, using to this end all pacific means: science, technological progress, and historical opportunities. American mission to the Ottoman Near East was, all in all, postmillennialist. It hoped that after (hence "post-") successful missionary efforts, the earth would be a much better place, ready for Jesus and his visible, powerful omnipresence (parousia). The distinction must, however, be taken with caution; it is an ideal type that does not sufficiently reflect both the variety and the openness of eschatological thought—be it labeled pre- or postmillennialist. Despite their generally postmillennialist stance, many Near East missionaries of the nineteenth century believed in the Christ's parousia once the millennium would begin, since he was its crucial cornerstone. Mission was preparation for parousia.

Whereas postmillennialism invited a secular translation of salvation and emphasized Enlightenment, premillennialism strongly underlined Jesus' agency, at the risk, however, of isolationism and quietism. In disillusioned distance from politics, it tended to be "apolitical" and at the same time more submissive to authorities than generally well-educated, politically engaged postmillennialism. Religious expectation of catastrophe is generally linked to a strong appeal to individual conversion, not to collective action. Some minor overseas missions founded in the second half of the nineteenth century in America were outspokenly premillennialist.[15] American premillennialism was informed by difficult personal or collective experiences. It distrusted the historical optimism inherent to postmillennialism; all the more so as President Andrew Jackson's Indian removal of the 1830s, the Gold Rush of the 1840s and 1850s, and the Civil War of the 1860s had revealed massive evil within American society. The Apocalypse of John, written in the first century, did not respond to experiences of historical "success," in any established sense of the word. It attempted to uncover and overcome contemporary, "unsuccessful," traumatic history by means of the Word of God and in the quiet certitude of Jesus' lordship. It referred not to an ideal past but to a future that had already begun. Today, the ordinary use of "apocalypse" or "apocalyptic" mostly points to spectacular changes and catastrophes in "last days." Where there is a tendency to catastrophism, a spell of coming catastrophes, and an according use of apocalyptical themes, I speak of "apocalypticism."

Also specific to American millennialism, but again not exclusive, was the connection, around 1800, of emerging American postmillennialist overseas mission with the postulate of the restoration of the Jews to Palestine and to Jesus. Jews had to return to Palestine as restorers of Israel and to Jesus, their king. Restorationists were Zionists *avant la lettre.* In contrast to the Zionists, however, they hoped that the Jews, to whom Jesus belonged so viscerally, would at last take him in and greatly take strength from him. This would happen either after their return to Palestine or before (as most restorationists expected pre-1800). Without coming to new terms with Jesus, restored Israel would lack the spiritual power and global acceptance it needed to be the nucleus of the Kingdom of God.[16]

The early American missionaries hoped, moreover, that the Muslims would come to new, Christian terms with Jesus, whom the Muslims already respected as a prophet. American missionaries did not, however, know much about the Muslim Jesus, and they knew little or nothing about Muslim eschatology, the reign of the *mahdi,* or of a *sahib,* a Muslim leader in apocalyptic times. It is striking that they did not know about the old traditions of Muslim expectation of Jesus'—Isa ibn Maryam's—second coming and final reign on earth. It is true that Muslim apocalypticism was, in the Ottoman world of that time, not as influential a current as it has been since the late twentieth century. The term *millennium* and direct biblical references could, in that time, scarcely be found in the Muslim context. The Muslim apocalyptic heritage, of which millennialism is an undeniable part, nevertheless existed; it became more topical with the Ottoman existential crisis of the late eighteenth century and the emergence of Islamism in the late nineteenth century. It has finally boomed, both in militant and quietist forms, since the Islamic Renaissance of the second half of the twentieth century.[17]

Eschatology in the Ottoman world is not a well-researched topic, at least not for the last two Ottoman centuries. It is, however, safe to say that in the

Ottoman nineteenth century there was no eschatological current comparable to postmillennialism or the restorationist movement. These predominantly Anglo-American currents were embedded in Western macrodynamics of expansion and stood in a particular Protestant relationship to Jewish legacy, the Hebrew Bible, and civil emancipation of the Jews. There were explicit apocalyptical feelings in the late Ottoman world, feelings of end times—religiously expressed or not—including the fear of Islam's corruption, the empire's fall, and the rise of non-Muslim "infidels." The feeling of threat and existential disorientation led to a longing for saviors. "Among the Muslims, too, there is no auspicious master [*sahib-i hayır*], to raise in their midst saying the way things are, or are not," complained an Ottoman student in Europe in a letter of 1896. He prayed, "Mercy, my God, give the community of Muhammed security and protection."[18]

"Last days" marked by disorder (*fitna*), before the messianic reign, were expected by Jews, Christians, and Muslims in premodern periods. Some Ottoman Muslims and Jews praised Ottoman sultans in the fifteenth and sixteenth centuries as blessed rulers who put order in the chaos of the last days, thus paving the way for the *mahdi,* Jesus, or the messiah who would restore the Jews to Palestine and establish the messianic kingdom. The broad apocalyptic dynamics of that period, in Europe and in the Ottoman world, were marginalized in the late sixteenth century with the exception of England.[19] In the mid-seventeenth century, a strong intracommunal Jewish movement emerged with Sabbatai Zwi from Smyrna. Zwi was declared the messiah, preached Jewish restoration in Palestine, and won over many Jews in Europe and the Ottoman Empire. At the cradle of the Sabbatian movement stood, among others, English millennialism: "In the home of his father . . . young Sabbatai heard the stories of English merchants about the Puritans who loved and studied the Scriptures, identified themselves with the Jews and looked forward to the Restoration of Israel."[20] Zwi's failure to lead the Jews back to Palestine together with his forced conversion to Sunni Islam contributed to a decline of traditional messianic expectation and piety among Jews. For many among them in Western Europe, it led to their final turning to European Enlightenment, including its modern ideologies (atheism, radical revolutionism, messianic nationalism, and socialism), but excluding a comprehensive modern rearticulation of religion and historical experience.[21] The strong long-term appeal of American millennialism, in contrast to premodern Jewish messianism (both personal messianisms), lay in its ability to reconcile Calvinist Bible reading, Enlightenment, and experiences of persecution, pioneering work, rise, and success. At the turn of the nineteenth century, Protestant millennialism, based on a powerful reading of both modern history and old prophetic traditions, allowed both coping with the past and projecting a markedly different future.

When Sayyid Qutb, at the beginning of his seminal Islamist manifesto *Milestones* (1964), wrote that "mankind today is on the brink of a precipice," he invited a radical revival of the original Muslim community that had to be the nucleus of God's reign on earth, because this community alone would be able to lead a Muslim world and global humankind devoid of spiritual values. "It is necessary to revive that Muslim community which is buried under the debris of the man-made traditions of several generations, and which is crushed under the weight of those false laws and customs which are not even remotely related to the Islamic teachings, and which, in spite of all this, calls itself 'world of Islam.'"[22] As for American missionaries before him, *revival* was a key term for Qutb, but linked to "salutary violence." Qutb had to compete with and demarcate himself from the strong transnational appeal of revolutionary socialism. Frantz Fanon propagated at that time social-revolutionary violence and its salutary community-founding impact among oppressed people.[23] Refusal of socialist atheism; disillusion over contemporary Egypt, where Qutb had grown up and experienced years of imprisonment; and embarrassment at the way of life in the United States, where he had lived for two years, led to his resolute turn to a "Muslim authenticity" beyond the existing Muslim world and culture. He seminally called for an Islamic revolution to overcome a present that he judged unbearable and unacceptable. But there was not much of a positive future, no modern Islamic or peacefully apocalyptic perspective, beyond the violent breaks that he asked for. His militant apocalypticism is reminiscent of that of the anti-Roman Zealots.[24]

Revival generally contains criticism of established religion, compared to an earlier Golden Age. In Qutb's case, the criticism is similar to that which American missionaries addressed to a Christianity they wanted to restore in the Near East to its "primitive purity," thus preparing for parousia. (This was the explicit ABCFM strategy after 1830.) In contrast to Qutb, whose influential writing began to combine elements of Qu'ranic anti-Judaism and European anti-Semitism, the American missionaries first used, not opposed, the existing global dynamics; and they gave the Jews a privileged, peculiarly "restored" place. The declared goal of both Qutb and the American missionaries was eschatological: "the establishing of the dominion of God on Earth" (Qutb). But they would not have agreed on the simultaneous necessity, as Qutb claimed, of pervasive war as "a movement to wipe out tyranny and to introduce true freedom to mankind," since the early church, which too had experienced jail, torture, and execution, had refused to call for it, opting for faith in God's agency.[25]

The rhetoric of salutary war nevertheless is part of American political globalism since World War I. That war marked both the beginning of a postmissionary U.S. globalism and the end of a century of religious and civil mission to the Ottoman Near East. President Woodrow Wilson in 1917 and President Franklin Roosevelt in 1941 justified the American entrance into world war by the necessity to fight against tyranny and for freedom. For a short time after Wilson, the U.S. approach to the Near East was reconceived in terms of realpolitik and oil needs. During and after World War II, however, U.S. diplomacy conceived its role toward the world again in terms of political globalism or "Wilsonianism." Millennialism, which is globalist by definition, now split into three conflicting, though related, directions: the nurturing, after Adolf Hitler and Joseph Stalin, of a (more or less) nonmessianist, informal "empire of the good" led by the United States against forces of the evil; the identification of Zionism and Israel, with which, for many Americans, the old messianist dictum of "building up Zion" came to converge; and a strong premillennialist current whose missionaries now came to the Near East, in particular to Palestine-Israel. Against this background, apocalypticism has strikingly boomed in American culture after the 1960s.

How can we grasp two centuries of American enlightened modernity, Bible belief, and hope for a "Zion" to build up? Are we dealing with a modern ideology, arguably the most successful, the strongest, and the longest lasting of the ideologies created since the late eighteenth century? Or are we dealing with spirituality, a universal language of the human heart, a historically and biblically inspired faith, a constant confidence in a constructive global future and the benevolent master of this earth yet to come (the source of this spirituality)? Does the millennialist mind-set end by masking with shrill religious overtones a cynical game of power and greed or go on promoting spiritual, social, and political freedom? These questions follow us throughout the book. It is important to elaborate on and examine tentative answers to these questions with regard to the concrete evolution of America's interactions with its Nearest East up to the late twentieth century.

CHAPTER 1

The United States and the Near East, circa 1800

For revivalist Protestants in Europe and America, the late eighteenth and early nineteenth centuries were the threshold of a new age, the "dawn of the millennium." Millennialism and modernity were, for them, synonymous. What historiography calls "modern times" in history, the period since the late eighteenth century, was for them "latter times," the eve of the Kingdom of God on earth. Seemingly unworldly biblical sayings made sense for their vision of contemporary history, since they refused to separate history from the apocalyptic history of salvation. They considered the two particularly inextricable with regard to the Near East.

Christianity, indeed, was at its end; the "times of the Gentiles" and their churches (and mosques) was "expiring," but not in the same way as for Voltaire and many enlightened celebrities in Europe, who saw the end of religion and Christianity because these had definitively become *infâme* and a curse to rational society. For the revivalists, Christianity had ended because the history of salvation opened a new epoch, with one particular new-old player: the Jews. Missionary America and Voltaire (who denounced anti-Protestant prejudices in France) shared antipapal resentments. Both agreed on the end of (Catholic) "Christian Europe," but not on the Bible, the Jews, and global history: Voltaire hated the Jews as much as the (above all, Catholic) church, and his modernity excluded any explicit legacy of history of salvation. In contrast, modernity and millennialism coincided significantly with the foundation of the United States; both shaped Christianity there much more than elsewhere. Both millennialism—preparatory to the Kingdom on earth, including the "restoration of the Jews"—and enlightened modernity shaped the early U.S. encounter with the Near East and coincided with the incipient existential crisis of the Ottoman Empire. At the eve of American modern times, Bible reading and understanding of the contemporary world overlapped to an unprecedented degree. Contemporary history, Near Eastern history, and the history of salvation were all meaningfully interwoven by the intellectual efforts made by early missionary America. In eighteenth-century continental Europe, by contrast, millennialism had a bad, nonconformist taste, linked to anti-Jewish reflexes, among the Christian majority.[1]

A small trade dating from British colonial times, notably with the Aegean Smyrna, was the first concrete connection between the United States and the Ottoman world. Clashes with corsairs made bad news in the American press and soon called the young U.S. Navy to the Mediterranean. But the first lasting American entrance to the Near East was missionary. It carried a peculiar legacy of Puritan spirituality and American historical experience to what were seen as the historically fascinating and prophetically promising "Bible lands." The American missionaries were expecting the fall of Islam, the fall of the pope (Catholicism), and the restoration of the Jews to Palestine and to Jesus. They considered these historical moves as necessary conditions for the achievement of the Kingdom of God on earth. They understood themselves as workers committed to this achievement that needed previous worldwide evangelization, the struggle for global Christian unity, and the restoration of Israel. The centrality of the Near Eastern world is self-evident in this whole vision. The most spectacular changes—the fall of Islam and the restoration of the Jews—had to take place there. From there, from a transformed, "leavened," and "regenerated" Near East, Zion, and the global Kingdom had to be built up.

From a Separate to an Entangled History

Around 1800, the United States was a confident young republic that had successfully established itself after a war of independence. The Ottoman state, by contrast, which formally controlled a huge area from the Balkans to Asia Minor, Syria, North Africa, and the Arabian Peninsula, had moved into an existential crisis. The Peace of Küçük Kaynarca in 1774 mirrored Russia's military superiority in the preceding war and marked the beginning of an Ottoman feeling of inferiority vis-à-vis Europe. It triggered for the first time reforms according to European models, at that time primarily for military improvement. From that period, the so-called Oriental Question—

the question of the future of a Near East in acute crisis—was and remained a constant challenge in international diplomacy.[2] In growing millennialist circles, the Oriental Question began to be linked to the newly so-called Jewish Question in the West. For certain authors, the Ottoman-Russian war of 1768–1774 would bring about the "final temporal restoration" of the Jews to the "Holy Land."[3] Since, after the independence of 1776, American ships no longer enjoyed protection by the British navy, the Congress voted in 1794 to create a navy "adequate for the protection of the commerce of the United States against [formally Ottoman] Algerian corsairs."[4] U.S. Marines were dispatched in 1804 and 1815 to punish and prevent attacks against American ships. Early on, the experiences with corsairs and North African vassals gave a bad impression of Ottoman rule to the American public.

Ottomans and Americans in general shared an attachment to religion, but not a similar attitude toward Enlightenment, social utopia, and millennialism. Both refused modern European atheism, however, and both remained attached to the religion of the scriptures. The French Revolution and its antireligious ideology met with deep suspicion in the Ottoman capital; only the Young Turks, nearly a hundred years later, would open themselves to modern European ideologies in addition to European expertise and technology. Ottomans and Americans would remain more or less immune to European socialism in the nineteenth and twentieth centuries. For American missionaries, there was no fundamental gap between the Gospel, scientific progress, democracy, social change, and enlightened belief in universal human commonality in contrast to innate difference. Ottoman state ideology and Sunni popular culture, however, were suspicious of all these modern achievements, seeing them in general as Western and atheist. Protestants in France and America interpreted contemporaneous antireligious actors as instruments of the Almighty; in particular, they warmly welcomed Bonaparte's occupation of Rome and arrest of the pope in 1798 as a divine punishment of the religious persecutions since the sixteenth century, for which they saw the Catholic leader responsible. In contrast to the continental European notion of Enlightenment, shaped by French thought and the French Revolution, in the Anglo-American world religion, prophecy, and Enlightenment did not stand in sharp antithesis to one another. The famous physician Isaac Newton's Bible studies on the restoration of the Jews are among many examples of this synthesis at the eve of the nineteenth century.[5]

Bonaparte's conquest of Ottoman Egypt in 1799 proved the vulnerability of the Sultan's empire and made it clear, politically and militarily, that at any moment the end of Ottoman power could be expected. This was an important stimulus for apocalyptic visions in a West that excluded religion more and more from the public space and relegated it to the private sphere. In contrast to some Jewish circles,[6] British and American restorationists did not accept the heir to the antiecclesiastical and atheistic French Revolution as a possible Cyrus—an imperial restorer of Israel, like the Persian king Cyrus in the sixth century B.C.E.—during and after Bonaparte's Near Eastern campaign. They hoped that Great Britain and, much later, the United States would take on this role. Moreover, in Puritan defiance of existing worldly power, they pinned their hopes on the Holy Spirit, not the genius of a brilliant emperor, for the transformation of the Ottoman world.

Bonaparte's Near Eastern campaign consisted of a mix of anti-British imperialism, mission of enlightenment, and recourse to the myths of ancient Rome and Egypt. He introduced not only modern arms but also modern science, in particular archeology and Egyptology, to the Near East.[7] The imagery of ancient Rome and Egypt and corresponding restorative myths contributed to his imperial self-representation and stood in stark contrast to the restorationist *imaginaire* and the evangelical faith in the rise of the powerless. Portraying himself as a new Alexander and liberator of Egypt, he used Islamic discourse in his attempt to win over the Muslims. But the instrumentality of religion was transparent, and the hearts of the Muslims were not won over. The project as it had been intended failed completely.[8] This *campagne orientale* on the eve of the nineteenth century stands paradigmatically for a masterly but soon aborted demiurgic renewal of the Near East by an occidental power, instead of by the people on the ground in synergy with Western forces. The challenge of a Near Eastern renewal, however, remained powerful for the European great powers, for the American missionaries, and for the United States after the world wars.

Even before Bonaparte's conquest, the British scientist and restorationist theologian Joseph Priestley had hoped for a post-Ottoman Palestine and formulated the myth of an empty but promising place, occupied by an illegitimate power: "Palestine, the glory of all lands, which is now part of the Turkish empire, empty and ready to receive you [the Jews]. But till the fall of this power, which, without deriving any advantage from it, keeps possession of that country, it is impossible that it can be yours. I therefore, earnestly pray for its dissolution."[9] Palestine was the place where entangled modern history became most visible against a background of both ancient history and the history of salvation. In the nineteenth century, Palestine became a principal "mission field" especially, and for the first time, of the Protestants; here the restoration of Israel should take place. Protestant mission in Palestine and the whole Levant combined millennialism and pragmatic work that applied Western achievements in education, health, technology, and science.

Paradoxically, and for several reasons, the modern Occident made Palestine much more of a "holy" land than it had ever been before. Not only the Protestant restorationists focused on Palestine, but the region became to an unprecedented extent the destination of pilgrimage and religious tourism from the West and from Russia in the nineteenth century. For modern Europe, and in particular for France, this compensated, often nostalgically, for the evacuation of religion from the public space; it was not tied to a vibrant millennialism as it was for many Americans.[10]

How to conceive at last of restored Israel without leading Jewish agency? Ultimately, in the late nineteenth century, after a few precursors, Palestine became the object of desire or the territory of an ethnic nationalism with a Hebrew biblical background. Zionism realized the restoration of Israel in Palestine, for which restorationists had so much prayed, in an unexpected manner. Eastern European Jews were its privileged actors.

Pre-missionary American Moldings

The missionary Protestantism of the early nineteenth century in the United States combined an unbroken belief in the Bible with the postulates of the Enlightenment. To this it added the successful American experience of what was widely acclaimed in the West as the most modern and democratic state on earth. Before the late eighteenth century, Protestant Bible readers and colonists in New England saw themselves as the "New-English Israel,"[11] Americans as "God's own people," and America as Canaan or "God's own land." These equations run through the writings of Cotton Mather (1663–1728), one of New England's most influential theologians and publicists, who began *The Great Works of Christ in America* (circa 1700) as follows: "I write the Wonders of the Christian Religion, flying from the depravations of Europe, to the American Strand; and, assisted by the Holy Author of that Religion, I do with all conscience of Truth . . . report the wonderful displays of His infinite Power, Wisdom, Goodness, and Faithfulness, wherewith His Divine Providence hath irradiated an Indian Wilderness."[12] Mather had eschatological expectations above all for America itself, not for the world and a Jewish Israel: "A Golden Age will arrive to this place [America], and this perhaps before all of our First Planters are fallen asleep." Americans were for Mather the privileged bearers of the biblical covenant, a "People which have proportionably [*sic*] more of God among them than any part of mankind beside."[13] In Cotton Mather's time, the communal life of the church was synonymous with the local public order. He had studied at Harvard College, the only university then existing in New England. Its offshoot, the Theological

Seminary at Andover, became a hundred years later a hotbed of missionary millennialism.

In a vein of America-centered millennialism like Mather's, but with a stronger sense of global mission, John B. Adams, one of America's founding fathers and its second president, wrote in 1765, "I always consider the settlement of America with reverence and wonder, as the opening of a grand scene and design in Providence for the illumination of the ignorant, and the emancipation of the slavish part of mankind all over the earth."[14] The mid-twentieth-century theologian H. Richard Niebuhr denounced church leaders such as the Presbyterian Lyman Beecher (1775–1865) for whom the institutions of New England had been "such as the world needs and attended as they have been by the power of God, able to enlighten and renovate the world." For Niebuhr, by such careless language that blurred the distance between God's and men's power, the "old idea of American Christians as a chosen people . . . was turned into the notion of a nation especially favored."[15] Religiously fed political rhetoric paid no heed to the fact that not state and nation but small churches, not American patriots and business-minded men but fatally persecuted Jesus–believers, were addressed in the biblical text of the Revelation. During the American Revolution, language of Enlightenment went hand in hand with strong biblical rhetoric, much in contrast to the French Revolution. From the old idea of America qua new Israel, a civil millennialist religion evolved in the late eighteenth century. Jews, who had also fought in the American War of Independence, could share in that civil religion. Based on a successful American historical experience, civil millennialism believed in American destiny and its mission of making the world a better place. Equal rights, wealth, and supraconfessional civil millennialism may explain why among American Jews, in contrast to European Jews, socialism and secular Zionism (at least until World War II) had little success.

The revivalist Jonathan Edwards and Samuel Hopkins, spiritual fathers of the overseas mission after them, both stood at odd with the rhetoric of religious nationalism. The patriotic clergyman Samuel Sherwood, too, distinguished between church and nation.[16] At the same time he emphasized the "American quarter of the globe" as "a fixed and settled habitation for God's church," and the war of the emerging United States against imperial Britain and conflicting forces as an apocalyptical struggle that would finally result in the "kingdom of our God, and the power of his Christ . . . to all the ends of the earth." From the beginning, as we see, U.S. wars had not only to be "just wars" in the Augustinian sense; they had to be apocalyptic wars that led to peace on earth. Sherwood did not yet use the expression "build up Zion" in the restorationist sense, as American missionaries to the Near East would soon understand it.

The great losses in the War of Independence against Britain; gaps between rich and poor, between officers and soldiers; and other interior tensions led to a desacralization of politics, or more precisely, according to the historian Nathan Hatch, to a partial turning away from postmillennialism.[17] After all, could the American Revolution be seen as millennialist when it did not liberate the slaves and did not treat the Indians as equals? For the post–Revolutionary War missionaries, the answer was clearly negative.

Visions of History: Restoration of the Jews and the Global Kingdom of Jesus

Since the end of the eighteenth century, the weakness of the Ottoman Empire had concretely enforced thoughts of a post-Ottoman order, or at the least an Ottoman reordering. This implied a number of restorative myths. Bonaparte's *imaginaire* combined the rationality of French Revolution with a kind of revival of ancient Egypt and Mediterranean Roman rule. The Ottoman reformers after him attempted to restore the heyday of Ottoman power in the sixteenth century with the help of European know-how. Representations of pre-Islamic Egypt, Babylon, Iran, Palestine, and Lebanon appealed to nationalists from the late nineteenth century onward. The return to early Islam appealed to the Wahhabite inspirers of the Saudi state builders in the early twentieth century.

In contrast to these attempts at restoring power and glory, the concrete modern idea of the restoration of the Jews, far beyond "Jewish homesickness," could be traced back to powerless and marginal Protestants of the sixteenth century. Unlike established Catholic and Protestant churches, both allied with secular power, American Protestants, mostly Puritans from England or members of free churches from the European continent, had undergone a long history of persecution. Their eschatological view of history was influenced by this experience. They read in the Bible and viscerally felt that their destiny was interconnected with that of Israel and the Jews, that both were part of a common history of salvation whose future they eagerly tried to understand. They anticipated groundbreaking reversals within a historical development toward the Kingdom of God on earth that would bring the oppressed and powerless their full rights. Often, this vision meaningfully included the restoration of the Jews to Palestine and to Jesus Christ.

Protestant minority groups in Europe, particularly in Germany and

Switzerland and, above all, in Great Britain, shared a belief in the prospect of Israel's restoration that had emerged during the troubled Reformation period; new contacts with Jews, especially Hebrew teachers, played a certain, though limited, role. The roots of restorationism go back to the birth of Christianity, rabbinic Judaism, early apocalyptic literature, and the prophetic books of the Hebrew Bible. Protestants in Britain and beyond had repeatedly envisioned, since the sixteenth century, the restoration of the Jews to Palestine and to Jesus, together with the "fall" of the pope and of Europe's whole system of power. "Wherefore wee need not be afraid to averre and mainteyne, that one day they [the Jews] shall come to Ierusalem againe, be Kings and chiefe Monarches of the earth, swaye and governe all, for the glory of Christ that shall shine among them," wrote the English lawyer Henry Finch, a zealous Protestant, at the beginning of the seventeenth century. "The Romane name (I will speake it, because it must one day be) shall bee taken from the earth, and the Empire shall returne to Asia, and again shall the East beare dominion, and the West be in subiection."[18]

Restorationist vision contradicted, or transcended, from the very beginning the idea of an American empire: in the words of a traveler in North America in 1759–1760 the "idea, strange as it is visionary," which had "entered into the minds of the generality of mankind, that empire is travelling westward; and every one is looking forward with eager and impatient expectation to that destined moment, when America is to give law to the rest of the world."[19] The rise of American power connoted in the eighteenth century the rise of the weak and religiously persecuted, who had escaped from Europe in the seventeenth century and remained threatened in their will to independence. That the birth of the United States succeeded in a situation "when nothing but hope and virtue could survive" (Thomas Paine) was for them like a flash of apocalyptic truth. It entered the American dream and civil religion to be evoked by political leaders up to now.[20] On the eve of modern times, however, in contrast to the idea of a rising Western empire, religious hopes began to be more than ever projected on the Near East. This was true even for Europe and Russia, where, in the nineteenth century, secular utopias successfully competed with churches and synagogues for first place in the people's *imaginaires*. Pilgrimage to Palestine, above all from Russia, took on dimensions it never had before.[21] In Britain and in the United States, the millennialist appeal had to vie much less with contradicting secular ideologies; in the United States in particular, it accommodated much better with the existing civil religion.

Protestant restorationism was groundbreaking. It put the Christian reader of the Bible in the place of the Jews and asked how they, the first receivers of biblical prophecies, would understand them. This, together with the Pauline belief in a still-valid Hebrew covenant, proved to be a strong argument for restoration. More than in a simple shift of global power from the West to the East, restorationists believed in the abolition of repressive power relations; pariahs both under Christianity and Islam, the Jews should be restored and reempowered as agents of that future Kingdom of which they had been, willingly or unwillingly, the passive witnesses since Jesus' times. Marginal for nearly three centuries, restorationism began to be established in English Protestant thought by the late eighteenth century. At the same time spiritual restoration, that is, conversion to Jesus, for the first time began to be thought of perhaps as not preparatory to the return to Palestine but following it.

At the same time the question was raised: which power would assist the Jews in their return home? Would the duty and honor fall to Britain or, as seemed possible in the 1790s, to revolutionary France?[22] The United States, then, was not considered a possible imperial Cyrus; American Christian patriotism at that time did not desire empire but stood at odds with British imperialism and the myth of imperial Rome. "We may be ready to wish that Providence would permit us to become a *great* nation; but the spirit of christian [*sic*] patriotism rather dictates another petition, that we may be a *good* nation. . . . May not united America ever vie in magnificence and splendour ancient *Rome,* and after stretching the arms of her power from one end of the world to the other, pillaging mankind and becoming rich with spoil, suffer the distress and ruin, which she shall have inflicted," the congregational minister John Allyn warned in a sermon preached in 1805 to the government of the state of Massachusetts in Boston (which was later to become the missionary center).[23]

Early Missionary Boston and the Restoration of the Jews

A hastening toward millennium, far from any imperial thoughts, shaped the quantitatively small but symbolically loaded interaction between America and the Near East in the early nineteenth century. "O when will Jesus take the kingdom, and reign from shore to shore! . . . That long desired day, is beginning to dawn. The Lord hasten it in his time," wrote Levi Parsons, missionary to Palestine, in his diary when he arrived in Ottoman Smyrna in January 1820.[24] A feeling of millennial dawn reigned in the missionary community. "We have now entered upon that period which is immediately preparatory to the Millennium," claimed a New England minister.[25] The

ABCFM pioneers and their successors understood their engagement as a response to the millennial challenge of building up, gradually and pacifically, the global Kingdom. The Reverend Noah Porter recalled a meeting of the American Bible Society in New York in the 1810s where "not more than two or three hundred people were present. There was, however, a deep-felt interest in the Foreign Missionary enterprise, here and elsewhere, at the time. The impulse that had been given to Christian feeling in our churches by the missions of the London Missionary Society . . . ; able writers on the prophecies in England and this country had brought the millennium near in the apprehension of leading men, both ministers and laymen, in the churches; and now that measures were instituted to embody them in the work, they were prepared to give these measures their ready and hearty support."[26] Millennialism fell on fertile ground in the young United States. There was a broad receptive public and a potential of young men and women ready to risk their lives for spreading the message of the coming Kingdom of Jesus.

The feeling, as an orator expressed it during the Fourth Annual Meeting of the ABCFM in 1813, was that "still the period is advancing; it is hastening; in which Christians will be most honourably united in the present world. The morning . . . will actually arise on this dark world, when all distinctions of party and sect, of name and nation, of civilization and savageness, of climate and colour, will finally vanish."[27] Later writings—for example, of William Goodell, an American missionary in Istanbul of the mid-nineteenth century—prove the ongoing vision of the contemporary era as a time of fundamental departures toward a universal humanity:

> The history of the world is only one black disclosure of the designs formed, the means used, and the projects executed or attempted, to subdue one another. . . . But within the last fifty years the minds of a few persons in a few countries have been turned to the subject of subduing the earth, and ascertaining what they could make out of it. . . . The very ends of the world are now brought together, and the moral effect of this among the nations is, that men begin to feel that they belong to one brotherhood. . . . What improvements may we not confidently expect in the next fifty years![28]

For Americans, the "dark world" of oppression and disorder was in particular the Ottoman world; hence, mission there was urgent. Napoleon's Eastern campaign and reordering of Europe had triggered an apocalyptic reorientation toward the Near East including, more than ever, the idea of the restoration of the Jews. In the 1793 *Treatise on the Millennium* by Hopkins, the spiritual father of the overseas mission, we find the restoration of the Jews only as an event of the past after Babylonian exile, not as part of the apocalyptic future. Hopkins's main emphasis was on the "reign of Christ and his church on earth,"[29] his main move being toward global evangelization and millennium, not restoration. This element spread in America after 1800 and was based on conceptions worked out in Britain in the preceding decades. Early missionary America was closely inspired by what millennialist thinkers had developed in eighteenth-century Britain, and this in turn was connected with a large transnational movement of pietism that, since the seventeenth century, had stood partly in opposition to established Protestant churches.[30] Despite its peculiarities, missionary America was part of a multiply connected transnational network, or "Protestant International," in place since the late eighteenth century and led by British organizations. This network sometimes cooperated with but often marked also critical distance from the leading "Protestant powers" and the cultural and racial ideologies of the time. Beside the ABCFM in Boston, the German-speaking Basel Missionary Society, founded in 1815, was among the important hubs of this network in the nineteenth century. An autonomous center, the Basel Mission nevertheless stood in close connection with the British Church Missionary Society.[31] In contrast to the restorationists in Britain, however, Americans were not attracted by the idea that their political power would help bring about the restoration to Palestine. Their millennialist mission of the early nineteenth century to the Ottoman world relied solely on vision, faith, commitment, and the perception of a window of historical opportunity.

Hannah Adams's book *The History of the Jews: From the Destruction of Jerusalem to the Present Time,* published in 1812, reflects the new impulses, the mental attitude, and the status of knowledge in Boston's early missionary circles on the Jews, the Ottoman world, and Islam. Critically pessimistic about the present time and both Christian and Muslim treatment of the Jews, Adams saw "the Christian world enveloped in darkness and ignorance; and in the professed disciples of the benevolent Redeemer violating the fundamental precepts of the Gospel; assuming a shew of piety as a mask for avarice, and a pretence for pillaging an unhappy people [the Jews]. If from the west we turn to the east we shudder over similar scenes of horror; wherever the Mahometan banner is erected, contempt and misery await the Jews." Without resentment, and not without humor, she stated that Christian mission among Jews had not succeeded up to then, adding, "The Jews, nothwithstanding the calamities they have so long endured, still look down upon all nations, and continue to claim the partial kindness and protection of heaven. The miracles, performed in favour of the first Hebrews, inspired their descendants with a contempt for those nations which the Deity never honored in the same manner."[32]

Adams shared with many of her contemporaries the conviction that "the history of the Jews exhibits a melancholy picture of human wretchedness and depravity," but more than the Jewish nonrecognition of Jesus, she blamed pitiless Christian and Muslim societies. Adams adopted the view of Jewish authors that "the preservation of the Jews as a distinct people, is an event unparalleled in the annals of history." Both she and the missionaries took this as a strong sign of divine loyalty and biblical truth. "The exemption of the Jews from the common fate of nations [i.e., dissolution], affords a striking proof of the truth of the sacred scriptures." While the conservation of Jewish peculiarity, the Jews' nonassimilation, was dismissed by many modern Europeans as Jewish traditionalism and "obstinacy," for missionary America it confirmed, on the contrary, the potential for the future history of salvation. Both Calvinism, the basic "software" of American Protestantism, and a specifically American millennialism challenged anti-Judaism and anti-Semitism from the outset.[33]

The American synthesis of Enlightenment thought and belief in the Kingdom of God made possible for Christians and Jews within the state not only equality but also a much more constructive interpretation of Jewish history than in Europe. In modern Europe, Enlightenment and its universalism were (partly) implemented in the restricted framework of secular nationalism that proved incapable of fully integrating Jewry. The anti-Jewish clichés of Voltaire, a father of the European Enlightenment, speak for themselves. What mattered, in turn, for the missionary community was faith or infidelity, among Christians and Jews. From this resulted skepticism toward an American "mixed society" that did not share in the same spiritual current of believers still longing for "a better country."[34] Adams's and the missionary community's genuine interest in, not to say love for, the Jews included the expectation of the Jews' final turn to Jesus. "Many pious and learned men have supposed that they [the Jews] will not only be converted to the Christian religion, but restored to Palestine, and placed in a state more splendid and glorious than ever," stated Adams somewhat prudently in her discussion of new books on the topic of the restoration, and on the question of whether conversion had to take place before or after the return to Palestine. She was a leading founding member of the Female Society of Boston, a branch of the London Jews' Society. The Female Society of Boston financed William Schauffler, ABCFM missionary to the Jews in Istanbul and Izmir.[35]

As spiritual children of Edwards and Hopkins, the first promoters of an American overseas mission distinguished between national and missionary interests and developed a global millennial perspective beyond the national experience. The foundation of the ABCFM in Boston in 1810 was, in a broad sense, part of the foundation period of the United States, a time of new departures on different levels in the late eighteenth and early nineteenth centuries. The Great Awakening, led by Jonathan Edwards, had begun in the 1740s, and the Second Awakening, with Samuel Hopkins, lasted from the late eighteenth century to the early nineteenth. For the revivalists, society was to be remade, in America and elsewhere, in anticipation of the coming global Kingdom. Many educational institutions were established at that time and voluntary organizations emerged, among them the American Bible Society, the American Anti-Slavery Society, the Boston Prison Discipline Society (for the reform of the prisons), and the ABCFM. *Disinterested benevolence,* a key term of the Second Awakening, called for unreserved consecration to the service of God and humankind, in marked contrast to individual and national egoism. According to Hopkins, one of the founders of the ABCFM, only "the extension of Christian love could bring nearer to humankind the millennium that would wipe out poverty, injustice and oppression."[36]

Before and after the establishment of the United States, the New World in America had proved not to be the golden age. Prophecy-believers, in contrast, hoped Palestine to be the starting point of the real Kingdom on earth and missionary America, its midwife. Politically, most of the ABCFM pioneers were progressive liberals; they belonged to groups that fought for the abolition of slavery, women's emancipation, the equality of the Jews in law and in public life, and the rights of the Indians. The ABCFM led an extensive fight against Indian removal policies. Humanitarian crusade and struggle for human rights were part of its gospel. "Will any bring it to the bar of God, when these wretched Indians point to us, as the cause of their ruin?" Levi Parsons, a young student at the Andover Theological Seminary, wrote in his diary before answering himself: "Reason, religion forbids."[37] Despite a common American patriotism that included elements of millennialist political religion, there was a break between Americans who believed in the untouchable dignity and equal rights of the Indians, Jews, African Americans, and whites, and those who did not. Sensitivity to and knowledge of host cultures had a high standing in the ABCFM, though it thought these cultures had, like any culture, to be challenged by the Gospel. American overseas missionaries of the nineteenth century were mostly graduates from or had begun their studies at universities soon to become prestigious, such as Harvard, Yale, and Princeton; they formed an intellectual and religious avant-garde. At the beginning they met considerable resistance within the churches and society to their "audacious projects" overseas.[38]

Millennialism was constitutive of the missionary project, and this, in turn, of American Christianity. Despite many strategic changes and interesting shifts, this main overseas mission lasted throughout the last Ottoman century (1820s to 1910s). The missionaries' performance supported a Christian identity and fed a belief at home that, without this mission, would have risked becoming a feeble credo and empty millennium talk. "Millennium; a term denoting, in its popular sense, a future felicitous state of the church and the world of a thousand years' duration, of which, while every one has some vague anticipation, almost no one has any clear and well-defined conception. No phraseology in prayer, in preaching, in the religious essay, or in the monthly-concert address is more common than that of millennial state, millennial reign, millennial purity, millennial glory, etc.," George Bush, a critic of millennialism and antirestorationist, wrote in 1832.[39]

"American Soul" and Indians, "Remnants of Ancient Israel"

A dark stain and serious challenge to the early missionary community was the treatment of the Indians in the United States. These native Americans were in a significant way the Orientals within one's own society, those who fundamentally questioned the American project because they lived another way and according to a different rhythm of life. For the early ABCFM, in particular for Jeremiah Evarts, its secretary in 1821–1831, dealings with the native Indians were the decisive evangelical test for the young U.S. society. In 1838–1839, significant parts of the Indian tribe of the Cherokees in northern Georgia and South Carolina were forcibly relocated, some of them in manacles. Around four thousand of approximately sixteen thousand relocated people died during the 116-day forced journey to "unorganized territory" west of Missouri, now Oklahoma, at a distance of around 621 miles. This was the so-called Trail of Tears, the particularly deadly archetype of several Indian removals from Florida, Georgia, Alabama, South Carolina, and Mississippi in the 1830s. It concerned about one hundred thousand Indians, of whom many thousands died; many more could not cope with the trauma and began a life of misery and alcoholism that was to last for generations.

The Indian Removal Act of May 28, 1830, had authorized the government to grant Indian tribes western prairie land in exchange for their territories, especially in the Southeast. The Removal Act was a departure from the policy of respecting the established rights of the Indians. Former general Andrew Jackson, the seventh U.S. president (1828–1836), implemented Indian removal as a top priority of his presidency. He is regarded as the man who established modern mass democracy combined with strong popular presidency in the United States. Jackson had experienced the American Revolution and was a military hero, having crushed the Indian tribe of the Creeks in 1813–1814. He perceived the Indians as erratic, inferior to the white settlers, and a threat to the national integrity of the young state. This threat was all the more critical in Jackson's eyes as many tribes had believed Great Britain was more likely to respect Indian property and had therefore been on the "wrong side" during the American Revolution and its wars. Indian attacks were a hard reality for many settlers already before and after these wars. Settler militias, in turn, over which governors had only partial control, were mostly rapacious and brutal. They ultimately proved to be a major instrument in hastening Indian removal.[40]

The Trail of Tears involved a tribe among the so-called Five Civilized Tribes. The Cherokees had managed to adapt their way of life in many respects to that of the white men, including, in some instances, slavery. They introduced European know-how, were successful farmers, formed a tribal government modeled on the U.S. government, developed an alphabet for their own Iroquoian language in 1821, and very quickly became literate.[41] Three aspects proved to be relevant factors of Cherokee removal: their regional autonomy, their wealth in terms of cultivable land and gold, and their success in finding their own, semiautonomous path in modern America. Jackson's Indianophobia and his fear of the secession of southern states if he opposed them was combined with the expansive greed of white Georgia in the 1820s and 1830s; with Georgia's will to be the only master of the territory; the pressure of its settlers; and the suggestive suspicion that the Cherokees were a fifth column and the missionaries to the Cherokees, agents of the North.[42] In December 1828, just after Andrew Jackson's election, the state of Georgia extended its jurisdiction to Cherokee land, on which gold had been discovered. This land, belonging to the Cherokees according to a treaty, was now mapped out for distribution to white citizens of Georgia. In (not only retrospectively) racist terms, the new Georgian jurisdiction forbade, among other discriminations, Indians to be "a witness or party in any suit where a white man should be defendant," or any contract between a white man and an Indian without testimony of two white witnesses. The purpose was to "render life in their own land intolerable to the Cherokee" and plunder them, as the anthropologist James Mooney (1861–1921) stated.[43] All this happened in the years before the final Trail of Tears. President Jackson feared that "independent, sovereign Indian nations would prove easy prey for manipulation by hostile powers." Anachronistically or not, removal was, in his view, "the only way to safeguard the Constitution of the United States and the nation's survival," historian Sean Wilentz states in his recent book on Jackson.[44]

Beside acts of individual and collective Indian resistance, a major obstacle to removal both on the local and the national level was the ABCFM. It had begun its work among the Cherokees in 1816, six years after the society's foundation in Boston in 1810 and three years before it sent its first missionaries to the Ottoman Empire. Identifying with the marginalized and oppressed, the early ABCFM's American Indian mission founded churches and schools "in the wilderness." When, in 1818, the Cherokees negotiated a new treaty "giving up a part of their ancestral domains," the ABCFM secretary "hurried to Washington and helped insure the inclusion of a clause granting the Indians perpetual rights to their remaining tracts in the South."[45] After an initial policy of assimilation especially to the English language, which they thought would help the Indians survive, the missionaries adopted a more integrative approach. They promoted the vernaculars and a bilingual Cherokee-English newspaper. They attempted to bring the Indians the best they had, or believed to have and to know. Since the Cherokees shared in this best, they were equals according to not only the abstract principle of human equality but also the intimate belief in the Gospel.

In a significant way, however, Indians and other nonwhites remained the "others" of American society. For the ABCFM, race and culture could not be a factor of discrimination; material envy, certainly not. The Gospel was unambiguous in these respects. The settlers' identification with old Israel, however, had been leading to ambiguous attitudes. The Cherokees' visible "progress in civilization" and acquisition of wealth spoke against all those who despised Indians as inferior, ABCFM representatives argued. Against prejudices among many Yankees, the ABCFM defended marriages between whites and Indians in the 1820s. For Jeremiah Evarts, the leading ABCFM secretary in 1821–1831 and an American patriot, American society was anti-Christian if it repressed and excluded the Indians.

More difficult than the struggle for mixed marriages was what Evarts considered to be the decisive test of the American project: to resist forcible Indian removal. Together with the missionaries on the ground, sympathetic publishers in New England, and some politicians in Washington, Evarts led an extensive fight against the removal policy of the Jackson administration after 1828—for Evarts, a struggle "for the soul of America." Under the pseudonym of William Penn, he wrote a series of articles that were printed by several papers and cited in congressional debates.[46] Despite these efforts, the Congress passed Jackson's bill for Indian removal in May 1830. Evarts nevertheless continued the struggle. "The people of the United States are bound to regard the Cherokees and other Indians, as men; as human beings, entitled to receive the same treatment as Englishmen, Frenchmen, or ourselves, would be entitled in the same circumstances. Here is the only weak place in their cause. They are not treated as men; and if they are finally ejected from their patrimonial inheritance by arbitrary and unrighteous power, the people of the United States will be impeached," he wrote in one of his last essays of November 1830.[47] Evarts died, exhausted, in May 1831.

At the end of 1830, Cherokees and missionaries held a meeting at Cherokee New Echota and adopted resolutions against removal. Staying on Cherokee territory without permission from Georgian authorities, the ABCFM missionaries Samuel Worcester and Elizur Butler were imprisoned. The ABCFM and those it had won for its cause in Washington, D.C., supported their appeal to the Supreme Court. On 3 March 1832, Chief Justice John Marshall declared the Cherokee Nation to be a distinct community outside the jurisdiction of the state of Georgia and ordered the prisoners dismissed from indictments.[48] Despite the Supreme Court, however, Jackson favored Georgia and wanted removal. Understanding this, the missionaries recognized their cause as lost, at least in the terms in which they had fought it until then, and did not back those Indians who opted for armed resistance. These Indians went on to kill the representatives of a minority Cherokee faction that had finally signed the pro-removal New Echota Treaty of 1835. The majority of the Cherokees remained in passive resistance.

"The soldiers came and took us from home," said a Cherokee woman recalling the eve of the Trail in autumn 1837:

> They first surrounded our house and they took the mare while we were at work in the fields and they drove us out of doors and did not permit us to take anything with us not even a second change of clothes, only the clothes we had on, and they shut the doors after they turned us out. They would not permit any of us to enter the house to get any clothing but drove us off to a fort that was built at New Echota. They kept us in the fort about three days and then marched us to Ross's Landing.[49]

The main agent of the relocation itself was the army. During the Trail of Tears the missionaries accompanied the deportees and rebuilt missionary stations in the West. But the deportation had broken the enthusiasm of a creative Cherokee renaissance in their homeland, and the ABCFM's previous fervor for Indians waned—the more so as the political commitment against removal and the acceptance of mixed marriages had not pleased all supporters of the ABCFM.

The Cherokee mission, and with it the vision of a modern, prosperous, self-determined future for that part of U.S. society on its ancestral soil, had been a crucial issue for the missionary community. This vision failed, however, and with it a particularly sensitive test of American millennialism in the United States. "This local fiasco was an omen of national things to come," concludes the American historian Ussama Makdisi in his recent book. "Andrew Jackson's campaigns against the Creeks and Seminoles, and the agitation by Georgia for the dispossession of the Indians, clearly anticipated the callous systematic expulsions of eastern Indians formalized by the Indian Removal Act, and with it the evisceration of an original American Board ideal to redeem America through its evangelization of the Indians."[50]

More than ever, it was clear that redemption—a substantial reign of Jesus on American soil including all people on the ground—was not to be realized in the United States. Missionaries to the Indians from the ABCFM and other organizations began to adapt more to the American mainstream and the exigencies of interior politics in accordance with the Bureau of Indian Affairs. "The Indian children are taught to speak English, taught the manners and ways of the whites, in a word: Americanized," stated a report of this bureau in 1882.[51] The dominant Christian civilizing mission explicitly included the destruction of Indian religious heritage. This was now far removed from the more interactive and integrative approach of the 1820s.

The painful Indian removal of the 1830s made those missionaries who were critical about Americanizing people—as was the ABCFM in general during the first half of the nineteenth century—focus even more on work overseas, in particular in the Ottoman world. "Going east," they believed, was their call, not "going west." The ideology of manifest destiny, which emerged in the 1840s, called to colonize the American West. Its emergence coincided with the dynamics of the California Gold Rush. This outburst of greed destroyed the very different rhythm of life Johann August Sutter had established in his large agricultural settlements together with native Indians and white settlers in the Sacramento Valley.

Overseas, the 1830s marked the beginning of the Ottoman reform period, or Tanzimat (1839–1876). Its prominent leader was the young sultan Abdulmejid, on whom the missionaries now set more hopes than on President Jackson, who had toughly taught the missionaries that the reign of Jesus was not of his American world. This lesson, however, would partly be forgotten. The missionaries did not consistently scrutinize their own home country as a seriously incomplete and deeply questionable, though impressive and instructive, project. Manifest dysfunctions of the Ottoman state and the technological backwardness of the Ottoman world also tended to induce a fallacious feeling of superiority in terms of religion and culture. Instead of fresh, open, and creative encounters, missionaries were tempted to impose their Calvinistic piety on the Near East and to consider, despite better wisdom, American culture as singular, exceptional, and self-sustaining.

CHAPTER 2

A Quest for "Zion" and Peace on Earth

Mission to the Bible Lands

At the beginning of the twentieth century, a London paper aptly observed that, despite the far stronger British presence in the eastern Mediterranean world, "the American people are more generally and keenly interested in Turkish affairs than are the people of Great Britain," relating this to the work of American missionaries in the Near East.[1]

The initial strategy of the American missionaries had followed the belief in the restoration of the Jews to Jesus and to Palestine. This Palestine-centric approach was soon replaced by an Armenia-centric strategy of "Christianity revived in Asia Minor," the main American missionary strategy in the Ottoman world before 1908. The somewhat romantic and utopian aspect of Israel's restoration made room for reassessed priorities according to experiences and observations on the ground. The Jews on the ground were not as accessible as were the Oriental Christians, in particular the Armenians. The Jews did not appear to be the first victims of injustice in the Old World, as had commonly been believed in early-nineteenth-century New England. The situation of the Armenians appeared clearly to be more alarming in the late nineteenth century; anti-Armenian pogroms of a far larger scale took place than even the anti-Jewish pogroms in czarist Russia. Bible translation, publishing, and school work for Armenian groups now prevailed. Beside the Oriental Christians, heterodox Muslims, particularly Anatolian Alevis, who could be accessed relatively easily, were counted as natives to become protagonists of the Kingdom to come. Despite important shifts and changes during the nineteenth century, the optimistic postmillennialist stance of the American missionary enterprise remained valid. Optimism prevailed in particular when Sultan Abdulmejid approved of the establishment of an Ottoman Protestant community (*millet*) and of modern reforms of all religious communities in his empire.

The harsh reaction of the Ottoman authorities to missionary contacts with Alevis (heterodox Muslims) and other setbacks during the second half of the Tanzimat, however, reconfirmed old American convictions that Muslim power could not be reformed. Protestantism, as represented by the ABCFM, was to become a main ideological enemy in the eyes of the post-Tanzimat Sultan Abdulhamid II, because it not only empowered the Oriental Christians but was also an important factor in the renaissance of Armenian, Syriac, and Alevi self-consciousness. For Abdulhamid, who wanted to reempower the *millet-i hâkime,* the ruling group of the Sunni Muslims, in order to strengthen the threatened empire, the missionary work was fundamentally subversive. Before examining the agency and interactions of American missionaries in the pre–Young Turk Ottoman world, however, we look at nonmissionary Ottoman-American relations.

The Ottoman Empire and the United States in the Nineteenth Century

For the Ottomans and the Ottoman government, the United States was *terra incognita,* not the land of dreams and symbol of progress and happiness that it became for late Ottomans and post-Ottomans from the late nineteenth century onward. America had never been a goal of Ottoman expansion, either symbolically or territorially. Since the eighteenth century in any case, the Red or Golden Apple, the early Ottoman symbol for going beyond the frontiers, for desiring and appropriating foreign Christian spaces, had lost its appeal. In vain had sultans of the fifteenth and sixteenth centuries desired to possess the seemingly weak and divided Western Europe that then turned overseas and expanded globally—a move from which the Muslim power was excluded.[2] On 9 November 1800, when an American vessel landed for the first time in Istanbul, there was general astonishment. A messenger of the Ottoman government asked whether America was in the "new world" beyond the Atlantic. The officials knew neither the location nor the flag of the United States. Before 1830, the Ottoman state was not interested in establishing official relations with that faraway, unknown country. Ottoman-American commerce in 1830 thus was more or less unilateral: the United States imported goods for $414,392 but exported for only $74,263.[3]

Since the late eighteenth century, the Ottoman political elite had been living with a feeling of crisis and deficiency, after having cultivated for centuries a blunt consciousness of superiority vis-à-vis the West. Now it turned to the European, not American, example of force and progress, in particular to France, in order to reorganize itself and gain new strength. Throughout the Tanzimat, the emphasis remained on army reform and administrative centralization. Ideologically, many of the reformers turned at the same time to what they believed to be the Ottoman heyday, the sixteenth century, and its Sunnitization of the state. In 1826 the strong reform sultan Mahmud II (1785–1839) destroyed the traditional elite corps, the Janissaries, who had resisted change and were religiously suspicious because tied to the Bektashis. This heterodox and specifically Ottoman order was also suppressed. With typical euphemism, the massacre of 1826 was officially called "Auspicious Event" (*Vak'a-i Hayriye*).[4]

After failed attempts in the 1790s, the United States tried again to establish diplomatic relations with the Ottoman state in the 1820s. The Greek war of independence in 1821–1830 temporarily made Britain, protector of the Ottomans since Napoleon Bonaparte, the sultan's adversary. Therefore, the sultan needed a new ally and military assistance and turned to the United States. Ottoman-American negotiations resulted in the Commercial and Naval Treaty of 1830.[5] Commercially, the United States now enjoyed the same status as the European powers. Diplomatically, the treaty paved the way for the establishment of consular services. Like most Europeans, Americans living in the Ottoman Empire enjoyed so-called capitulations: they were exempt from certain taxes, and American consuls, not Ottoman courts, took care of most of their legal matters. Conflicts would arise when former Ottoman subjects, mostly non-Muslim, naturalized Americans, returned to the Near East, or when, from the late nineteenth century onward, Eastern European Jews immigrated to Palestine via the United States.

In 1831, Captain (Commodore) David Porter, the first American chargé d'affaires after the treaty was signed, took office in Istanbul, where he stood in close relationship with the early missionaries.[6] A secret article of the treaty of 1830 planned the construction of warships for the Ottoman Empire, but this was not endorsed by the Senate. Thus there was no step toward a special relationship with the extra-European power, as Sultan Mahmud II had hoped. The political situation in his empire changed dramatically when the troops of the Egyptian khedive (viceroy) Muhammed Ali conquered Ottoman Syria in 1832, threatening Anatolia and the Ottoman capital. This authoritarian, modernist restorer of Ottoman Egypt had gained power following the French withdrawal from Egypt at the beginning of the nineteenth century.

The French finally supported this promising Ottoman-Egyptian reformer, while Britain again took on the role of a protector of the sultan in the 1830s. He was obliged, however, to accept free access of British products and to declare reforms in his empire. Against this backdrop, the Ottoman reform period (Tanzimat) began in 1839, when Mahmud II died and was succeeded by Abdulmejid. Abdulmejid promised in the founding declaration of the Tanzimat, the *Hatt-ı Şerîf* of Gülhane, "perfect security for life, honor, and fortune." This comprised a regular tax system and a system for the levying of troops that was intended to rectify, once for all, the widespread public irregularities and insecurities. Ideologically, the *Hatt-ı Şerîf* looked back to the "former strength and prosperity" of the empire and invoked the "glorious precepts of the Koran" and the "support of our prophet" Muhammad, as a contemporary ABCFM missionary rightly observed.[7] Muhammed Ali had ceded in 1839 to a muscled British ultimatum backed by Russia, Prussia, and Austria-Hungary.

The United States remained, until 1917, outside the game. American diplomacy would not be ready to join in when Sultan Abdulhamid II, after the British invasion of Egypt in 1882, requested American mediation in the conflict. The same was true in a different constellation, when, in 1896, Britain called for American participation in concerted political efforts toward the Ottoman government, which it held responsible for the large-scale anti-Armenian massacres of 1894–1896. Yet, despite political abstinence, Ottoman-American commerce grew. A renewed Treaty of Commerce and Navigation was concluded in 1864. Imports from the Ottoman Empire always exceeded American exports, but these too grew. In the late nineteenth century, however, exports suffered from the severe competition of the European powers and the absence of strong American diplomacy. Not until the end of the century did U.S. diplomacy begin to struggle more seriously for its economic interests in the huge Ottoman world. This new policy of commercial diplomacy led to increased American exports, and in 1906, a U.S. embassy was at last established in Istanbul. Nevertheless, missionaries, not traders or diplomats, remained the main American players in the Ottoman world until the early twentieth century.[8]

Beginning a Mission to Palestine

The restorationist factor and the orientation toward the Ottoman world had given the old American millennialism strong new impulses; it had broken the fixation on North America as the promised land and on the Americans as the new Israelites. For the first time, it led to a concrete encounter between the Puritan tradition of New England and the Islamic world. Restoration of Israel was important, but it was not the mission's only motivation. The American mission followed a general move toward the millennium and parousia, however these would ultimately be realized. Accordingly, the American Turkey Mission was open to readjusted strategies, though without renouncing the original ideas of the early nineteenth century.

Levi Parsons and Pliny Fisk, both twenty-seven years old and graduates from the Theological Seminary at Andover, Massachusetts ("which orthodox Congregationalists had begun as a counter to Unitarian influence at Harvard College"),[9] were, in 1819, the ABCFM's first missionaries to the Near East. At a meeting held at Andover in fall 1818, the Prudential Committee of the ABCFM had requested the young men to prepare for such a mission.[10] In the months before his departure, Parsons desired "to keep my attention fixed exclusively on the mission to Judea; to employ every moment, to engage every feeling for a spiritual crusade to the Holy Land," as he wrote in his diary. The task at hand was "to aid the children of Israel on their way to Zion." But as the soldier in the army of Israel that he perceived himself to be, he had distressing conflicts of mind when he compared himself to self-confident young Americans who did not worry about prophetic wisdom. "The boldness and fortitude of the men of this world are sufficient to put to shame the disciples of Jesus. . . . The sinner in his opposition to the Gospel laughs at difficulties, and moves forward with unyielding resolution. Not so with Christians. Slothful, covetous and timorous, they forget their high standing in the armies of Israel." To the young missionary, many things were not clear at all, and could not be. A few weeks before his departure, Parsons entrusted to his diary that "I find many predictions, many precious promises; yet my mind remains in darkness," and that he needed "more perfect knowledge of his [God's] revealed will in regard to the Jews."[11]

In those months Parsons had the opportunity of preaching to American natives. Interestingly, an Indian chief alluded to the Puritan myth, still spread in the mission to the American natives, that they might be the remnants of the ten lost tribes of ancient Israel. (The hopeful recovering of the lost tribes, an element of the restoration myth, was to play a role among pioneering missionaries in the Levant.)[12] The chief gave Parsons an oral message to deliver to "the Jews, their forefathers in Jerusalem." In response to those Americans who believed the natives to be incurably inferior in terms of race, mind, and civilization, and therefore to be repressed, Parsons and the ABCFM pointed to the Gospel and what they considered the fruit of mission, "the intellectual, moral and spiritual improvement of the Indians, especially of their children and youth, wherever they have enjoyed the benefit of the instructions of missionaries."[13]

On 31 October 1819, just before their departure, Fisk and Parsons preached in the overcrowded Park Street Church in Boston: Fisk on "The Holy Land: An Interesting Field of Missionary Enterprise," and Parsons on "The Dereliction and Restoration of the Jews." The sermons reflected the religious and intellectual socialization of both men, recalling Hannah Adams's writings, but they were more affirmative. "Admit that the Jews are to be restored to their own land. . . . Destroy, then, the Ottoman Empire, and nothing but a miracle would prevent their immediate return from the four winds of heaven. . . . Their return will be welcomed with universal rejoicing."[14] Parsons meant this literally, as future real history, not figuratively. His vision combined the restoration of the Jews and the access to power of the slain Lamb, a metaphor for Jesus. These were two sides of the same coin of the salvatory, prophetic future. "The ransomed Jew, as he ascends the hill of Zion, will mingle his songs with the whole Church militant and triumphant, saying, Worthy is the Lamb that was slain to receive power," Parsons preached. The undiminished distinctiveness of the Jews, despite persecution both under Christian and Muslim dominion, confirmed the veracity of the universal prophetic perspective of which the Jews were a manifest monument. "So long as Mussulmauns [Muslims] consider it a *duty* to persecute them, every artifice will be employed to increase their wretchedness, and to add horror to despair itself. . . . And while one judgment has followed another in rapid succession; judgments which must have blotted out the *existence* of any *other* nation under heaven, the children of Israel have been continued by an invisible hand, as a standing monument of the veracity of God."[15] By benevolently working for the restoration of the Jews, the missionaries gave them back something of the amazing grace they had received through the Gospel, the finest legacy of old Israel, Parsons argued.[16]

In a similar restorationist vein were the instructions of the Prudential Committee to the missionaries. The committee emphasized the millennial dawn and defined the missionaries' work as preparatory to and an agency of the coming Kingdom:

> The Jews have been for ages an awful sign to the world. But the period of their tremendous dereliction, and of the severity of God, is drawing to a close. You are to lift up an ensign to them, that they may *return and seek the Lord their god and David their king.* They will return. The word of promise is sure;—and the accomplishment of it will be as life from the dead to the Gentile world. The day is at hand. The signal movements of the age indicate its dawn.—It may be your privilege to prepare the way of the Lord. . . . He is your Leader

> and Commander. That Land belongs to Him. There again he will establish his throne, and will reign from sea to sea and from the river to the ends of the world.[17]

As these words show, the establishment of the reign of Jesus, the sole owner of Palestine and soon to be acclaimed king of Jewish Israel, stood in the very center of the worship and instructions that inaugurated the American Near Eastern mission.

The view of the Muslims, articulated on the same occasion, was partly positive in a dogmatic perspective and wholly negative in a historical one. In the eyes of the second missionary to Palestine, Pliny Fisk, they "assert the unity of God, the immortality of the soul, and future rewards and punishments. They have, indeed, much of truth in their system: but their customs, established by the usage of centuries, the despotic nature of their government, the prominent articles of their faith, and the very genius and spirit of their religion, shield the Mahommedans almost impenetrably from the influence of Christianity."[18] The first American missionaries believed that the Muslims had "much of truth in their system" and that they were to be won over for, not ruled out by, the Kingdom. At the same time, Islam was little known to them. It represented for Americans both backwardness with regard to the Enlightenment and depravation in religion, politics, and culture. They knew generalities about Muslim religion and history; they did not ignore the medieval role of Muslim civilization for philosophy and science, when "Christendom was involved in darkness and ignorance," as wrote Hannah Adams. All religion, however, even if monotheist, that did not promote the access to power of the "Lamb" but maintained religious dependencies was vain and void, according to Revelation as read by the missionary community. Another ABCFM member, the Yale president Timothy Dwight, stated in 1813 that "the Romish cathedral, the mosque, and the pagoda, shall not have one stone left upon another, which shall not be thrown down."[19] The missionary community knew little about Muslim eschatology and seems not to have studied Ignatius Mouradja d'Ohsson's insightful *Tableau général de l'empire othoman* of 1788, which was based on Ottoman sources and conveyed a pro-Ottoman argument. Its erudite author, an Ottoman Catholic Armenian and dragoman of the Swedish embassy, largely dealt with religion, including the second coming of Jesus as expected by Muslim teachers: "The *imams* have subordinated this man-god [Jesus] to his [Muhammad's] priestly authority declaring him his vicar and last of the universal caliphs who will come at the end of the times in order to exercise in his name the rights of the priesthood and the supreme power upon all the peoples of the earth."[20]

Fragile First Experiences

Pliny Fisk and Levy Parsons sailed on 3 November 1819 to Smyrna, whence they undertook travels to Greece, Egypt, Palestine, and Syria. Parsons died, ill and exhausted, as early as 1822 in Alexandria, Egypt. Fisk settled in Beirut in 1825 and died the same year, also from fever. This was a painful and modest beginning, compared with the goals; "the children of Israel" in particular were still far from being led "to the Saviour of the world" in the Holy Land.[21] To a large extent, the young missionaries' expectations remained unfulfilled. Nonetheless, important first encounters, experiences, and acquaintances were made and reported to Boston.

Fisk's and Parsons's steps on the ground were fragile, tentative, exploratory. English missionaries from the Church Missionary Society (CMS) and the London Missionary Society took care of the inexperienced young Americans after they arrived in Malta at the end of 1819. The mid-nineteenth-century Catholic writer Thomas W. Marshall called Malta, a British crown colony since 1814, "a symbol of Anglo-Saxon might, which . . . has been for more than a quarter of a century the head-quarters of Protestantism in the Levant. Nearly forty years ago Mr. Jowett [of the CMS] had recommended it to English missionary societies as a centre for their operations . . . for thirty years an eruption of tracts and Bibles has flowed out of Malta, and covered both shores of the Mediterranean."[22] In the 1820s, Malta was a center and a refuge for American missionaries on their way to the Near East. To the two newcomers, the American consul declared the Ottoman Empire to be "rapidly decaying" and stated that it "must fall." But Parsons remained skeptical. "We may desire to see this empire in ruins, and Zion triumphant, but our heavenly Father may appoint for us a very different portion."[23]

Arriving in Izmir in January 1820, Fisk and Parsons came for the first time in contact with the Ottoman world. They explored the city, its region, and its rich New Testamentary past. They saw everything more in terms of eschatological imminence than of biblical erudition, in which ABCFM members after them were to excel. Parsons was concerned, not to say obsessed, with prophecy, in particular with the book of Revelation, including its dark sides. "The time of slaying the witnesses is not yet arrived, the servants of God still prophecy in sackcloth. . . . The time will be short, the witnesses will rise, and the whole world yield to the dominion of Jesus." He asked "how to avoid the conclusion, that distresses far more aggravating than have yet been known, are in reverse for Zion."[24] Tied to the feeling of imminent catastrophe yielding "to the dominion of Jesus," his view of other people was informed by the fear that they were lost. "A Christian who possesses the smallest share of the spirit of primitive saints, must weep when he beholds this great city [Izmir] given to idolatry and to the power of a false prophet. . . . How certain their destruction!"[25] This young first American missionary to the Near East was, in contrast to those after him, overwhelmed by visions of destruction on the road toward redemption.

From the British, Fisk and Parsons learned the distribution of Bibles and tracts as a "method of doing good in Turkey," to "prepare the way for building the walls of Zion."[26] The young men's missionary strategy, as outlined in Boston on 31 October 1819, had been vague, open, and optimistically comprehensive. "Let the Mahommedans of Judea embrace Christianity, and they would with great ease diffuse it through the surrounding Mahommedan countries. Let the Jews of Judea embrace the Messiah, and they would with ease and efficacy make known to their brethren every where, that they had found Him of whom Moses in the law, and the Prophets did write. Let the Catholics of Judea learn the simplicity of the Gospel." Even if the focus of early mission was on the restoration of the Jews, the seminal idea that Oriental Christians should be made missionaries was present from the beginning. "Let the Greek and Armenian Christians add to what they now have of the true religion, such doctrines and feelings, as we may hope they will receive from reading the Bible. . . . It may be expected, that they will furnish some of the best of missionaries, and engage in effective measures for reviving knowledge and piety in all Western Asia."[27]

With a letter of recommendation from an Armenian merchant to Armenians in Jerusalem and Jaffa, Parsons left Izmir for Palestine, hoping to distribute there Bibles to pilgrims. "Jesus Christ holds an undisputed title to this land consecrated with his blood," wrote Parsons in February 1821 on his arrival in Jaffa.[28] Again, an apocalyptical prospect determined his feeling that contrasted with the more postmillennialist orientation of subsequent missionaries to Turkey:

> The prospect is, that Turkey must be drenched in blood. How terrible is God in arms. . . . To all who seek the prosperity of Zion, the present commotions will be viewed as the developments of those eternal counsels which secure all kingdoms to Christ. Since the illustrious days of the Apostles, there have never been more evident displays of the determination of God to visit and redeem these sacred shores. Let us admire and tremble and adore.[29]

He felt that Ottoman Turkey would soon end in blood.

Though Parsons repeatedly anticipated it in his diary, there was no concrete risk of his own martyrdom. In an existential and subjective sense, however, this young man was indeed sent out as "a lamb among wolves." Doubts and sickness, much more than open enemies, made him suffer and wish "to view death near."[30] The *Memoir of Levi Parsons, First Missionary to Palestine from the United States* can be read as evidence of both a deeply fragile and a highly significant first encounter of millennialist America and Ottoman Bible lands, one that led to religious limits and existential aporia but was nevertheless deeply desired.

Parsons died young and anxious, not "in a good old age, an old man and full of years" like successful biblical patriarchs. "How much Christians who are in health should pray for their brethren on a dying bed! I need many prayers to-day. I cry out in my distress," the young man wrote a few days before he died. "Shall I ever see Jesus as he is? Will Jesus make my dying bed? Let me not doubt." On his own "dying bed" in Alexandria, he complained "how dreadfully solemn" it was "to remain fixed between two worlds, between time and eternity, between a mortal and an immortal tabernacle!" To his brother L. he confessed that his "most bitter pangs, as I view eternity, arise from the thought of an *eternal* separation from *one* whom I have ever loved as my own soul. Farewell."[31]

The ABCFM presented Parsons as an offering of the American churches to the service of God and his death, as little heroism as lay in it, as a reason to rejoice. "Such a man the American churches sent forth as their first messenger of peace to the inhabitants of the Holy Land; as a pledge that they are bound to fulfill obligations long deferred;—as an offering of first fruits to the ancient seat of sacred learning and divine manifestations; an offering, as we have abundant reason to believe, 'well pleasing, acceptable to God,'" the ABCFM Annual Report for 1822 read. "Far, very far from our hearts be all murmuring or repining, on account of this early removal. Let us rather rejoice when we behold so bright a display of christian virtue."[32] Parsons was among the best "fruits" Christian America could give, the report continued; "his piety [was] child-like, ardent, equal; and his consecration to the divine master entire and universal." Whereas antiabsolutist, revolutionary Europe "killed" its fathers, there was no similar intergenerational break in early missionary America. A striking aspect of the pioneering Near East mission is the intergenerational confidence, the both trusting and creative obedience of the younger toward the elders. They were ready to be obedient martyrs of the Kingdom they and their spiritual fathers and mothers believed must be built.[33]

Armenians instead of Jews, Ottoman Reform instead of Fall

Fisk's and Parsons' experiences and encounters, letters and reports, were carefully studied in the ABCFM, and the mission accordingly adapted. Particularly satisfying encounters had been made with the Armenians. "To some Armenians, who made application for tracts, I said, 'perhaps some of my friends will pass through Armenia with bibles and tracts for sale.' 'We shall rejoice' they said, 'and all will rejoice, when they arrive,'" Parsons had reported when in Jerusalem in May 1821. "If a missionary could return with the pilgrims to Armenia, his trunks of books would pass without exciting any suspicion, and he would receive the greatest assistance from those who accompanied him. I earnestly hope that after the next Passover, some person will be prepared to undertake the interesting service of making known to the churches the moral state of Armenia."[34] The idea of Armenia as a missionary field had already been studied in American missionary circles in 1819 but had not been seen then as a priority.[35] In 1830–1831, however, Henry O. Dwight and Eli Smith were sent by the ABCFM to research the conditions of the Armenians and Syriac Christians in eastern Anatolia and in the neighboring regions of Georgia and Persia. Their report of more than seven hundred pages, published in 1833, formed the basis of knowledge for the missionary approach to those regions and their Christian inhabitants.[36] After his tour, Dwight joined William Goodell in Istanbul in 1832, and eighteen years later he published a work that documented the new strategy of *Christianity Revived in the East; or, A Narrative of the Work of God among the Armenians of Turkey.*[37] With the Armenians, the mission experienced a real spiritual encounter, because many Ottoman Armenians were already reorienting themselves spiritually and culturally. "The good work among the Armenians has been steadily advancing. . . . The work of regeneration has absolutely commenced," Goodell wrote in 1835. "We have seen nothing like this, nothing to be compared with it, since we left America, now almost thirteen years ago."[38]

The ABCFM strategy therefore changed in the 1830s; the conversion of Muslims and Jews was more or less abandoned, and the prospect became less apocalyptical. The "revival" of the Eastern Christians and their empowerment emerged as central issues. In contrast to the pragmatic and more success-oriented Americans, British and some German-speaking Christians remained loyal to the direct goal of Jewish restoration. The London Society for Promoting Christianity amongst the Jews, founded in 1809, had begun its work in Palestine in the 1820s, but it was able to settle in Jerusalem only after the Egyptian army had invaded Syria and established comparatively liberal rule. The society benefited from the foundation of a British vice consul in Jerusalem in 1839, among whose duties it was "to afford protection to the Jews generally."[39] The establishment of the Anglo-Prussian Protestant bishopric in 1842, by agreement of the king of Prussia and the British government, strengthened the London Society, whose infrastructure served as the basis of the bishopric in Jerusalem. Its first head was Michael Solomon Alexander, born in 1799 as a son of a rabbi in Posen. The opposition of the rabbis—the Ashkenazis even more than the Sephardis—to the mission and its successful hospital was fierce. The rabbis held economic power since they distributed the alms from which an important part of the Jewish community in Palestine lived. The London Society's men on the ground described the rabbis' rule as a slavery in spiritual, psychological, and economic terms.[40]

The Swiss missionary Samuel Gobat succeeded Alexander upon the latter's death in 1846. Gobat feared that the London Society and its milieu in Britain projected philo-Semitic wishes on a few potential Jewish converts instead of working where doors were open, in particular among Palestinian Arabs; Jewish reappropriation of Jesus' unique spiritual power was reserved for more eschatological days. Gobat readjusted the focus of the bishopric during his long period of office until his death in 1879. Among others, the influential school Talitha Kumi of the Kaiserswerther Diakonissen was founded in his time. Both missionary America after 1830 and the Anglo-Prussian bishopric under Gobat put the restoration in a more distant future. In the mid-nineteenth century, only a few pietist farmers, in particular from southern Germany, believed in the immediate "restoration of Israel and the coming of the Lord."[41] They settled faithfully in Palestine and considered it "a high honor to be their farmers and wine growers once the faithful Israelites [Jews] will be called priests of the Lord and servants of our God."[42] (Note the sharp spiritual contrast to Hitler's disfigured anti-Semitic "thousand-year empire.") Despite his readjustment, Gobat continued to hope that "Israel would be converted and restored, and that from this all peoples would be blessed." But he remained skeptical about conversions of Jews and refused to publish devotional stories of such conversions.[43]

From a different, but complementary, side, Hannah Arendt's bold analysis of British Prime Minister Disraeli sheds light on the ambivalent fascination of nineteenth-century Britain for the Bible, (the Jewish) race, salvation, and world dominion. This critical analysis is relevant also with regard to the United States of the late twentieth century (see Chapter 5). The "Holy Land mania" that arose in the United States in the second half of the nineteenth century was of a different but equally exoticizing character.[44] It stood in contrast to missionary faith and pragmatism, but it helped maintain a broad public interest in the Near East and Near Eastern mission and was a strong sign of the Near East's constitutive importance with regard to American religion and identity. "The East! The birth-place of history, the cradle of religion. There *was* Eden; and there is Ararat, Bethlehem, and Calvary. Jerusalem is the mother of us all. A home-feeling have we towards all the prominent places of Judea," wrote the Reverend William Adams emphatically in 1853, introducing a book by William Goodell. "Our hearts have an inalienable property in those localities, which are associated with our religion."[45]

The ABCFM missionary Goodell had arrived with his wife, Abigail, in Beirut in 1823, shortly after Fisk and Parsons. In 1831, they settled in Istanbul instead of Jerusalem. "When we left America, it was to go to Jerusalem. That was our destination; but we have never been there," Goodell wrote in a letter of March 1865, just before sailing back to America permanently. "Now we set our faces toward the New Jerusalem, and I hope we shall not fail of arriving there."[46] Successfully settled in Istanbul as a father, preacher, and translator, he had a different life experience and a less apocalyptical view of history than Parsons. He became a translator of the Bible into Armeno-Turkish (Turkish with Armenian letters). Not the revolution, but the renovation of the Ottoman world; not the sociopolitical remaking of the Ottoman world as a whole, and "in blood," as Parsons had written, but its spiritual empowerment from within, by its Christians, stood before his eyes. "But those dark times [1820s] have passed away, and can hardly be expected to return. The sun is up at Constantinople, and, with the enlightened policy of the present reigning Emperor [Abdulmejid I], nobody can make it again dark," he wrote in 1853.[47] The spirit of political and legal reform prevailing during the first half of the Tanzimat, from 1839 until 1860 or so, changed the ABCFM's attitude toward Ottoman power. The initial view of Muslim power was not fundamentally revised, but hopes were set on the Tanzimat and pioneering work undertaken. Enterprising men and women made pragmatic use of the doors opened by the Tanzimat, founded many mission stations and important institutions, and penetrated eastern Asia Minor in the 1840s and 1850s. Beside teaching and preaching, like his brother in faith Goodell, Henry Dwight began to edit in Istanbul in 1855 *Avedaper* ("Bringer of Good News"), a weekly religious newspaper in the Armenian language.[48]

By the mid-nineteenth century, not Jerusalem, Palestine, and the Jews but Istanbul, Asia Minor, and the Armenians were the primary focus of the ABCFM. When in 1870 it gave up Syria to the new American Board of Foreign Missions of the Presbyterian Church (ABFMPC), the ABCFM abandoned only a fraction of what it had acquired while in Asia Minor.[49] A revised prophetic vision was not elaborated. Instead of the conversion of Jews and Muslims, which had proved to be infeasible, the most hope was set on "Christianity revived in the East," above all on the "great work of reform" among the Armenians. They were the keystone of the postrestorationist, revivalist strategy that was now to serve as a lever for the reform of the Ottoman system. The fall of Islam, in the sense of the Ottoman Empire, was no longer a desired perspective; the goal was now reform. This was to take place comprehensively via the "spiritual revival" of the Oriental Christians and a general democratization. The example of the new Protestant community (*millet*) of 1847, backed by the Protestant International, its exemplary constitution of 1856, and the constitutional dynamics afterward in the Ottoman Empire, would, the missionaries hoped, ring in a general democratization.

Not surprisingly, the traditional churches, challenged by a small but dynamic and self-confident Protestant competition, felt threatened. The establishment of a separate Protestant *millet* in 1847, confirmed by imperial edict in 1850, was the initially unintended result of the ABCFM's related work in Istanbul. The heads of the *Rûm* (Greek Orthodox) and Armenian Apostolic (or, as called in Ottoman sources, Gregorian) mother churches had reacted vigorously against the ABCFM's strategy of revival and had banned those who adhered to the Protestant teaching. Therefore, the Protestants needed their own community, both in ecclesiastical and in civil terms. After 1850, the missionaries drafted a democratic constitution for the new Protestant *millet,* which they wished to be modern and seminal for the Ottoman society.[50]

A Seminal *Millet* Reform?

Shortly after the Young Turkish revolution of 1908, the Armenian American author Leon Arpee wrote that "free government in Turkey now promises to be a permanent thing." He asserted that when "the history of the regeneration of Turkey is written, a large place will be given to the Armenians of that Empire."[51] He believed the reorganization of their *millet* in the preceding decades to have led to a dynamism that proved seminal for the whole empire.

After the close of the Greek war of independence and the Ottoman-Russian war, French and Austrian diplomacy had pressed for the return of exiles and the establishment of a separate Catholic *millet;* in 1828, after the battle of Navarino, the Ottoman Catholics had been persecuted and relocated from Istanbul. The establishment of the *Katolik milleti* in 1831 was, however, nothing new with regard to the contents of the *millet* itself. The head of the *millet* was again a patriarch (a separate civil head existed only until 1846), the organization itself hierarchical and clerical. In this respect, the establishment of the *Protestan milleti* was different and innovative. Again, as in 1831, diplomatic pressure, this time from the British ambassador Stratford Canning, paved the way for the establishment. Canning stood in a close and protective relationship with William Goodell and the small missionary Protestant community. In 1854, the Protestants in Istanbul drew up the Protestant Constitution, or *Nizamname,* that was put into force just after the proclamation of the Reform Edict (*Islahat Fermanı* or *Hatt-ı Hümayun*) in 1856. The Reform Edict made official the hitherto largely informal *millet* system[52] and, interestingly, demanded its reform toward a modern representative system for which, implicitly, the *Protestan milleti* had set the model. In the Reform Edict we read:

> All the privileges and spiritual immunities granted by my [Abdülmecid I's] ancestors . . . to all Christian communities or other non-Muslim persuasions, established in my empire under my protection, shall be confirmed and maintained. . . . The temporal administration of the Christian or other non-Muslim communities shall, however, be placed under the safeguard of an assembly to be chosen from among the members, both ecclesiastics and laymen, of the said communities.[53]

The modernization of the *millet* interestingly accompanied the effort to create suprareligious equality and commonality. The edict therefore often used religiously neutral notions to designate the subjects of the empire.[54] This has led me to call the political thought of the Tanzimat a notable attempt toward an egalitarian ethno-religious plurality, instead of the traditional hierarchical plurality.[55] The thought was probably too avant-garde to be fully implemented at that time. The Ottoman reformers as well as Sunni Muslims in general were too closely attached to their imperial tradition. Even if they may have misread their sources, some reformers, in particular the Young Ottomans, a small group of intellectuals, made sincere efforts to reconcile early Islam and the idea of representative government.[56] The reality of the nineteenth century, however, was that Christian, not Muslim, Ottomans excelled in applying that idea, and instead of powerful modern synergies, polarization and destructive envy resulted in the Ottoman society.

Compared to all other *millets,* that of the Protestants was a grassroots organization, even if it profited from American missionary inspiration and British diplomatic protection. This grassroots feature and a strongly transnational character explain important differences from the "national" *millets* dominated by religious hierarchies. Also, compared with the pre-Tanzimat shape of the *Katolik milleti,* the constitution of the *Protestan milleti* twenty-five years later breathed a liberal and democratic air. No patriarch headed the Protestant *millet,* only a civil agent, or *vekil* of Ottoman nationality. He, like the other employees of the *Protestan milleti*'s central organization, was elected each year by an assembly of representatives of the local Protestant groups. The most salient point is the separation of church and civil *millet.* A person who claimed membership in the *Protestan milleti* was not necessarily a member of any Protestant ecclesiastical organization yet benefited from the care of the *millet* organization and the protection of the Ottoman government. In the traditional *millet,* there had never been a separation of *millet* and church membership. Anyone who renounced the church renounced the *millet.* The Protestants therefore believed that the separation ensured a new freedom of conscience in religious matters. According to Henry Dwight in 1860, "A silent, though deep and thorough revolution is going on in the minds of the Armenian people in regard to their civil rights." Copies of the *Protestan milleti*'s constitution were circulated throughout the country in the Armenian and Ottoman languages.[57]

Even if being *Prote* (Protestant) was regarded by many Muslims and non-Muslims as opprobrious, heretical, and subversive, both in the capital and the provinces, modernity, freedom, and progress were broadly associated by Muslims and non-Muslims alike with American Protestant agency in the second half of the nineteenth century. The positive image, particularly in the countryside, was due to the missionary schools, hospitals, and factories. *Prote* and progress also meant a new, much more independent and public role for girls, whom the missionaries provided with a similar education to the boys. Moreover, as "Bible women"—teachers, nurses, and so on—they could take on roles outside the family and beyond traditional patterns, but also beyond new nationalist trends. "Those of the village who embraced Protestantism were pulled away from Armenianism. . . . Protestants were no longer Armenians; they were 'Prod,' illegitimate, apostate," complained a non-Protestant Armenian from the village Parchanj in the province of Mamuretülaziz.[58]

The traditional *Ermeni milleti,* called Gregorian according to St. Gregor the Illuminator, the spiritual father of the Armenian church, was numerically much more important than the *Protestan milleti.* The Reform Edict, again, formed the basis of its famous National Constitution, or *Statut organique* or *Nizamname* of 1860, confirmed by imperial edict in 1863. The Reform Edict was also the basis for a similar reorganization of the other two non-Muslim *millets,* the *Rûm* and the small Jewish *millet.* These new *millet* constitutions form the immediate background for the first Ottoman Constitution of 1876.[59] Thus, at the high noon of the Tanzimat, we observe a democratic reorganization of the *millet* system approved by both the Ottoman state and new, more democratic Armenian elites. These had won over the oligarchy of the *amira,* or aristocracy, of the eighteenth and the first half of the nineteenth centuries. In the Armenian Constitution we read, "[Principle] 5. The administration [of the Armenian community] . . . must be representative. 6. The foundation of representative government is the principle of rights and obligation, or the principle of equity. The authority of such government is derived from the majority of votes, which is the principle of legitimacy." The Armenian Constitution vested the entire administrative power of the community, both civil and ecclesiastical, in a representative body chosen by popular vote, as was already the case for the Protestants. The General Assembly counted 140 members and met twice a year. In contrast to the Protestants, however, a fixed number of clerics were members of the assembly, and the assembly took cognizance of both civil and ecclesiastical matters. Further, the patriarch was both bishop and civil head of the *millet.*[60]

The contemporary Armenian American Arpee believed wholeheartedly in an inclusive, pluralist Ottoman Turkey. For him, the Armenian Constitution of 1860 had commenced a new era for Turkey as a whole; the Armenian experience of self-government in the Ottoman world was to be extended to the whole Ottoman population. "During the decades immediately following 1860 the Armenians developed a system of public instruction which placed a good common-school education within reach of every Armenian child, male or female, and the best of foreign educational institutions in Turkey began to feel keenly the competition of their higher school of learning." Arpee's assessment of the reform of the *millet* system was highly positive: "The distinctions of class disappeared, and Armenian society recognized no supremacy but that of personal merit and education. . . . They developed a new democratic and national spirit, and learned to cherish the principles of a free republic within the absolute monarchy of the Sultan's empire."[61] A genuinely revolutionary liberalism in religion, education, culture, and politics emerged at the intersection of American mission and Ottoman reform. This was the case among the Armenians in Asia Minor and with regard to Lebanon, as Ussama Makdisi has identified concerning the religious and intellectual biography of Butrus Bustani, a Maronite converted to Protestantism.[62] With regard to representative government, however, one also has to keep in mind the general European, and especially French, influence on the whole Ottoman reform process.[63]

Whereas in multireligious Mount Lebanon the new liberalism went together with a "long peace," established thanks to a duly negotiated autonomy in 1861,[64] in Asia Minor it soon clashed with a traditional understanding of Muslim monopoly both locally and in central government. In the eastern provinces of Asia Minor, which were inhabited mainly by Kurds and Armenians, the centralization of the Tanzimat had destroyed old power structures, in particular Kurdish principalities, without building up a functioning administration beyond the towns. Lawlessness in the countryside was the result. To this situation the weaker, mostly unarmed Christians reacted by appealing to the representatives of the European powers, sometimes via missionaries; by organizing self-defense; and, finally, by forming revolutionary groups. The Ottoman state, in particular Abdulhamid II and the Young Turks after him, perceived the Armenian dynamism after the mid-nineteenth century as a threat to, not an opportunity for, the state. Looking back to the Armenian *Nizamname* of 1863, the Young Turk regime communicated in the official news agency *Milli* of 16 August 1916 that "this constitution has been the principal reason for the strength of the Armenian revolutionary organisation and for the efficiency of its activity. Because the power was concentrated in the national Assembly composed by men elected by the people. Thus all institutions . . . and the representatives of the clergy became members and organs of the [revolutionary] committees."[65] In this misleading way, the regime justified its abrogation of the Armenian Constitution following the physical destruction of the Armenians of Asia Minor.

Discovering Heterodox Islam: The Case of the Alevis

The possibility to adhere to the *Protestan milleti* and thus to enjoy the protection of the *millet* chancery, and if necessary, of British diplomacy, proved to be highly attractive. When Alevi tribes in eastern Anatolia applied for such a membership and wanted to become *Prote,* however, the Ottoman state reacted harshly to what it feared to be a splitting up of the Muslim community. Despite the willingness of the local Protestants to welcome the Alevis into the new community, British diplomacy was not inclined to press the case. The Americans learned that the Reform Edict of 1856, despite its wording and their expectations, did not mean free ideological competition and religious liberty for everyone; rather, it meant more religious liberty for members of the *millet.* With regard to the period before 1856, the Turkish Ottomanist Selim Deringil guesses that "the new atmosphere of religious freedom for Christians caused a panic among Muslims, who felt that their hitherto dominant position was threatened, making them more prone to force Christians to convert."[66]

By the mid-nineteenth century, the Sunnis in the capital and the provinces of the Ottoman Empire could feel that a new dynamism in education and spirituality was at work beyond their reach, calling the traditional order and its corresponding power relations into question. Nothing was more sobering for the Muslim claim of splendid religious and political sovereignty than Muslims who wholeheartedly preferred American to Ottoman teaching and a modern *millet* to the *ummah,* the community of Muslims, whom only coercion and threat could keep from converting. In 1856, in an address to the British ambassador Stratford Canning, the missionaries had expressed far-reaching hopes that "blest by social prosperity and religious freedom, the millions of Turkey will, we trust, be seen ere long sitting peacefully under their own vine and fig-tree." By 1864, however, Arpee writes that "the Turkish government was employing restraining measures, and that, too, with the knowledge and sanction of the British Ambassador, Sir Henry Bulwer. Ten years later the Grand Vizier definitively declared that the Hatti Humayun provision for religious toleration did not contemplate Moslems."[67]

The Alevis, or *Kızılbaş,* as they were most often called in Anatolia until early twentieth century, had opposed their integration into the imperial Ottoman state body during the fifteenth and sixteenth centuries. In the early sixteenth century the *Kızılbaş*—so called because of their red headgear—had pinned their hopes on the Persian Shah and Sufi poet Ismail and had rebelled against the sultan and become, in Ottoman eyes, traitors and public enemies. In this context, the Ottoman Empire under the sultans Selim I and Suleiman turned definitively to orthodox Sunnism. The Alevis had internalized the Shiite version of Islamic founding history, including the "passion" of Kerbela. They venerated Ali (ibn Abî Tâlib), Muhammad's son-in-law, more than Muhammad and remained attached to unorthodox Sufi beliefs and practices that were widespread in Anatolia before the sixteenth century. Religious propaganda by the *Ulema,* the religious hierachy led by the Sheykh-al Islam in the Ottoman capital, reviled the Alevis as immoral unbelievers without holy books (*kitapsız*) and therefore worse than Christians or Jews. They had to live at the edge of society and in remote regions, notably the Dersim (the Alevis' heartland between Sivas, Erzurum, and Harput, renamed Tunceli in 1936) and Elbistan, southwest of the Dersim. Marginality did not mean complete exclusion but rather an inferior status within the system. Without mosques, the villages inhabited by Alevis were clearly recognizable, before Sultan Abdulhamid II and his successors up to the present day constructed unwanted mosques for them.[68]

The relationship between the Protestant missionaries and the Alevis began shortly after the establishment of the Protestant *millet* in 1850. It was one of mutual sympathy, some shared values, and common hope for a new age. The reality, however, fell far short of the great expectations. Missionary enthusiasm for this people and curiosity about them remained nevertheless constant. In 1911, Henry Riggs, born of missionary parents in Sivas in 1875, wrote, "The more one learns of this strange and attractive religion, the more the question is forced upon him, What is the source of this religion, and what the history of these simple, ignorant people, who possess so much that their wiser neighbours have not?"[69] It is amazing to hear a member of the expansive missionary movement of that time referring to a non-Christian religion in these positive terms. It shows refreshingly that even if American patriotism and Protestant culturalism had begun to take on more weight in the ABCFM of the late nineteenth century than among the pioneers previously, who had known slavery and Indian removal in the United States, many missionaries did still not yield to the spell of American exceptionalism. The quest for the universal Kingdom motivated the hopeful transgression of limits, authentic encounters on the ground, and genuine sympathy beyond the bounds of doctrine. Without "reaching the Muslims," it was clear, Jesus' Kingdom, the main goal of mission, would be an illusion. Heterodox groups now seemed to be the long-searched-for open door to Islam.

In the 1850s, the missionaries of the ABCFM were probably the first outsiders to enter the close endogamous community of the *Kızılbaş*. They were perhaps the first non-Alevis to be admitted to the secret religious assemblies called *jem* that were led by *dedes* (hereditary priests) and combined prayer, sermon, popular court, and religious dances of both sexes.[70] They were deeply touched by this "unique people," their wholehearted hospitality, their fine tenderness during the *jem,* and their persistent wish to be instructed by the missionaries. They appreciated their spiritual songs, by which they transmitted their faith and philosophy, and the *muhabbet,* the "graceful dialogue," to which Alevis gave particular importance. The Americans were surprised that the *Kızılbaş* declared themselves to have the same faith as the missionaries and that, with no hesitation, they willingly participated with the visiting missionaries in their prayers and Bible readings, saying "that from their remotest ancestors it has been handed down to them, that in the last times a Christian teacher shall come to instruct them." The Alevis' veneration of and prayers to Ali, often called *şâh-i mardân* (king of mankind), made the Americans wonder about the identity of Jesus and Ali as claimed by Alevi *dedes;* about the identity of their Sufi notion of *insan-i kâmil* (complete human being) with the Son of Man of the New Testament; and about the council of the forty saints in heaven—the model of the *jem*—which, after his ascension (*mihraj*), Muhammad could join only when he had acknowledged his own humbleness and the *insan-i kâmil's* superiority.

Americans with Puritan roots, moreover, could easily understand the Alevis' ambivalent attitude toward state authorities, as the sultan-caliph, or "prince of this world," was still seen by the Alevis in the old tradition as Yezid (Yazîd I. ibn Mu'âwiya), the sixth caliph, responsible for the tragic murders of Kerbela in 680 C.E.[71] From the Alevis, the American missionaries could have learned in good time that a strong criticism of the Ottoman system and established Sunni Islam did not exclude the respect for Muhammad and Muslim religion.

In the 1850s and 1860s, the ABCFM missionaries were pleased to know that locally powerful *Kızılbaş* chiefs offered protection to the young Protestant communities in their local conflicts with the Armenian Church or Sunni neighbors. They marveled to hear about a Kurdish *Kızılbaş* chief near Tchemishgezek who proclaimed himself a Protestant and continued stubbornly to do so without ever having been in direct contact with the mission. This Ali Gako and other *Kızılbaş* in the regions of Harput and Sivas, who began to call themselves Protestants, had mostly learned from their Armenian neighbors about the new Protestant movement. Serious problems between missionaries and Alevis, especially conflicts with *dedes* who felt uneasy vis-à-vis Protestant self-assurance, occurred only seldom. However, "superstition" was a frequent matter of discussion, and attendance at missionary schools led to tensions within families.[72]

With the Alevis, the ABCFM discovered nominal Muslims desirous of fundamental reforms because, according to the missionaries, they suffered more under the existing conditions even than the Christian minorities. Once evangelized, this "noble race, true children of nature" seemed an ideal agent of the change the missionaries hoped to promote in the Near East.[73] The attempt by several *Kızılbaş* groups to redefine their identity and social role, however, touched vital interests of the Ottoman state. In a letter from Adiyaman, the missionary George Nutting suggested a special charter (*firman*) for the *Kızılbaş* based on the *Hatt-i Hümayun* of 1856. Nutting's idea, however, was no more than wishful thinking. The state strictly opposed extending to the *Kızılbaş* the protection offered by the new Protestant *millet* or establishing a new *millet* of Alevis who, though heretics in the eyes of the officials, were nominal Muslims; their possible explicit turn away from ruling Islam made the officials panic. In the view of the missionaries on the ground, the people involved definitely needed protection, but Western diplomacy would never have been ready to press for an engagement of this kind, even if missionaries had vehemently pleaded for it.[74]

As a result, the Americans found themselves compelled to reduce their contacts with the Alevis to a minimum in the 1860s and 1870s. In the region of Sivas, they came to fear for the lives of their native employees and of the Alevis concerned. The ABCFM could not help the Alevis gain any improvement in their precarious social position. Repression by local officials and Sunni neighbors as a response to their Protestant inclinations intimidated them. Only a handful of Alevi children could attend the mission schools. Yet many Alevis in the eastern provinces of the empire continued to avow that they were *Protes,* a term that apparently meant for them social and scientific progress in accordance with the precepts of their own religion of the heart. Alevis and missionaries maintained sympathetic relations, but the former knew that they had to stand on their own.[75]

Sultan Abdulhamid, Antagonist of Missionary America

Representatives of the ABCFM had lobbied at the Congress in Berlin in 1878 for efficient reforms toward religious freedom, in the sense they had understood the Reform Edict of 1856, and backed the Armenian claims for greater security in the precarious eastern provinces where the Ottoman-Russian war of 1877–1878 had brought chaos to an already precarious and tense situation. The security postulate resulted in article 61 of the Berlin Treaty. After the congress, the ABCFM strategists in Boston declared that a "new era" had begun, that the Ottoman world could now better be evangelized than ever, that the great powers now highly esteemed the social force of Protestant Christianity, and that Protestant England would establish security for life, property, and law in the Ottoman eastern provinces through an agreeable protectorate.[76] These were illusions. The handful of military consuls dispatched to the eastern provinces after 1878 could never offer anywhere near the kind of protection that would have been necessary. Its political engagement and militancy for human rights, added to all its flourishing work on the ground and its religious challenge, made the ABCFM an archenemy to Sultan Abdulhamid II and contributed to a disagreeable and tense atmosphere. At the same time, Abdulhamid admired the United States, which he considered modern and prosperous and more distinctively Christian than contemporary Europe. Analogously, he desired a modern and distinctively Islamic Ottoman state.[77]

In the 1880s the young sultan Abdulhamid II and the imperial elite were marked by the Ottoman-Russian war in the Balkans and eastern Anatolia in 1877–1878. Abdulhamid saw this disastrous war as a failure of the Tanzimat, since the reforms had apparently not enabled the empire to prevent or to win this war. In contrast to the Tanzimat, the young sultan began to carry out a sociopolitical strategy oriented toward the restoration of the *millet-i hâkime* and, more generally, the *ummah:* that is, the restoration of Islamic strength, unity, and confidence in the face of the danger of the final disintegration of the empire. This Islamism was by no means the same as the declared promotion of social, legal and political equality during the Tanzimat. Abdulhamid's Islamism mobilized the masses and demanded allegiance to the sultan-caliph. A highly developed system of spies detected all possible enemies. This fin de siècle Islamism can be called a Muslim nationalism that worked toward Muslim cohesion and empowerment within a modernizing state. It gave Muslims priority with regard to imperial ideology and identity, the access to and contents of public education, religious facilities (e.g., the Hijaz railway), and the resettlement of Muslim refugees (*muhacir*).

Abduhamid implemented more effectively than any reformist before him centralizing concepts in infrastructure, administration, education, and health. He tried actively to integrate the Alevis and other heterodox groups such as the Yezidis into the *ummah,* that is, to Sunnitize them. He succeeded in reintegrating the Sunni Kurds by giving numerous tribes the status of privileged cavalry units, the *Hamidiye.* Therefore they called him *Bavê Kurdan,* father of the Kurds. Sunni Kurds had been frustrated by the pre- and early Tanzimat state, which destroyed the age-old Kurdish autonomies. Abdulhamid sent his own *Hanafi* missionaries to central and eastern Anatolia to mobilize the Muslims for his politics.[78]

Even if Abdulhamid's politics of incorporating Alevis and Yezidis did not win them over, it isolated them successfully from the ABCFM. Protestantism as represented by the ABCFM, which fundamentally called into question the traditional Muslim cohesion and power, became a main ideological enemy, especially as it appeared to be a major factor in the renaissance of Armenian and Syriac self-consciousnesses and seemed to have the ideological potential to win over groups of nominal Muslims or to initiate something like an Alevi renaissance. For historical reasons, the relationship between Alevis and native Christians, at least in eastern Anatolia, was much more intimate than that between Alevis and Sunnis. A Protestant-influenced, educated, and consolidated Alevi community would stand side by side with the Armenians and ultimately promote common political ideas such as social equality and regional autonomy. Abdulhamid, who informed himself seriously about the eastern Alevis, already feared such perspectives, which were to become a Young Turkish nightmare on eve of World War I. In fact, an Alevi-Armenian alliance would have gravely challenged the demographic and political predominance of the established system in central and eastern Anatolia.[79]

Abdulhamid also saw danger in missionary attempts to reach the Kurdish people. Since the early Tanzimat, Sunni Kurds had been confused about their social and political role and looking for new orientation, for which reason the sheiks rose to the new role of politico-religious leaders. The ABCFM also tried to work among Kurdish-speaking people but was unable to do so because "Hamidism had reached an acute stage as against Armenia and Koordistan." Printed Gospels in Armeno-Kurdish (Kurmanj-Kurdish written with Armenian letters), for Kurdish-speaking Armenians, and later in Arab-Kurdish, as well as modest Kurdish village schools and Christian instruction, appeared as dangerous attacks on Islamic unity and as germs of ethnic self-consciousness.[80] In this perspective, the missionary work of the Protestants was subversive and seditious *(fesâd-pezîr),* as Yıldız Palace documents state repeatedly from the 1890s onward. Catholic mission was not seen in the same way; it had earned the reputation of being loyal to the government, and it profited from the diplomatic rapprochement between the sultan and the pope in the late 1880s.[81] Despite a growing anti-Protestant atmosphere in the Hamidian administration, however, in the 1880s and the early 1890s the ABCFM extended and cultivated what were prosperous missionary "islands" in a precarious Ottoman world: schools, hospitals, printing and publication, and the evangelical communities. Muslim resentments against these successes, coupled with social envy and, above all, with resentments against the Armenians for their dynamism in general and their recently founded revolutionary movements in particular, made an explosive mixture in the 1890s.

Rightly and wrongly, Abdulhamid saw the Armenian dynamism as connected with the American input on the ground. The Armenians had been the most dynamically developing group in the nineteenth-century Ottoman Empire. They had experienced an educational boom, thanks to their own institutions and to those of the missionaries. They had successfully implemented the democratizing *millet* reform according to the Reform Edict. In Ottoman literature, theater, journalism, medicine, science, jurisprudence, and commerce, Armenian men and women played a prominent role. Armenians had begun to take on functions within the state of the Tanzimat; they imbibed Ottomanist ideas of a reformed, pluralist Ottoman state under the rule of modern law. In contrast to the Orthodox Ottomans *(Rûm)* and the Christians of the Balkans, Armenians were called *millet-i sadîke,* the "loyal nation." This changed, however, when sultan Abdulhamid II considered the Tanzimat a failure and began to implement interior politics of Muslim empowerment; obstructed the reform in the six eastern provinces demanded by the Berlin Treaty (art. 61), because he feared losing them like the Balkans; and removed Armenian functionaries in eastern Anatolia.

In that context revolutionary Armenian groups emerged: Armenakan, founded in Van in 1885; Hnchag (or Hinchak), founded in Geneva in 1887;

Tashnag(sutiun) or Armenian Revolutionary Federation (ARF), founded in Tiblissi in 1890. The program of the Hnchag postulated an independent, socialist Armenia, in collaboration with the Kurds. The Tashnag, or Armenian Revolutionary Party (ARF), the strongest party after 1900, struggled for a renewed reform process and equal political rights for Muslims and non-Muslims. It would stay side by side with the Young Turkish Committee of Union and Progress (CUP) after the alliance concluded at the 1907 congress of Ottoman opposition parties in Paris.

While advocating equal rights for the Armenians and empowering them, missionary America strongly condemned revolutionary violence and the schemes of history based on such violence. Revolutionary Armenian violence included retaliation against tribal, mostly Kurdish, incursions and targeted both Armenian notables and Ottoman functionaries. "They terrorize their own people by demanding contributions of money under threats of assassination—a threat which has often been put into execution," wrote Cyrus Hamlin, a former ABCFM missionary and afterward the founder of the Robert College in Istanbul, in 1893. Hamlin had met the cofounder of the Hnchag, Nishan Garabedian, alias Rupen Khan-Azat. He describes him as an elitist revolutionary desperado who was ready to spread much blood but, despite his high intelligence, lacked any sober projection of the future. "We must stand aloof from any such desperate attempts, which contemplate the destruction of Protestant missions, churches, schools and Bible work, involving all in a common ruin that is diligently and craftily sought," concluded Hamlin.[82]

A Social Earthquake: The Armenian Massacres of 1895

Revolutionaries who belonged to a non-Muslim "ruled nation," *millet-i mahkûme,* challenged the *millet-i hâkime,* the Muslim ruling group, and its head, the sultan-caliph. Militarily this was not very important, but symbolically it appeared as a sacrilege. When European powers pressed for reforms—in 1878 and again in 1895, after the 1894 massacres of villagers in Sasun who had refused to pay taxes—rumors spread that the *gavur* (infidel) wanted to establish a Christian kingdom in eastern Anatolia. In autumn 1895, some one hundred thousand Armenians, mostly men and boys, were massacred by local Muslims and transregional gangs who claimed to act in the name of the sultan. ABCFM missionary Corinna Shattuck reported in a long letter from Urfa "the indescribable sickening odors from the great holocaust, in the Gregorian church, where 3000 having gone Saturday night for refuge, perished. Some were killed by the soldiers and mob who forced entrance. More perished by the flames made by 25–30 tins of Kerosene spilled on people, mattering, and on everything combustible." She estimated five thousand, the British vice consul G. H. Fitzmaurice eight thousand Armenian dead in Urfa in December 1895.[83]

The massacres began after the sultan had signed, under international pressure, a reform plan on 17 October 1895. He was able to influence Muslims on the ground through an informal network of sheiks and agents, but it is not clear to what extent he did so and with what orders. Generally, however, the state did not protect the victims; social envy, an Islamist discourse, impunity for murderers and robbers, and a policy of exclusive Muslim empowerment were to condition later massacres.[84] The mass violence of 1895 had a complex historical setting and can be seen from different perspectives. What happened was not an "intercommunal war" between native Christians and Muslims or Armenian nationalists and Islamists; the general picture was that of unilateral, large-scale pogroms and massacres, not bilateral fights. In one perspective, the massacres were the bloody expression of a clash between a threatened Sunni hegemony and Western, particularly American Protestant, modernity. American modernity included a millennialism that abrogated Muslim sovereignty over the Bible lands. The prosperous missionary islands and the *millet* institutions seemed to be harbingers of this vision. A dynamic development, cosponsored by Protestant diplomacy, had taken place since the Tanzimat and was bearing its fruits among non-Muslims. Many Muslims considered this the preparation of a new order in which, they feared, an outclassed *millet-i hâkime* would definitively lose its traditional dominance and self-esteem. No Ottoman group stood more clearly for such modern dynamics than the Armenians.

Missionaries had warned for a long time that a highly destructive anti-Christian potential existed in their regions. The mass violence of 1894–1896 deeply affected the groups to which the missionaries were closest and also led to destruction within missionary compounds. "The end we see not. We are in a thick cloud, but God lives and we will trust him, tho' all expected help from man fail," Shattuck wrote at the end of her letter. For the first time, it seems, American Protestant self-confidence, postmillennialist optimism, and related strategies were seriously questioned—together with "the seeming indifference of so-called Christian nations." This terrific blow and the accompanying humanitarian challenge nevertheless brought the different denominations together. The ABCFM and the Armenian Apostolic (Gregorian) Church now cooperated in humanitarian aid and other matters. New German and Swiss Protestant organizations arrived on the scene, and new missions emerged that were, in contrast to the ABCFM, of a clear premillennialist strand. For them, the Belle Epoque both in the Old World and in America was doomed to judgment. (In this perception of the contemporary world, these mission groups differed little from the European socialists, who expected bloody class struggles before the coming of the perfect, classless society. They refrained, however, from revolutionary violence.)

For the premillennialist groups, the Armenian massacres were signs of bad apocalyptical times, not an accident, albeit a most troubling one, along a postmillennialist road toward the Kingdom. In 1880s New York, the Christian Alliance and the Evangelical Missionary Alliance (later the Christian and Missionary Alliance) were founded by Albert B. Simpson, a Presbyterian minister who had left his ministry and begun to focus, as an independent evangelist, on the neglected masses of immigrants. In the United States of the fin de siècle, in particular in New York and among its Jewish immigrants from Eastern Europe, a strong movement to evangelize the Jews emerged that was premillennialist, in contrast to the postmillennialist restoration current of the early nineteenth century. Part of this movement was the later American Board of Missions to the Jews. It was founded in 1894 as the Brownsville Mission in Brooklyn, New York, by the Hungarian rabbi Leopold Cohn, who persevered, together with his family, against strong Jewish resentments. The American Board of Missions to the Jews would be one among many premillennialist agencies in Israel after 1948. As early as the 1890s, the Christian Alliance and the Evangelical Missionary Alliance sent missionaries to Syria, including to Palestine and its Jews. Of a similar character—marked by a consecrated evangelical Christianity and sharp eschatological, generally premillennialist conscience—was the German-speaking Hilfsbund für christliches Liebeswerk im Orient, founded in Frankfurt in 1896, which sent humanitarian help and missionaries to Asia Minor, where experienced ABCFM workers introduced them. A similarly minded German newcomer at that time was the Karmelmission for Jews and Arabs in Palestine.[85]

The Armenian massacres of the 1890s gave birth not only to new missions but also to a transnational human rights movement, in which America and American missionaries played a leading role. An effective political Anglo-American cooperation in favor of the Armenians was considered but did not crystallize. Nevertheless, for the first time the idea of an armed struggle in the Old World for the great cause of civilization began to germinate in American political thinking. The task at hand was "to stand side by side and shoulder to shoulder with England in support of a great cause—in a necessary struggle for the defence of human rights and the advancement of Christian civilization. That a great cause of this sort is now presented by unhappy Armenia I cannot doubt," Secretary of State Richard Olney put it in 1896, after warning in 1895 of a "partnership in the cost and losses of the struggle [over the fate of Turkey] but not in any ensuing benefits."[86] In contrast to the emerging U.S. imperialism in the Pacific and the situation a hundred years later, America played in the late Ottoman Near East the role of a "Good Samaritan for God." "America called by Armenia" stood out not only from "the Turk in his iniquity" but also from the "powers that cowardly combine," wrote the American author and educator Henry van Dyke, who was close to the ABCFM, in a poem of the time.[87]

After 1895, a consensus arose within the ABCFM that missionary work had to be more compatible with a constructive project for the entire Ottoman society, and that its liberal criticism of the Ottoman authorities must not be misunderstood by revolutionaries as a license for violence. The missionaries continued to plead for solutions on the ground. "It seems clear that hope that has been placed on Europe has been misplaced, and that no human source of help remains except the Sultan and the Turkish government. It seems then plain that the only course remaining for those who are not able to leave the country, and not willing to accept the Moslem faith, is to secure the confidence of the Government and persuade it that all rebellious movements have ceased, that so some tolerable *modus vivendi* may be secured," wrote a missionary in Van with regard to the Armenians.[88]

The ABCFM's Eastern Turkey Mission (ETM), which worked in the region where most rural Armenians lived, felt compelled to proclaim in 1904 that "the E.T.M is a hand laid upon that portion of the empire, not to snatch it from the Turk, but to dispense Gospel blessings upon it that shall make the Christian populations thereof more loyal to the home of Othman [Osman, founder of the Ottoman dynasty], more law-abiding citizens, more sincere and evangelical in their faith, more intelligent, honest and progressive tradesmen and artisans and in short, genuine and manly Christian men, and cultivated, spiritual and womanly Christian women."[89] The ABCFM's antinationalist as well as antiseparatist stance was sincere. It resulted at different times in disciplinary measures against or the exclusion of revolutionary students. Nevertheless, many missionaries found it an unhappy situation to preach loyalty in a system that they often considered intolerable. With regard to the effects of American education, a younger missionary doctor in Van, Clarence Ussher, wrote sarcastically in 1904:

> The effort has always been and is to train Armenians to love their country and to be loyal to their government, but every thought that leads a man to respect himself and distinguish himself from a beast leads him to rebel inwardly against being treated as a beast. Every

> particle of education and every thought of America and her institutions tends, in this sense, to unfit Armenians and others to live quietly under existing oppression. As our work has touched many thousands of lives we are forced to say that a very large number in this vilayet are so unfitted to consider themselves as mere beasts.[90]

The ABCFM remained uneasy under the Hamidian system, with which missionary America stood fundamentally at odds in many respects. Abdulhamid made absolutely no attempt to punish the perpetrators of 1895–1896. The main problem for the Hamidian authorities was not the supposed cooperation between ABCFM and Armenian nationalists (such accusations were merely a diplomatic trick played against the missions) but the very fact that the American missionaries promoted a successful modern Christian education. Therefore the Muslims again turned out to be not strengthened, as had been Abdulhamid's aim, but weakened. The empowerment of the Christians stood in the way of the Hamidian politics of Muslim unity through new institutions, schools, the *Hamidiye* regiments, and a mission spreading Hanafi Sunnism.

Hypothetically, peaceful synergies could have been created between Abdulhamid and missionary America. Beyond the sensitive issue of education, in the second half of the nineteenth century members of the Protestant International had established charitable modern institutions for a multireligious clientele: successful hospitals and innovative works such as ABCFM member Corinna Shattuck's School for the Blind in Urfa or the Swiss Quaker Theophilus Waldmeier's Asfuriya hospital for the insane in Lebanon.[91] Abdulhamid and the Protestant International claimed to be God-fearing; the policies of both were supra-(ethno-)nationalist and articulated social perspectives in religious terms. The way these terms were given, however, could hardly be compatible. The American missionaries saw in the Hamidian system a harmful, even murderous combination of Sunni dogmatism, arrogance of power, corruption, and authoritarian tradition. Abdulhamid had suspended the constitution and obstructed efficient reforms in the eastern provinces. For him, this was the defense of Muslim rights. Did not the "Christian powers" implement imperialist politics in their own colonial dominions without putting them to the test of human rights? Behind the altruistic commitment of missionaries, the apprehensive sultan-caliph feared an imperialist agency that threatened both the political and symbolic foundation of his power.

CHAPTER 3

Dream and Trauma

Missionary America and Young Turkey, 1908–1923

In 1908 the U.S. Progressive Era met the era of the Young Turks. Postmillennialist missionaries met the stark patriots of the Committee of Union and Progress, of whom most believed in positivist progress. Americans and Young Turks both set high hopes on "Young Turkey," but in different terms. Missionaries and Young Turks had shared independently of one another the conviction that a reactionary despotism and "fanatical Islam," as represented by the Hamidian system, were among the main reasons for the catastrophe of 1895 and other problems in the country. In contrast to the CUP, however, "true religion" for the missionaries was not the attribute of an *ancien régime* but the motor of a future-oriented mind. The CUP aspired to shed the tyrant's blood and take its place, whereas the missionaries rejected revolutionary violence. They observed the problems not from the center of power in the capital but much more from the grass roots in the provinces and from a transnational internationalist perspective. Americans believed in civil society building, which their education would now promote as a priority, and in diversified federalist administration; the Young Turks focused on a strong, sovereign, and unified centralist regime. The term *Young Turks* designates the broad oppositional, constitutional movement against the sultan Abdulhamid II but is mostly used as a synonym for the strongest political group within that opposition, the CUP. This conspirational committee took partial control of the empire in 1908–1909, then full control in 1913, and led the empire to World War I in 1914. Most leaders of the Turkish War of Independence (1919–1922) and the Republic of Turkey, founded in 1923, had been members of the CUP until 1918.[1]

The Ottomans' entry into World War I by the will of leading CUP members put Turkey in a position of profound antagonism to the ABCFM. During World War I, the Young Turk regime destroyed Christianity, above all Armenian Christianity, in Anatolia. This destruction killed the American social utopia of 1908, destroyed the "revived Christianity" of the nineteenth century, and shattered the century-old American hope of a millennium peacefully built up in the Bible lands. Levi Parsons's somewhat forgotten apocalyptical vision of 1821, "that Turkey must be drenched in blood," was now fulfilled; but what would follow now, if not total hopelessness? Those cast as the principal actors of eschatological change since the 1830s, the native Christians and primarily the Armenians, had become the victims of mass murder and expulsion. Therefore, missionary America suffered serious damage between 1915 and 1923. It lost its principal friends and clients and most of its concepts. Even its readjusted visions for Asia Minor and the Near East after 1918 were utterly defeated at the peace negotiations of the victors in Paris and Lausanne.

Young Turkish Hopes and Fears

With regard to backgrounds, networks, places of socialization, and intellectual history, the Young Turks lived in a different world from that of the missionaries. The Young Turks' language of culture and education was French, whereas the language of the missionary Protestant International of the nineteenth and twentieth centuries was English. The Young Turks felt themselves to be part of the "wretched Ottoman nation" (*biçare millet-i Osmaniye*) and, they hoped, its saviors. Whether willing partners or in critical opposition, the missionaries were indelibly part of a globally leading "Protestant world" formed by the United States, Great Britain, and Germany. Whereas the Young Turk educated elite was strongly influenced by more or less atheistic French positivism and German biologism, including social Darwinism, the missionaries combined their belief in science and progress with biblically inspired views on human beings and society. Could these differences be overcome? Was there enough common ground for promising and long-lasting collaboration? The ABCFM and CUP both disliked Abdulhamid's system and militant Islam. Both shared notions of progress, modern education, and the equality of women. Both focused on reform, constitutional government, and civic equality. They did not, however, share the same priorities, social loyalties, and historical-religious references.

The Young Turks came mostly from the middle class, often lower middle class, and from outside the Ottoman capital, but they had generally studied at the elite state schools in the capital. The primary concern of the first Young Turks in the 1890s was how to save the Ottoman Empire, considered as the last defense of the Muslim world against imperialist European powers. This was particularly true for the "Turks" (used synonymously for Muslims) from Russia who lived as émigrés in Istanbul, the seat of the caliphate. Deeply politicized and partly traumatized, this stratum had cultivated an exclusive Turkish Muslim solidarity at an early stage. It was among the circles of Turkish-speaking Muslims from Russia that, from the outset, Islam was integrated into Turkish nationalism, and Turkism was born. This prepared the way for the general ethno-national awakening among educated Turks in the 1910s, the corresponding broad movement of the *Foyers turcs* (*Türk yurdu,* Turkish home, and *Türk ocağı,* Turkish hearth), and the strongly Turkist mind-set of the young educated elites during the wars of the 1910s.[2]

Whereas the influential movement of the *Foyers turcs,* founded in 1911, had a strong ethno-national Turkist molding, the CUP, founded twenty-two years earlier, was nationalist in an Ottoman Muslim sense. Significantly, both movements originated at the Military Medical School (*Mekteb-i Tıbbiye-i Askeriye*) in Istanbul. At the end of the century, this school was the meeting point of three elements fundamental to the Turkish national movement of the following decades: Western science, elitist political conspiracy, and the military institution. During the first fifteen years or so, the CUP remained relatively open. But the hard core of the committee, including the two military doctors, Bahaeddin Şakir and Nazım, would exhibit a pronounced anti-Christian and Turkist tendency from as early as 1906, while using a language suited to winning over the non-Muslim opposition and Western opinion for tactical reasons; the political language employed within the conspiratorial group, however, was substantially different. After 1910, the non-Muslim communities within the empire began to be described as religious, racial, and class enemies.[3]

At the Military Medical School, most students had more or less lost their religious faith. Nevertheless, they remained profoundly attached to Sunni Islam, both as an identity and as a culture, as well as to the idea of Islamic unity. They began to view Islam more and more in terms of ethnicity, coupled with Turkishness, rather than as a theological confession and ethical reference. Ludwig Büchner, Ernst Haeckel, Carl Vogt, Emile Boutmy, and Gustave Le Bon were among the influential figures they most idolized; the strand of French positivism connected to the revanchist right exerted a particular influence on them. This reception focused on the progressive but antidemocratic, antiegalitarian, and antihumanist elements, emphasizing the inequality of different races and cultivating contempt, or at least elitist paternalism, for the sheeplike masses. Shaped by deep anti-Christian and anti-Western resentments, this interpretation left aside the idea of a "church of humanity" that had been as dear to the father of French positivism, Auguste Comte, as to the materialist Büchner—especially as many Young Turks had, in their European exile, strongly missed the modern suprareligious human solidarity they had hoped to find there.[4] Büchner, one of the icons of the Young Turk intellectuals, had himself been a doctor, as well as a materialist and a Darwinist.[5] To him, reality equaled nature, as described by scientists, and impersonal nature replaced God. Man was nature's product, determined by the laws of nature, by race, and by the "law" of the survival of the fittest. Such trendy doctrines, which strongly appealed to the youth around 1900 and for which idols like Büchner seemed to stand, were cultivated both in the elite schools in the Ottoman capital and at universities in Europe, where many Young Turks had fled in the 1890s. The missionaries refused these doctrines as both antibiblical and antihumanistic but could not escape difficult discussions in their colleges if they did not want to appear as fundamentalists. The best known example is the debate on Darwinism in the Syrian Protestant College in Beirut in 1882, seven years before the CUP was founded.[6]

One of the CUP's first members, an émigré from Russia, was Ali Bey Hüseyinzâde (Turan) (1864–1940), who had been born in Baku. He introduced his naive young fellow students at the Military School of Medicine to the history of ideas, particularly Western ideas. According to Yusuf Akçura, another well-known intellectual from Russia, Ali explained his move to Istanbul in 1889 with these words: "I'm a Turk, I'm a Muslim. Turkey is a Turkish and a Muslim state. Therefore Turkey is more my home than Russia." After his flight from Abdulhamid's police, Ali published the journal *Füyuzat* in Baku in 1906–1907; it coined the seminal slogan "Europeanize, Turkify, Islamize" and called for a revolution in Turkey.[7] Following his return to Istanbul in 1911, Ali obtained a post as a senior consultant and, on the initiative of Talat, a leading CUP member, was elected to the CUP central committee. The same year he became engaged in the Turkist movement of the *Foyers turcs* and their journal *Türk Yurdu.*

In 1913, at their congress in Petit-Lancy (Geneva), members of the *Foyers turcs* declared Anatolia to be their national motherland (*anayurt*), or "promised land," as the Turkist ideologist Tekin Alp would later write. Turkists could accept the end of the Empire—provided the Turkish nation was awakened and saved. In Petit-Lancy they agreed "how beneficial in political and economic terms it would be to create in Anatolia a homogeneous and concentrated unit of the Ottoman Turks." They were unanimous that "Anatolia was the homeland [*anayurt*] which would guarantee the political existence of Ottoman Turkdom." They planned "to make the Turks the owners of Anatolia and, supported by established men of various trades, to lead the way on behalf of the Turks who were as yet unaware of the salutary works aimed at guaranteeing their existence. And they swore solemnly that, being on the road towards the great national ideal, they would make Anatolia their national home."[8] For most Young Turks in leading positions before the Balkan wars of 1912–1913, when they had spoken about nation it was not about an imagined ethno-nation to be awakened and constructed but first and foremost about the *millet-i hakime,* the "ruling nation" of the past, now in a wretched state (*biçare*) and to be reempowered.

The key figures of the regime after 1913 pragmatically managed the explosive synergy of *millet-i hakime* ideology and Turkist ideal; they ensured the *Foyers'* close dependence on the government. Both the ethno-national and the imperial project excluded the equal integration of non-Muslims. During World War I the CUP and its sympathizers saw themselves engaged in a total struggle—a secular apocalyptical war—to maintain the empire and to strengthen the nation in both senses. For the Turkist current, which, after the Balkan wars, blended anti-Christian class and racial struggle,[9] the transformation of Anatolia to the national home of the Turks was the priority, whereas pan-Turkism wanted additional expansion toward Central Asia.

Progressive Era, Mission, and Young Turkey

Against the background of Abdulhamid's era, the American missionaries considered the Young Turk revolution on 24 July 1908 (i.e., the forced reinstatement of the Ottoman Constitution) a great relief. The Young Turk revolution was for the *Missionary Herald* a "nation's sudden conversion," comparable to the conversion of Saul to Christianity, becoming the apostle Paul.[10] American missionaries had learned a great deal about the Ottoman world since 1819 and possessed long-standing experience on the ground but had known very little about the oppositional Young Turks until 1908. This lack of knowledge may be one reason for the high and sincere expectations that particularly the ABCFM but also many other generally well-informed groups and individuals held at the beginning of the Young Turk period. For the Turkish author and nationalist Halide Edib (Adıvar), "It looked like the millennium."[11] Whatever came after, a strong desire for reconciliation, an authentic potential of hope and utopia, erupted in 1908 among Ottoman Muslims, Christians, and Jews.

"It looked like the millennium" was also the feeling of many contemporary American missionaries. Again a new era was proclaimed in specific missionary terms, an era of peaceful progression toward, this time, a democratic Ottoman Near East. The main change from the ABCFM's perspective lay in a new holistic approach that had already germinated, but had not yet been proclaimed and implemented, during the Hamidian period. The Turkey mission now meant, in the words of James Barton, the foreign secretary of the ABCFM and a former missionary at Harput, the "advancement of the kingdom of God in Turkey" by building up a plural, equal, and liberal "Ottoman nation." In schools and the press, the task of the mission was to promote "modern Ottoman citizenship," polyethnic "constitutional patriotism," "civic force," "progress," "humanitarian leadership," and "moral contagion" instead of conversion. Such were the new watchwords of the Turkey mission after 1908—words that were again emphasized on the important platform of the interdenominational World Missionary Conference in Edinburgh in June 1910.[12] Missionaries whose grandfathers had anticipated, in religiously apocalyptic terms, the imminent fall of the Ottoman Empire now loudly promoted in secularist terms a particular Protestant form of Ottomanism, that is, belief in the coexistence of different communities and ethnicities. They did not share in the growing feeling of a Social Darwinist "apocalypse," a final struggle of nations, which young nationalist elites in Europe believed to be increasingly inevitable in the early twentieth century. In their optimism, however, the American missionaries to some extent ignored relevant signs of the time and put their message at risk. Their projection of the future, their message of the Kingdom, lacked a serious consideration of the dark sides of the late Ottoman situation and the Belle Epoque in the Old World.

ABCFM Foreign Secretary James Barton was enthusiastic about the new era; "Never before in the history of Moslem and Christian intercourse," he wrote shortly after July 1908, "have believers in these two religions so drawn together and publicly demonstrated their purpose to exalt patriotism above creed and love of country above religious hatreds. A long step has been taken toward a better understanding between Mohammedans and Christians as these hitherto widely separated classes join in a common purpose to make the constitution a success. This fact alone reveals unmeasured possibilities for the future." This leading ABCFM representative set particular hopes on the alliance of the ARF (Tashnagsutiun) and the CUP. "We have reason to expect that the so-called revolutionary Armenians will now . . . unite their efforts for a free Turkey, which is already beginning to be."[13] Barton's book

Daybreak in Turkey[14] exemplifies the optimistic belief that a modern Ottomanist civil society could soon be achieved and that America's mission, the ABCFM, had a privileged role to play in it—in contrast to counterproductive European pressures and intrigues. From Macedonia to Mesopotamia, there now existed the most promising mission field, Barton argued, and he emphasized the ABCFM's right to play a key role.[15]

The Young Turk revolution of 1908 had reinstated the constitution and parliament and put the fragile CUP-Tashnag alliance to the test of the turbulent Second Constitutional Era. The declared equality and political visibility of Armenians, however, including vociferous young Armenian nationalists, disturbed many Muslims. During the Islamist counterrevolution of April 1909 in Istanbul, Armenian members of parliament were among those who saved CUP representatives from violent attacks. The renowned writer and lawyer Krikor Zohrab, for example, saved Halil (Menteşe), a prominent politician in the CUP and afterward in the Republic of Turkey. During the massive pogroms in Adana in the same month, CUP officers, however, failed to protect the Armenian victims. These local pogroms recalled the Anatolia-wide ones of 1895–1896; some twenty thousand people lost their lives, among them about one thousand Muslims, the rest being Armenians. Both local authorities and troops officered by Young Turks sent from the Dardanelles committed atrocities in April 1909. In other places, however, such as Urfa and Mamuretülaziz, the authorities under the influence of Young Turks resolutely resisted those who wanted to plunder and murder the Armenians again. Despite serious setbacks the electoral alliance of CUP and ARF persisted until 1912. Many Armenians, however, preferred the more pluralist and liberal party İtilâf.[16]

The First Balkan War, beginning in fall 1912, caused the Ottoman Empire to lose most of European Turkey, including Salonika, the headquarters of the CUP, for good. While blaming the İtilâf cabinet (July 1912–January 1913) for the defeat, the CUP claimed to be the only truly patriotic force. The CUP's coup against the İtilâf cabinet, of which Gabriel Noradounghian was the foreign minister, led to the establishment of a dictatorial one-party regime in 1913. Through its Special Organization (*Teşkilat-i Mahsûsa*), the CUP regime conducted boycott and terror campaigns against the *Rûm,* expelling more than a hundred thousand from the Aegean coast in spring 1914. The CUP-ARF alliance had been concluded in Paris in 1907 on condition that security and equality would be established and that stolen Armenian land in the eastern provinces would be restored, but the CUP proved to be too weak and, finally, unwilling to return land against the will of the agas and tribal chiefs. Co-opting them to their regime, the CUP preferred these reactionary representatives to their Armenian comrades with whom they had shared important ideals. At the same time, it began to sponsor the Turkist movement, which was scarcely compatible with a pluralist Turkey.

The rise of Turkism was paralleled by a rise of anti-Christian resentment. "The events of the past five years, culminating in the Italian and Balkan wars, have added to this feeling of contempt [of Christianity as a religion] a feeling of bitterness. The Moslems of Turkey do not feel that Christian Europe has given them a fair opportunity to work out their career as a modern constitutional state," Howard S. Bliss, the president of the Syrian Protestant College in Beirut, wrote in 1913.[17] Despite decisive catastrophes for the empire in the Balkan wars of 1912–1913, the American missionaries remained confident on two points. First, the revolution of 1908 had been a highly promising moment in world history, both as a peaceful revolution and as a time of fraternization between different religious groups. Second, the American institutions taught what was needed for the new era, that is "right government," "real brotherhood," and "mutual toleration." Charles T. Riggs of the Bible House in Istanbul, the ABCFM's nerve center in the Ottoman Empire, wrote in 1913 that "the effects of the true missionary aim and teaching were seen in our schools and colleges, where, right through the bitter, cruel war, Turk and Bulgarian, Greek and Serbian, Jew and Armenian studied side by side in peace, expressing mutual regret for the outbreak that was so contrary to the principles embodied in those institutions."[18]

The representatives of the ABCFM believed that it could, through its institutions of higher education, do "more towards the settlements of the Eastern question than the joint action of all the European Powers."[19] Since the late eighteenth century, in diplomacy and far beyond, the Eastern Question had designated the challenge of how to conceive the future of the insecure Ottoman world, which was in particular for religious American millennialists a mysteriously promising place, whence light was to come—*ex oriente lux*. The ABCFM's "secularist turn" in the early twentieth century caused its missionary scope to converge with the conviction that America had to bring "a light unto all nations." It tended no longer to rely on and trust the resources it found on the ground to work with and to combine those creatively with its own commanding input. It was far now from Parsons's self-doubts and tentative steps of eighty years before. More than ever, the ABCFM felt sure that its work in Turkey was supported by the political leaders at home. The *Missionary Herald,* its journal, proudly quoted in March 1909 an address by President Theodore Roosevelt in which he praised the ABFCM policy of making Muslim students "good citizens" and making "them vie with their fellow-citizens who are Christians" for the development of a democratic "New Turkey."[20]

Translating Millennialism into Civic Commitment

Probably nowhere else, surely not in the Muslim world, did missionaries identify so much with a broad societal departure as did the ABCFM's missionaries to Turkey after the Young Turk revolution. The Ottoman Muslim world was now a promising Ottoman nation for which evangelical Christianity had to pray. The ABCFM's Ottomanist reorientation after 1908 did not mean that it distanced itself from the fundamental postmillennialist stance and revivalist reading of the Bible. The "Ottomanist approach" was more secular than the strategy of "Christianity revived in the Near East," but both shared the missionary commitment to hopeful reforms of the Ottoman state leading to pluralist equality (versus the traditional hierarchical plurality or modernist homogeneity). Parallel to the Social Gospel movement in the United States, which addressed the dysfunctions of American society, this approach took general social issues more seriously.

Explicit eschatological and restorationist language seem largely to have faded away after 1900, or perhaps even earlier; few missionaries would explicitly have approved of the apocalyptic terminology the ABCFM had used in the early nineteenth century. These terms, however, were not formally revoked. The Kingdom to be established remained a key term. Though the attitude toward Islam evolved significantly, the missionary community did not arrive at explicitly new or integrative terms, nor did even convinced Ottomanist missionaries after 1908. Islam was still seen primarily as a deficient monotheism, not as a religious experience in its own right, with resources to be discovered. Nevertheless there were important changes, and steps toward changes, in the early years after 1908. These had partly to do with non-Protestant students in American colleges who claimed full religious liberty based on the principles both of the Young Turk revolution and the liberal and critical spirit that was taught in the American colleges. In the Syrian Protestant College (later, the American University of Beirut), more than a quarter of the students were Muslims. They highly desired American education but not religion. In the 1908–1909 academic year, they protested against obligatory "presence" ("participation" was voluntary) during worship services in the college chapel and during Bible lessons. In order not to antagonize its Muslim clientele, the college finally changed its rules, but it still insisted that each student be morally educated. World War I deprived it of the opportunity to make first experiences based on a new, religiously more pluralistic and individualistic college policy.[21]

Some American missionaries from the Ottoman Empire were present at the World Missionary Conference in Edinburgh in 1910. In the relevant discussions on the Ottoman Near East, they expressed much more self-criticism than, for example, one could read in the *Missionary Herald,* which addressed itself to a large public at home. The strong focus on Christian minorities and the unsatisfying relationship with the Muslim majority, as well as a failed approach toward Islam as a religion and too-close ties with Western governments, were openly questioned. All agreed that Americanizing or Europeanizing people could not in any way be the purpose of Christian mission. On the contrary, mission was supposed to offer an "antidote" to the bad influences, including imperialism, of Western civilization.[22] A lofty tone was set in many discussions and reflections of that short period before World War I. Howard S. Bliss, the president of the Syrian Protestant College, pleaded for a new, sincere, and "politically correct" vocabulary concerning Islam:

> We must, in the first place, approach Islam with the humbling, not to say humiliating realization that our difficulties in the approach have been largely created by ourselves. . . . One result of this effort to approach Islam in the spirit of sympathy and appreciation will be to prune our missionary vocabulary of many disfiguring and irritating words. We shall not talk about "modern crusades"; we shall not speak of Islam as a "challenge to faith." Except indeed as applied to our struggle against weaknesses and temptations common to humanity, we shall drop the whole vocabulary of war.[23]

This last sentence corresponds exactly to the Sufi definition of spiritual *jihad.* The struggle against the missionaries' own ethnocentrism accompanied a strongly internationalist spirit that, occasionally, criticized American policies in harsh terms.[24]

Various innovative projects were put forward. Edward B. Haskell of the ABCFM station in Salonika developed a plan for social work. He criticized European Turkey Mission because its appeal had been "chiefly on traditional lines," and the American missionaries were not "sufficiently in touch with the view point of their natural allies [*sic*], the socialistic and other liberals of the country." He found fault with the fact that the Young Men's and Young Women's Christian Associations could not reach people outside Protestant circles. "All atheists, skeptics, Moslems and Jews, are barred from active membership in the Y.M.C.A. by the rule that active members must have accepted Christ 'as God and Saviour.'" Therefore he proposed the establishment of an interreligious club called "Loving Service" or "Brotherly Service," hoping that all those "who cannot unite on a basis of [religious] *belief,* might respond to a call to service and unite on a basis of *action.*" The new club's credo had to be the "recognition of all men as brothers, and the practice of the law of love by and towards all," and it was the "duty of those of us who grasp this truth to begin acting on it at once and trying to persuade others to act upon it." For Haskell, this movement should nevertheless be "religious" and "guide the socialistic and other liberalism into spiritual channels." Above all, it would be favorable to weld "together the discordant elements of Turkey and to strengthening the New Régime. Hence it ought not to be discouraged by the Government."[25] Haskell and his colleagues emphasized "religion" as a pivotal source of spirituality and humanism, and therefore a foundation of civic responsibility in the late Ottoman world. They were ready to call into question barriers of doctrine to social intercourse because they felt their own piety could be an obstacle to brotherly love and action.

For the ABCFM, the few years after 1908 were a time of experiments and new conceptual fermentation, terminated abruptly by World War I. The urgent and leading idea was "how to reach Turks," that is, the Muslims. A multireligious Young Men's Club that "reaches Turks" was created in Caesarea (Kayseri). "Facts to ascertain the missionary problem in the Turkish Empire," that is, information on the social and ethnic context of each missionary station, were collected by the Bible House; Haskell's "Plan for Social Work"[26] was developed. But there was not enough time to implement fundamental change. In fact, many missionaries were probably not ready to do so.

In retrospect, it was a period of illusions. That holds true for the benevolent assessment of contemporary nationalisms, including that of the CUP; it concerns too, as already mentioned, the "forgotten" gap between missionary and nationalist ("jingoist") America; between Gospel and culture; between the good message and realities of coercion, exploitation, and violence. There was illusion insofar as the "growing spirit of nationalism" in Japan, China, India, and Turkey fundamentally did not want the foreigner—not only because of imperialism but also because of religious resentments and the challenge to national identities. The missionary think tank in Edinburgh was partly conscious of this; because Christian mission was universal in its aim, its report reads, it was seen as "antagonistic to the intense national spirit of Japan, which many Japanese are taught to regard as divine both in origin and in world-wide mission." Similar things could be said of Turkist or Islamist Ottoman admirers of Japan far beyond the era of Young Turkey. Nevertheless, for the commission in Edinburgh, in "some respects the recent Turkish revolution [of 1908] has been the most remarkable which has ever taken place in any nation," not least because of the "fraternising of members of different religion." The mentors of the worldwide missionary movement firmly believed that their mission could side with the Asian national awakenings, because Christianity was "universally indigenous." Those who held positions of responsibility in the ABCFM wanted to believe all the more in Ottoman patriotism as it signified in their view a progressive, supradenominational civic sense. They did not, or did not wish to, take into account the fact that their ongoing challenge of identities and promotion of Christian values simply met with hate: with open or disguised hate among Turkist nationalists, and with particular resentment among Muslims who felt treated as inferior religiously and excluded from the dynamics of the Western world. The thinking in Edinburgh revealed itself as wishful that "Christianity must show . . . that the so-called Christian nations really believe in Christianity, and that, although they are still far from attaining to the Christian position, they are yet in the lead in character among the nations."[27] World War I brutally contradicted this wish but offered a welcome window of opportunity for those believing in social Darwinism and wanting to implement according policies.

ABCFM-CUP Interactions

In intellectual and political terms, there were obvious divisions between the Young Turk elite and the American missionaries from the outset. The missionaries—and with them, the whole Protestant International—were very critical of the trendy doctrines of the European fin de siècle. The CUP movement and its clubs, however, as they emerged after July 1908 in all the provinces, varied and were not yet under the strict control of the center. The center itself proclaimed Ottomanism, though leading CUP members held contrary beliefs. The provincial clubs mostly behaved in a very friendly way toward the ABCFM and its institutions, and vice versa, in 1908–1909; American missionaries were respected as "pioneers of progress" and invited for talks and discussions. The elderly missionary Herman Barnum, in Harput since 1858, was among those invited. "The Society of Union and Progress, as its name indicates, has for its object the union of the different hitherto divergent races into one patriotic body of Osmanlis [Ottoman citizens], and also the awakening of enterprise and thrift," he wrote in March 1909. Was this an authentic perception, or did he optimistically take some of the CUP's proclamations at face value? Private enterprise was primarily a postulate of Prince Sabahaddin's League of Private Initiative and Decentralization, a rival of the CUP. "The parent society is in Salonica, but there are branches in all the important towns throughout the country," Barnum continued. "This city [Harput] has a strong society of this order, composed of its best citizens, Turks, and Christians, upon an equality." In similar positive terms Edward Riggs described the opening of the "Club" in Marsovan (Merzifon) in October 1908 in which two professors of the local American College participated actively.[28]

The Reverend James L. Fowle was enthusiastic when he met with two CUP members, Tahir Bey and Faik Bey, on 14 September 1908 in Caesarea (Kayseri). "I confess that my faith has been weak. I did not expect in my lifetime to see Turks, Armenians, and Greeks mingling as brothers, or to hear Moslems speak in a Christian church in praise of liberty for all and equality before the law." Fowle listened to a speech by Tahir in the Greek church in Kayseri, which was crowded with Turks, Greeks and Armenians. Tahir started with the apostle Paul's words on love (1 Corinthians 13), which the Greek priests had chanted in Turkish; he conjured up an Ottoman coexistence in full liberty, equality, and mutual respect. Soon after, he made a similar speech in the Armenian Gregorian church. There Faik talked with Fowle.

> As soon as I told him I was an American missionary he spoke most cordially of the work done by the Americans and the English in teaching the principles of real liberty in this land. He told the Armenians that it was through our efforts that they (the Armenians) were better able to understand what liberty and equality meant, and thus they, first of all, had been ready to make sacrifices for it. He said openly to them, "You owe all this to the American and English missionaries." He spoke, too, in the highest terms of our schools and colleges. This was all said in the simplest, sincerest fashion, with no hint of flattery. It does not need to be said that I was as surprised as I was delighted.

For Fowle, this was "nothing other than the birth of a genuine Ottoman nation." He did not question Faik's exaggerated and ambiguous praise of the missionary impact for the Armenians.[29]

One could cite many more examples of the kind but may also note that the big names of the CUP's Central Committee were not present when the cordial encounters took place in the provinces. The American missionaries were most optimistic from 1908 on, more optimistic than the Catholic and Protestant missionaries of other countries, such as Switzerland and Germany, even if they too felt and warmly welcomed the singular spirit of July 1908.[30] The differences had to do with the postmillennialist expectations of the Americans and the excellent role they saw for themselves and their flourishing institutions in Young Turkey.

The ABCFM showed its ongoing loyalty toward Young Turkey and the CUP even during and after the anti-Armenian pogrom of Adana in April

1909. William Peet, the head of the Bible House in Istanbul, headed an international aid committee under the honorary chair of the grand vizier and the patronage of the sultan. Despite much friendly interaction between the ABCFM and the Ottoman authorities, in particular with the new Vali of Adana after August 1909, the CUP member Ahmed Jemal (later Jemal Pasha), initial rifts became clear. Jemal primarily wanted a strong state, plainly sovereign in educating the orphans of Adana as "Ottomans"; the ABCFM perceived this as an attack on both communitarian cultural rights and the very possibility of providing a Christian education. The Protestant missionaries began to realize that, against the background of what had happened in the 1890s, they not only analyzed the anti-Armenian violence differently but also had a divergent understanding of Ottomanism. Theirs was a (naive?) liberal civic sense; the CUP's was a growing state-centered authoritarianism. Still, the ABCFM directive was "to be very careful not to antagonize the Young Turk party" and to be "a little careful" about what to publish. Eager to show their loyalty to the new authorities and their faith in Young, or "New," Turkey, the American missionaries took assertive action against politicized Armenian students in their institutions. Some went so far as to put blame on the Armenian revolutionary youth in Adana.[31] Serious-minded observers saw the opportunities of 1908 to be gravely endangered by violent anti-Christian reactions of a Muslim elite and mob who feared being the losers, as well as by *millet* members who placed too much trust in a lasting European Belle Epoque, helpful Western agency, and historical progress.

Mutual Perceptions

American missionaries hoped that the "last shall be first," that the Turks "may surpass the Armenians in their appreciation of and devotion to the principles of real liberty and genuine civilization," and that thus the long desired conversion of the Muslim majority might finally take place in largely secularist terms.[32] The reality Young Turk observers began to discover in the provinces, however, revealed obvious gaps between gloomy Muslim and charming Christian quarters, the latter often with institutions promoted by the ABCFM. An aggressive depressive feeling overcame even otherwise upright young men. In March 1910, the journalist and tireless traveler Ahmet Şerif of *Tanîn,* a paper close to the CUP, wrote after visiting an American school in the town of Hajin where a majority of Armenians lived (some 150 km northeast of Adana, today renamed Saimbeyli): "From the faces of the schoolgirls and schoolboys life and vitality burst forth. Let us not lie: I did not feel admiration for this, but jealousy. I did not want to see this. Men were coming from America and I don't know where, and creating in the most remote villages of Turkey models of civilization. Sad and ashamed as an Ottoman, I left." Şerif observed, too, that the Armenians of the district of Hajin were loyal toward the government, wishing nothing more than justice and a well-functioning administration, and that they lived in close contact with their Muslim neighbors. With some satisfaction the missionaries read Ahmet Şerif 's texts, particularly his observation that provincial Armenians were more loyal to the Young Turk government than were Muslims.[33]

In a very different place, Samsun on the Black Sea, the same journalist thought he discovered the same reality, this time without any ties to the ABCFM—if not for a final remark that the Christian students had the opportunity to attend the American College at Marsivan for higher education.

> It is as if a general orphan-like spirit floats over the [Muslim] quarter. Laziness, an apathic attitude toward life is the character that appears among the Muslims. In contrast, if you enter the quarter of the Christians, your heart feels happiness; you find superbly constructed houses, which testify to proprietors interested in life, and to their beautiful disposition, and clean and broad streets. In contrast to the immobility of the Muslims, the Christians are always on the move. In this respect, they enjoy the good things of life much more. . . . The difference is even more obvious in regard to education. Whereas the Christian citizens generally know how to read and write more or less, the Muslims are very much behind.[34]

A strong feeling of inferiority and obsession by Muslim decadence emerged in this Young Turk observer. During a journey in Ottoman Albania, Şerif noted that the children of remote villages attending beautiful missionary schools took "pride in Americanism [*Amerikalılık*], whereas they were Ottomans like their fathers and forefathers before them." With bitter self-criticism, the Young Turk journalist concluded that these facts "clearly show us the collapse of our morals, and what now are our own duties. We must agree with those [missionaries and others] who say that [Muslim reactionaries], who cannot penetrate the sources of Islam, to true humanity and general fraternity, . . . are an obstacle for progress. Yes, with our blindness and insolence we merit such libels."[35]

Like Abdulhamid, however, the jealous Young Turk journalist began to single out the missionaries as "the fundamental foes of our Ottoman and Muslim identity [*Osmanlılık, İslâmlılık*]. They always work against this identity." Even if, "thanks be to God, no Muslim was made Protestant," there were many Muslims who, under American influence, "had, in effect, forgotten that they were Muslim and Ottoman," Şerif concluded.[36] There was deep resentment and a distressing feeling of exclusion. The Americans believed in a new Ottoman world that, in the Young Turks' eyes, was new indeed, but it was not their world. Theirs was passing away, they feared. How could they calmly bid farewell to it, if the future looked strangely American and they themselves felt excluded? Departing from Beirut, in June 1911, Şerif looked back from the ship: "The city in front of us is a picture of a passage [from one era to another]. My eyes automatically turned to the American Protestant Establishment [Syrian Protestant College, later AUB] and remained fixed on those great, majestic buildings. But they could not penetrate inside the walls. There is the spirit of today's Beirut, in these and similar buildings. There, a young world is nourished. But this nourishment is poison to Ottoman identity [*Osmanlılık*]."[37] In the minds of the CUP people, the divorce was consummated. Mission was Western and Christian, thus part of Western liberalism and imperialism; the CUP's path had to lead in the opposite direction. Missionary work, even the most humanitarian help, was seen as part of an evil force that came from outside and strove for an unwanted future—unwanted because it fundamentally questioned what they believed to be their irreducible Ottoman, Muslim, Turkish identity. This was an essentialist concept and, as such, a dead end: the Young Turks' blind spot. But nevertheless it was a psychological reality to be carefully dealt with—since most of them were not ready or able to emancipate themselves from it.[38]

The weekly *The Orient,* published by the Bible House after April 1910 and printed by H. Matteosian in Istanbul, contrasted with *Tanîn. The Orient*'s masthead indicates Charles T. Riggs as its editor. This paper sought to be a secular interface, reaching out to a more general Ottoman public. It covered Ottoman news, regularly including events in parliament and a review of the Ottoman press, and sometimes of the treatment of Ottoman issues in the international press. In particular, however, it addressed those interested in Protestant issues both within and outside the Ottoman Empire. It is true that as early as the World Missionary Conference in June 1910, a certain skepticism had been expressed about a Young Turk progressiveness that linked European atheism and its "armoury" with anti-Christian Islamism.[39] The CUP's secretiveness was also criticized early on.[40] However, while a fundamental antimissionary and anti-American stance was already explicit in the CUP journal *Tanîn,* the American missionary optimism about Young Turkey, including a benevolent attitude toward the CUP, prevailed in *The Orient* until 1912. The ARF's instrumental attitude toward the church was criticized no less than atheistic attitudes among CUP members. Furthermore, American and other missionaries were the fiercest critics of European politics in the Balkans, seeing that they destabilized the fragile Young Turkey.[41] The missionaries paid much attention to the question of the *muhacir* (Muslim refugees from the Balkan) and their settlement in Asia Minor. When the American Red Cross, which stood in close contact with the ABCFM, brought the refugees humanitarian help, this was an opportunity to show that the Americans took "deep philanthropic interest in people of another race and religion."[42]

With regard to the education of women, the ABCFM believed itself to be pioneering a movement perfectly agreed to by the Young Turks. It was a wonderful feeling for Joseph Greene, who had been a missionary to Turkey for fifty years, when on 18 September 1908, during an assembly in Bebek Park, Istanbul, he listened to a talk by Prince Sabahaddin to which many Muslim girls applauded enthusiastically, pulling off their veils. Sabahaddin, himself a Young Turk but in opposition to the CUP, eloquently supported the education of girls. In that year more than fifty Muslim girls attended the American College for Girls in Scutari (Üsküdar). According to missionary teacher Mary Patrick, in 1911 "all prominent Turkish patriots at the present time express themselves with great enthusiasm regarding the necessity for the higher education of Turkish women."[43] Under the title "Are We Dreaming?" the journalists of *The Orient* satisfactorily reported on the emerging women's movement and the fact that its new journal, *Kadın Dünyası* (Women's World) had reproduced a photo with unveiled Muslim women on its front page—without indicating that the photo had been taken a few years earlier in the American missionary school in Scutari. American schools were strongholds of "Occidentalism" (*Batıcılık*). To be Western despite the West was the poignant slogan of the patriotic Ottoman women's rights groups that emerged in the 1910s.[44]

The Orient's lead story of 31 January 1912 dealt with the CUP politician Ahmed Rıza, for a long time a leader of the Young Turk movement, whom the sultan had elevated to the rank of senator. The article used laudatory terms to describe Rıza: "He has been fearless and impartial in his treatment of the Deputies, and has upheld the tradition of parliamentary law and usage to a degree that most men in a similar position would have found impossible."[45] A week later, the front page was devoted to the parliamentary elections. A critical attitude toward the CUP began to crystallize. In Izmir, an organized "great crowd of hooting, jeering Union and Progress partisans" had broken up an election meeting of the liberal Lütfi Fikri Bey. *The Orient* concluded, "The Unionist machine is a powerful one, and those who get in its way may expect a tough struggle."[46] The elections in April in fact turned out to be *sopalı seçim,* that is, the CUP won by means of coercion, threats and beatings (*sopa*). Considered illegitimate by the opposition, the CUP cabinet was forced to resign in July, and the parliament was closed in August 1912. *The Orient*'s review of the year 1912 in the first issue of 1913 saw the "fate of the Union and Progress party" as "variegated, the darker shades predominating." As hopeful as ever, even during the Balkan wars, the men in the Bible House nevertheless anticipated "the real and effective solution of the vexatious Balkan problem, and the consequent inauguration of an era of peace and prosperity for that storm centre."

Henceforth the editorialist of *The Orient* criticized the CUP openly as undemocratic and incompetent.[47] He commented negatively on the coup d'état of 23 January 1913, when the CUP had begun its dictatorship.[48] Nevertheless, the same editorial ends by expressing eschatological hopes with regard to a new generation of students in the ten American colleges of the Ottoman Empire, that "the lives of all these students may be transformed by the power of the living Christ, and leaders for the cause of righteousness may be prepared, that the Kingdom of God may soon come." Perhaps in their sermons (which I did not access) the representatives of missionary America spoke more openly about the catastrophes to come, or of Jesus to come as judge of this world. All publications, however, were careful in combining criticism with hope; they never used catastrophist language. On the contrary, they tended to suppress the dark side of the Revelation. A constructive tendency prevailed, advocating peaceful historical evolution toward the Kingdom. At the beginning of the critical and, for the Ottoman Empire, decisive year of 1913, Charles Riggs wrote in *The Orient* that it was "fitting that all unite in humble supplication that the turning and overturning [in contemporary history] may result in the incoming of His kingdom."[49]

On Crumbling Ground

Now more focused on elite education, the missionaries felt more than ever that there was limited receptivity for their spiritual message, or rather, to the language and forms of piety that they employed to carry the Gospel. Modern education and a new scientific language were successfully spreading, but new forms of piety that took into account the transreligious Sufi heritage of medieval Anatolia, for example, had not developed. The forms of piety had remained Calvinistic, the religious language, to a large extent, American evangelical. How to teach a universal Gospel in a late Ottoman situation, where religious affiliations had become deeply politicized? The challenge was enormous. Not only spiritual disinterest among their clientele and prejudices on the Muslim side caused the ABCFM's failure to transmit a strong message in the crucial period after 1908.

Missionary archives reveal open suffering on the part of mission teachers due to lack of interest in their message. Young men in the Ottoman Empire, Christians, Muslims, and Jews, saw education mostly as an instrument for a professional career or a political commitment. Young women had a more holistic orientation, and their understanding of the deeper concerns of missionaries was generally better. They were more willing to translate spiritual content into their social lives.[50] Men were subject to rather different, perhaps more compelling group dynamics. They were focused on successful careers and politics and often subscribed to positivist and biologist views of the world, according to the zeitgeist. Individual spirituality and care for human relations and good neighborliness were hardly attractive because not professionally promising: so it seemed, and so it proved to a large extent, in the period of the world wars.

For Ahmed Şerif, the missions represented a strange, impenetrable world. This world was American, not Ottoman, despite the ABCFM's insistent claims to the contrary. Missionary America did not make him feel "true humanity and general fraternity"—for him, the source of Islam, even if the missionaries paraphrased their Gospel in these same words. Theoretically, there was some common ground between the missionaries and the Young Turks, even in religion; but in the reality of those days, estrangement, distrust, and hate prevailed. Both for Turkists and Turkish Islamists, religion was highly political and tied to nationalism. In 1910, the military *müfti* Fahreddin of Edirne had put it in these terms: "Turkness and Islam are one. If Islam disappears, one can no more speak about [Turkish] nationality. The missionaries are the bacillus of cholera that poisons our nation's existence."[51] The CUP elite feared losing everything: the final remnants of cultural self-confidence and social dominance together with the last remains of Ottoman rule and sovereignty.

There was a basic social envy on the part of many Sunni Turks and Kurds directed against the native Christians and the foreign missionaries. The CUP increasingly considered the native Christians as "foreign," unassimilable elements among a Muslim majority in Asia Minor. The political language of important CUP members from 1912 onward took on a new, strongly Turkist flavor.[52] Obvious gaps between Muslims and Christians partly due to missionary assistance, hate, and envy, coupled with anti-imperialist plot theories, formed an explosive mixture. Faced with growing anti-Christian resentment in Anatolia and daily anti-Armenian violence in the eastern provinces, Ottoman Armenian leaders, notably Krikor Zohrab, addressed European foreign ministers with a view to implementing reforms in eastern Anatolia according to the Berlin Treaty. The reform plan, drafted by the jurist André Mandelstam, chief dragoman at the Russian Embassy, was thoroughly revised with German participation and, under European pressure, signed by the Ottoman government on 8 February 1914. The plan divided the eastern provinces in a northern and a southern part; put them under the control of two powerful European inspectors, to be selected from neutral countries; prescribed to publish the laws and official pronouncements in the local languages; provided for a fair proportion of Muslims and Christians in the councils and the police; and demobilized the *Hamidiye.* For many international observers, both contemporary and later, such as the American historian Roderic Davison, these reforms were a compromise where no one lost out. There was hardly any other way of creating pacified and functioning multiethnic eastern provinces. After such bloody events and governmental failures as had followed the Congress of Berlin, the establishment of a balanced system under effective international control seemed unavoidable.[53] Jemal and Talat Pasha, however, filled later dozens of pages in their memoirs to justify their contrary viewpoint—that is, to explain why they regarded the reforms as an open door for Russia and wanted to obstruct them.[54]

The CUP was particularly suspicious of the Alevis, especially the eastern, mainly Kurdish (*Zaza*)–speaking Alevis. This suspicion increased rapidly on the eve of World War I, as the CUP now sided openly with Abdulhamid's Kurdish irregulars, the *Hamidiye Alayları* (renamed *Aşiret Süvari Alayları*), and with other tribes. From their establishment in the early 1890s on, the *Hamidiye* had been a plague for the local Armenians and Alevis. Many Alevis had adopted political and social ideas similar to the Armenians, welcoming international reforms. The Young Turks interpreted the close relations between Armenians, Alevis, and missionaries as the result of unscrupulous, subversive propaganda on the part of the Protestants and Armenians and as a dangerous threat to the Turko-Muslim unity for which they strove.[55] The publishers of *The Orient* saw the problem of the Armenians in the eastern provinces not as "one of autonomy nor of any change of laws, but merely one of the enforcement of law." They agreed that if the Ottoman government was chronically "unable or unwilling to guarantee these loyal [Armenian] subjects such basal [*sic*] rights [security for life and property and honor], then they must appeal to Europe to take measures to enforce the provisions of the Berlin treaty relating to security and order in these provinces."[56] Despite many single instances of violence, missionaries on the spot did not note such comprehensive social tensions, even after fall of 1914, as to make them fear mass murders by local perpetrators, as they had in 1895. In their perception, the mass violence of 1915 had clearly been instigated by the center.[57]

The ABCFM's positive attitude toward international reforms, its opinion that not foreign influence but the neglect of great domestic problems and promised reforms had weakened the country, and news from missionaries on the spot about ongoing anti-Armenian violence were understood by the rulers as detrimental propaganda, just as Abdulhamid had seen these twenty years previously. Nevertheless, some warning voices among CUP members themselves focused on the "bitter experiences" of the Armenians, the ongoing persecution, and the government's inability to carry out reform in the East. These voices, however, could not stop the increasing anti-Armenian and anti-Christian attitude in which resentful forces both on the spot and in the center of power converged.

"Let us for a moment put ourselves in the place of the Armenians; let us judge of the facts soberly according to their ideas, their point of view," wrote journalist Hüseyin Cahit (Yalçın), an influential CUP member and colleague of Ahmed Şerif. "Let us not be hypnotized by *our way* of thinking. . . . Let us establish among the various elements of our country a brotherhood born of really liberal agreement; otherwise we must lose all hope of safety." Cahit reacted to Ottoman dailies that violently accused the Armenians of appealing to international diplomacy, instead of to the national authorities, for efficient reforms. "Living in a dream and floating about in abstractions, we have been too blind to see realities," Huseyin Cahit continued. The road through the Sublime Porte and the Chamber of Deputies being "a blind alley, they [the Armenians] are compelled to look wherever else they can for a door of safety." For himself, however, the Young Turk Cahit had made the same choice as the CUP—as he put candidly and significantly in these terms: "Rather than enjoy reforms under pressure of the European States, I should prefer for my country the rule of despotism."[58]

The CUP's choice to go to war in August 1914 was codetermined by the intention to avert the Armenian reforms, which they declared to be the first step toward regional autonomy and Russian hegemony. In reality, the CUP wanted to maintain and expand its own unchecked, if unconvincing, rule. In September, the Ottoman government cancelled the implementation of the reforms and, with it, the only practicable hope of the Armenians in eastern Anatolia. Requisitions during the general mobilization hit the Armenians particularly hard; most of their sympathies were logically with the *Entente* and against war, especially as from August 1914 onward, the Ottoman propaganda war had a strong pan-Turkist and pan-Islamist touch and therefore excluded the Armenians.[59] On November 14 the Sheikh ul-Islam declared the Ottoman *jihad* on Germany's side.

Seminal Catastrophe, 1914–1918

Having held dictatorial power since 1913 and all being between thirty-two and forty-two years old, the leading CUP rulers considered war a remedy for the problems of the empire. They believed in a necessary and salutary war, as did young nationalist elites in France and Germany in the summer of 1914. Not these elites, however, but the responsible generation of their fathers, who held the highest power positions, lacked the strength to resist a general war that ultimately caused four decades of massive bloodshed in the Old World.

The belief in war put the CUP in yet more contrast to the missionaries. Most of the missionaries could never accept political violence or war as a part of the "nature" of human history. "Why all this carnage and butchery?" Charles Riggs, the editorialist of *The Orient,* asked during the Second Balkan War. "Primarily because modern civilization continues to teach the barbarous arts of war; because the state trains men to take a gun and stand up in front of his brother man and murder him by legalized murder." The idea of necessary and just, not to say salutary, apocalyptic war did not at all pervade the missionary community on the ground. Riggs finished his editorial on an eschatological note, with unorthodox socialist connotation: "They [the nominally Christian nations] will probably continue to do these things [war and arming] until the Church of Jesus Christ, or, shall I say, Socialism or some other kind of 'ism' can teach the nations the way of peace."[60] Faced with Social Darwinist readiness for total war among European elites, other Protestant intellectuals—for example, the young Karl Barth, who joined the Swiss Socialist Party in 1915—attempted to integrate into their political theology what they saw as socialism's truth with regard to social realities, as well as its utopian potential for peace and social justice.

In the eastern provinces of the Ottoman Empire, the people and the missionaries understood the drive toward war when in August 1914, after the secret treaty with Germany, military requisitions began. Dr. Daniel Thom, a longtime missionary in Mardin, wrote to William Peet on 16 August 1914:

> "War is hell" and it seems to me the Powers that have rushed into it headlong, regardless of life or limb, are finding it out to their sorrow, and the end is where? Even here, with no declared war we are finding it *"hell."* . . . The Government has robbed the city, and the country around, of its men, of its animals, of its money, leaving the thresh-

> ing floors loaded down with a richer harvest than has ever been laid upon, to rot where they are, for lack of men and beasts to tread them out and care for them. The millions that will be lost to the people and the Government cannot be estimated. Such suicidal conduct of a government I have not seen, during this variegated life I have lived. Other brains than Turkish are navigating this ship of State, through the rapids, and on the rocks, to be dashed to pieces, and helplessly wrecked, then will come in the foreign firms and bargain for the salvaging. Poor Turkey, poor Turkey, going it blindly, with a man at the head of the army, whose name is LIGHT [Enver], but he has certainly turned on the dark slide on his lantern, and is rushing head long, pell-mell over the precipice, to sure destruction, was there ever such blindness?[61]

This was strong and perspicacious language, even if—like many Americans—Thom tended to see too much direct German agency at work in the Ottoman Empire in those days. The attribution of martial decision making to German influence arose from the perception that such chauvinist, autodestructive conduct must be "foreign," not Ottoman, among those who had put their full hopes in a new Ottoman nation and knew very little about the political and intellectual biographies of the CUP leaders.

The CUP had considered the Armenian appeal to the European diplomats in 1912 an act of high treason and judged the ARF's refusal, in August 1914, to conduct a (suicidal) guerilla war against the Russians in the Caucasus side by side with the Special Organization similarly. Young Turk officers began to speak openly of the need to destroy the Armenian community, though most Ottoman Armenian men served loyally in the army. In a letter published in February 1915, Enver Pasha praised Armenian soldiers of his Caucasus campaign. But his disastrous defeat at Sarıkamış at the end of 1914 and his brother-in-law Jevdet's subsequent unsuccessful campaign in northern Persia led to high casualties, epidemics, and a brutalizing war on the eastern front on both sides, and both efforts had included Armenian militias. Many Armenians fled to Russian Armenia, among them several thousand young Armenians who became volunteers in the Russian army. After the catastrophic Ottoman military failures, the propaganda in spring 1915 spread the thesis of a general Armenian rebellion. The documentary record, however, including recently published Ottoman army sources, does not support the propanganda.[62]

The first Ottoman victory, at the Dardanelles on 18 March, saved the Young Turk leaders from depression, and according to the Austrian military attaché General Joseph Pomiankowski, who often accompanied Enver, it stimulated them to exercise a "brutal chauvinism" against Christians in general and Armenians in particular. Decisive meetings of the CUP Central Committee were held for which Dr. Behaeddin Şakir, the head of the Special Organization in eastern Anatolia, came back to the capital. In the night of 24 to 25 April, security forces began to arrest, torture, and murder the Armenian elites throughout Anatolia, starting with Istanbul. On 24 April also, a telegram from Talat Bey, minister of the interior, to Jemal Pasha, military governor of Syria, announced that henceforth Armenians should be deported not to Konya, as had been the case with the Armenians from Zeytun in March, but to northern Syria.[63] Without mentioning the Armenians, a provisional law, published on 1 June, allowed force against the population and mass deportations if national defense was at issue. (The parliament had been closed on 13 March.) The main removal of the Armenians from eastern and western Anatolia and the province of Edirne toward the Syrian deserts took place from June to October 1915.

In eastern Anatolia, men and youngsters were mostly massacred on the spot, with those in the army separated into labor battalions and killed. Women and children endured starvation, mass rape, and enslavement on their marches. Deportations from the west included the men, and the victims partly went by train. Several hundred thousand destitute deportees arrived in Syria in summer and fall of 1915. They were not resettled, as had been promised, but strictly isolated in concentration camps and starved to death. Ali Fuad, the governor of Deir ez-Zor, who had helped the deportees to make a new life, was replaced in July 1916 by the hardliner Salih Zeki. Those who survived until summer 1916 were massacred, apart from between 100,000 and 150,000 whom Jemal Pasha had settled in southern Syria and formally converted to Islam. Widely varying numbers are proposed, but the most reliable figure is that more than half of nearly two million Ottoman Armenians alive in 1914 were killed in 1915–1916. International holocaust and genocide scholars, beginning with Raphael Lemkin, saw that destruction as a paradigmatic genocide of the twentieth century.[64] The destruction of the Ottoman Armenians was legally and symbolically completed on 11 August 1916 when the Armenian community's National Constitution (*Nizamname*) of 1863, the backbone of a menacing Armenian dynamism, according to the official news agency *Millî*, was abolished.[65]

Few deportees had been able to escape and disappear to Aleppo. More important was the escape to Erzincan and Erzurum, occupied by the Russian army in 1916. Thousands of Armenians had found refuge among the Alevis in the mountainous Dersim in 1915 and were able to cross the Russian lines in 1916. Others had fled beyond the eastern front and returned with the advancing Russian army, which retreated after the October Revolution in November 1917; unable to stop the return of Young Turkish Ottoman rule at that time, Armenian militias acted brutally toward the Muslim population. The Republic of Armenia, declared on 28 May 1918, hoped to regain a part of northeastern Anatolia via diplomacy, but the related Treaty of Sèvres was not implemented. Enver's uncle Halil (Kut) threatened to annihilate the Armenians even in Caucasian Armenia. Soviet troops finally prevented eastern Armenia from being crushed by the Turkish nationalist forces that advanced toward Erivan in 1920. Armenia, however, lost its independence. Approximately 150,000 Armenian refugees, resettled in Cilicia after 1918, fled when the French forces retreated in 1921.[66]

After the Turkish entry into World War I, and irrevocably when, in spring 1915, systematic anti-Armenian policies began, the ABCFM considered itself to be in an emergency situation in its interactions with the CUP government. The "absolute obedience to the laws of the land" in the relationship between missions and governments, which had been "accepted mission policy," was now called into question; civil disobedience, particularly with regard to refugees, became legitimate. With regard to Turkey and relevant experiences in the 1890s, the report of the commission concerned in Edinburgh had stated anticipatively that "where Government itself becomes an instrument of violence and massacre, the ordinary principles governing the relations between Missions and Governments cannot be applied, because one of the related terms has ceased to carry its true meaning."[67] Tacy Atkinson, an experienced nurse in the ABCFM hospital at Mamuretülaziz, had razor blades smuggled into prison in June 1915 so that at least a few of those who were to be murdered outside the town could cut their ropes and flee to Dersim (today's Tunceli). Dersim was a region of Alevis, the only place relatively safe for the persecuted Armenians. Concerning the risk she herself ran in this and other illegal actions, she wrote, "I am not one bit afraid of prison, nor of anything man can do, nor of death, if it be necessary, but I am afraid of sin, and this is sin." She said she believed she would one day find herself in a common heaven with the man in charge of the local Red Crescent Hospital, a Muslim, who also did all he could to help Armenian deportees.[68]

Henceforth, the encounters of missionaries with CUP officials during World War I were strained confrontations between opposing systems of reference and different generations: elderly missionaries versus relatively young CUP actors; men of biblical beliefs and ethical values versus men of action, saviors of a world, "heroes"; missionaries functioning as Freudian superegos versus Nietzschean hyperegos of (would-be) *Übermenschen*. The following relationships can all be analyzed in these terms: Clarence D. Ussher's interaction with Enver's brother-in-law Tahir Jevdet, attorney *vali* in Van, in 1915, whom Ussher had known as a child; Floyd P. Smith's relationship with, and expulsion by, Mehmed Reshid, *vali* of Diyarbekir; George P. White's confrontation with the governor, military officers and, indirectly, with Minister of War Enver Pasha in Marsivan; William W. Peet's mostly indirect interactions with leading CUP members in the capital; the German missionary Johannes Lepsius's famous interview with Enver Pasha on 10 August 1915; and the German missionary Johannes Ehman's interactions and interviews with Sabit Bey, *vali* of Mamuretülaziz, in May–June 1915.[69]

The missionaries now understood painfully and more than ever that Jesus' reign was indeed not of *this* world, despite all their clever strategies and constructive efforts. Striking otherness, precise if mute accusations, skilled observation and documentation, and help for groups the regime wanted to destroy led the CUP to loathe the missionaries. If they had dared and had not feared the consequences, the CUP leaders on the ground would have treated the missionaries "like the Armenians," as they put it threateningly on several occasions. The ABCFM was most hated for its symbolic capital, its quasi immunity, and its representing America. Enver Pasha is a good example of this attitude. Even if he felt compelled to make some public shows of respect for the ABCFM, since its services to the Ottoman world and to Ottoman soldiers in its hospitals were unquestionable, he considered the missionaries as fundamental enemies. What a strange tension, therefore, when, during a visit in mid-July 1916 to Mamuretülaziz, Enver kissed Henry Atkinson, the twelve-year-old son of Tacy Atkinson and the late Dr. Henry H. Atkinson, and gave him a war medal as a symbolic reward for the American hospital staff's great services in Mamuretülaziz on behalf of wounded Turkish soldiers.[70] Dr. Atkinson, the founder of the hospital, had died in autumn 1915, "sick at heart, not wanting to live any longer on this wicked earth," as his wife wrote, after he had made a tour of inspection at Lake Gölcük, where the corpses of about ten thousand murdered women and children lay.[71]

Missionaries reacted in three different ways during the catastrophe. Many experienced and shrewd missionaries, particularly long-standing ABCFM members, had no doubts as to the criminal nature of the CUP's war regime. They used their international network and their prestige on the ground to protect themselves, to witness events, and to provide, where they could, humanitarian assistance to needy people, as did Peet in Istanbul, Ussher in Van, Mary L. Graffam in Sivas, and Jakob Künzler in Urfa.[72] (The protective capitulations had been annulled in September 1914.) Second were those who trusted authority or trusted Germany behind Turkey, such as the German Ehmann, who suffered a dramatic breakdown of his faith when the destruction began in June 1915; he nonetheless recovered. Third, younger missionaries and women, who were close to the victims, often despaired of life—such as Francis H. Leslie in Urfa (both missionary and consular agent responsible for the internees, who committed suicide following a mental breakdown, after Vice Consul Samuel Edelman left him alone with dangerous assignments in Urfa), the German missionaries Helene Laska in Harput and Martha Kleiss in Bitlis (who died in despair), and the Swiss teacher Beatrice Rohner (who had a mental breakdown and did not recover until years later).[73]

In many locations the missionaries observed the CUP policy and its actors on the ground. The observation was particularly dense in Mamuretül-aziz, where it led, after many detailed reports, to the establishment of a list of fifty-two local culprits.[74] Henry Riggs, teacher at the ABCFM's Euphrates College, observed during the summer of 1915 the transit camps of the deportees through a telescope and wrote that "for most of the women and children was reserved the long and lingering suffering that massacre seemed to them a merciful fate—suffering such as was foreseen and planned by the perpetrators of this horror. I speak guardedly and state as a fact this horrid indictment of the Young Turks by whom the crime was committed."[75]

A relatively young witness was Floyd Smith, a doctor who had been with the ABCFM in Diyarbekir since 1913. Until the first weeks of Dr. Reshid's governorship, beginning in March 1915, Dr. Smith had enjoyed close relations with the government. He confirms the government's precarious position in view of the general problem of desertion before the arrival of Mehmed Reshid:

> The vali was superseded early in March. By getting a large force of police and gendarmes the new vali [Reshid] succeeded in apprehending the larger part of these men. He soon started the imprisonment of prominent Armenians using as justification the false statement that they were sheltering deserters. . . . Most people had weapons in their houses in remembrance of the event of twenty years ago, but I feel positive that there was no idea of a general uprising. About the first of April a proclamation was posted demanding arms. Men were imprisoned right and left and tortured to make them confess the presence and place of concealments of arms. Some went mad under the torture.

Confessions were extracted under torture so that an Armenian close to the ABCFM was made to sign an absurd document saying that the ABCFM was preparing an insurrection in Diyarbekir and that its agent, Dr. Smith, was an Armenian.[76] Expelled, Dr. Smith was made to leave before the final drama started: the murder of the Christian population without, in this case, deportation. The government confiscated the property of the ABCFM in the city. The very rapid and voluntary deterioration of the relations between local functionaries and the ABCFM, an organization rooted in the *vilayet* of Diyarbekir for three generations, was a strong sign of the "new spirit" of Social Darwinist demographic engineering that the CUP emissary, the military doctor and *vali* Dr. Reshid, brought with him to the eastern provinces in the spring of 1915. In applying the Law on Abandoned Property of 25 May 1915, Dr. Reshid founded a commission for the administration of the Armenians' property. As in other places, instead of its declared goal, namely, the protection of the property and goods of the deported, the commission served to transfer these to the Muslim majority.[77]

Thanks to its experience, its institutions throughout Asia Minor, and its broad network, the ABCFM understood early on the comprehensive nature, beyond any expectable wartime measure, of the anti-Armenian policy that evolved in spring 1915. At many places missionaries were present during the first phase of the Armenian genocide, that is, the massacres and removal in Asia Minor in 1915. This was much less the case during the second phase in 1916, when the survivors of the deportation were starved to death in camps in northern Syria and the still surviving, massacred. ABCFM treasurer and informal head William Peet, in the Bible House in Istanbul, was among the best-informed persons of what was going on in the provinces; he stood in familiar connection with members of both the German and the U.S. embassies.[78] On 14 July 1915, Peet cabled to Boston that there were many urgent requests but that ABCFM relief funds were exhausted. Two months later saw the establishment of a humanitarian organization, later called the Near East Relief, in which many missionaries and helpers of different countries, beyond the leading ABCFM, began to work together.[79] This organization, together with the ABCFM, the German organization Hilfsbund für christliches Liebeswerk im Orient, German diplomacy, American diplomacy, and Swiss connections in Aleppo and Basel supported the humanitarian aid undertaking led by the teacher Beatrice Rohner in Aleppo in 1916–1917. Partly protected by Jemal Pasha, the military governor of Syria, and together with local Armenians, she built up legal orphanages and communicated illegally with the deportees in the camps. She was the only missionary in a position to write down an expanded testimony of the second phase of the genocide.[80] With money sent by Peet, Rohner had done a magnificent job with Armenian orphans in Aleppo and among thousands of deportees in the Syrian camps, before she broke down when the regime closed her orphanage in February 1917. Her orphans were sent away into government orphanages.[81]

During World War I, humanitarian assistance of any kind to the targeted Christian populations was understood as intolerable resistance to the will of the rulers. Little children in particular were a bone of contention: if they survived but were not assimilated to the Turko-Muslim identity, they continued to bear a heritage considered subversive. With regard to unchecked national sovereignty, also in the realm of spirit and symbols, the ruler were correct when they saw the missionaries as adversaries and a particular thorn in their flesh. In an article Hasan Enver Pasha wrote for Ottoman newspapers in 1918, this retired general, who had studied in Paris and been an Ottoman intelligence officer in Europe, Cuba and China, denounced the missionaries as "fighters and representatives of all America" and opined that for "their religious fanaticism, the Americans basically do not like Muslims," even do not wish "any Islamic state to exist upon earth." Against all evidence, Hasan Enver argued that by entering World War I in 1917, America aimed "to wipe us off the face of the earth." America wanted "to wage war against Turks and Muslims, in order to save Christianity in the Near East," he wrote, although he knew that the United States observed strict neutrality toward Turkey. His sentence contains an eloquent ellipsis: Eastern Christians were not to be saved but destroyed. He furthermore accused the missionaries of setting Armenians, Kurds, and Syrians against their Muslim rulers and urged that Turkey should profit from the state of war to eradicate the ABCFM.[82] Here is the entire document of this early, well-articulated anti-American viewpoint, which in the 1910s may additionally have germinated in acquaintances with German friends such as the orientalist and propagandist Max von Oppenheim, and the officers Hans Humann and Bronsard von Schellendorf, both friends of Minister of War Enver Pasha:

> Protestantism is the ruling religion in America, and religion is considered a very important issue. In view of their religious fanaticism the Americans generally do not like Muslims. Obviously for political reasons and allegedly on behalf of civilization and humanity, they accuse the Turks of cruelty and barbarism. In reality they cherish an aversion against them that is founded in their national mentality. While the idea of crusade has mostly died out in today's Europe, it continues to live on in America in spiritual terms. If the Americans had their way, there would not be a single Islamic state left on earth. As is well known, this religious ambition is implemented nowadays under the name of "religious missions." The Catholic missionaries do not benefit from

> the recognition, the public importance and the national sense of mission that the American missionaries enjoy. The American missionaries are the champions and representatives of the whole American people. American missionaries have for a long time been silently and secretly settling down in the Ottoman lands, with very little notice being taken of them. They started with their activities in Rumelia and especially in Anatolia. They incited and stirred up the Bulgarians, Armenians, Kurds, and Syrians against the Turks, while allegedly protecting and defending them. All are aware of the support enjoyed by the Armenians from the Americans, but less well known is the extent of their influence on the Bulgarians and the Christians of Syria. During a stay in America we became certain that the Americans had succeeded in forming an entire U.S.-based colony of Syrians that is anti-Turk. For us, it is very dangerous that, in the name of freedom, the American government is now participating in the world war. After all, America's ultimate ambition is to obliterate us from the earth. And even while they are unable to do this, they will by no means give up this project. Now there are people among us who think that, in view of such a situation, it would be appropriate to respond with humanity, generosity and politeness, that is to close our eyes. But it must be absolutely clear to us that nothing can dissuade the Americans from these religious efforts. In the same way as you have to fight a fire effectively, we must in this regard exploit the state of war in order to eradicate completely the Americans' right of intervention in our country. We must not blind ourselves to the fact: one of the reasons driving the people and the public opinion of America into this conflict is to wage war against the Turks and Muslims in order to save Christianity in the Orient.

Whereas Hasan Enver, the son of a converted Pole, had already served under Abdulhamid, Minister of War and CUP member Enver—he was thirty-three in 1914—belonged to a resentful young elite that saw itself called to save the empire, and, in Enver's case, to wage war in order to rescue a Turkish-led Muslim world. It understood that missionary America radically challenged Islamic power. It denounced the missionaries' work, purportedly carried out "in the name of civilization and humanity," for being a purely political instrument of anti-Islamic or anti-national forces. What a different perspective it might have had if the CUP committee governement had opted for armed neutrality in World War I, and for constructive cooperation with missionary America, which, after 1908, had followed a strongly pro-Ottoman policy—even if its members on the spot began only then to adopt more humble and sympathetic approaches to Muslims and to the Ottoman society as a whole.

Squandered Visions, Lasting Seeds?

However one looks at it, whomever one blames or not, World War I was a catastrophe for the Ottoman world, causing a terrible loss of population and establishing a fatal connection between mass violence, nationalist renewal, and political culture. It was also a catastrophic failure for missionary America, which had hoped to play a leading role as a peaceful civic force in Young Turkey. The failure was all the more painful when, after World War I, the ABCFM was also unable to implement its vision of a new order. A set of ideas had been developed, and they were adapted to the new situation in 1918. Key concepts were federalism; return of the Armenian and Kurdish refugees, in nonacceptance of the results of coercive and violent population policies; an American mandate over the whole of Asia Minor or even beyond; and the installation of a new liberal government. The national independence of native peoples was not a primary goal of Wilsonian and missionary "Protestant diplomacy" in the Near East, nor was "clamorous Armenianism" or political Zionism.[83] James Barton had proposed as early as January 1917 an American "mandate for the Ottoman Empire with Armenia forming one of six federated states within the whole."[84] Barton and the missionaries' anti-Islamic attitude, however, turned out to be reinforced after the experience of war policy and its partly Islamist rhetoric. Such attitudes had been partly questioned previously in the Belle Epoque.

Caleb Gates, the president of Robert College and a former missionary at Harput, argued when the Peace Conference in Paris began, "The attention of the Peace Conference should be centered upon giving the Turks a good government rather than upon delivering the Armenians and Greeks from Turkish government. Because it will be of little profit to establish an Armenia, more than half of whose people will be Turks, if alongside of this new State there remains a Turkey of the old type. . . . To save the Armenians and Greeks you must save the Turks also."[85] Clarence Ussher prepared plans for the return of refugees, Armenians and Kurds, to the eastern provinces. Returning from Russian Armenia, where he had fled from Van during the war, Ussher arrived in the Ottoman capital in spring of 1919. There he was in touch with Ali Kemal, the minister of the interior; Grand Vizir Damad Ferid Pasha; and Kurdish liberals. For his plan, he prepared letters to local notables in Ottoman Turkish. These letters were signed, and probably written, by Seyid Abdülkadir, the president of the Society for the Rise of Kurdistan.

"Doctor Ussher of the American Help Committee is coming these days into your region. It is the only desire and goal of that organisation [Near East Relief] to help in the name of civilisation and humanity, without distinguishing between races and religions, in order to still the needs of all groups and to remedy their distress caused by the war," we read in one of these letters, dated 11 April 1919.[86] But the letters were not sent.

Ussher did not go east but, first, west, and he arrived at Paris in June 1919. Beside him other American missionaries attended the Peace Conference. Ussher's ideas are representative of those of many other members of the missionary community:

> Suggestive Summary. 1. One mandatory for the entire Empire. 2. Internationalize the waters from the Black Sea to the Mediterranean. 3. Make Constantinople a free City. 4. A foreign Commission to control all governments, thereby eliminating the question of religious control of the state. 5. Declare absolute religious liberty for all, including Moslems. 6. Grant statehood for those sections showing fitness for same, and govern all others as territories under central government. Pre-war racial predominance should be a paramount consideration in fixing boundaries of states. 7. Establish a central representative governing body under control of mandatory. 8. Define qualifications on which territories will be admitted to statehood and make ability to read and write essential to the franchise.

Ussher did not advocate a tabula rasa of the existing system, as the Kemalists did a few years later, and he did not hold religious feelings in contempt. In another paper of 1919 he explained, "To abolish too suddenly an organized system of government from a recognized center might produce anarchy. The various nationalities of Turkey including the Turk, have been clamoring for a change in the government and a common prayer of the Turks was 'Allah Sahabi geundersen' (May God send us a master). The time has come for that 'Sahab.'"[87] Ussher's anti-Islamic stance nonetheless was clear and corresponded, in a way, with that of many CUP members and Kemalists, who also saw Islam as a hindrance to progress and modern civilization. During those years, however, they desperately needed and exploited Islam in order to mobilize the people, particularly the Kurds, behind them. Since the fin de siècle they had taken Islam as a constitutive, distinctive element for defining Turkish ethnicity.

In contrast to the Turkish nationalists, Ussher wanted the crimes of the war regime to be examined and no particular ethnic element to dominate the others. Istanbul should become a center of international organization and solidarity, if possible the center of the League of Nations. His criticism of Turkish rule had to do with bitter experiences during World War I but turned out to be sweeping.[88] Ussher's vision for the future was nothing but a unitary, ethno-nationalist state; it was a confederation of autonomous regional entities.

> Recent experience in the Caucasus demonstrates the extent to which such disintegration will retard the development of each. Prosperity depends on inter-communication and freedom of trade; while the autonomy of the Empire should be preserved, the government should be completely re-organized under one mandatory, eliminating all Turkish control, except locally. The existing machinery of administration can be gradually modified so as to bring about the reform without shock or violence. Local self government can be granted as the people show themselves fit for responsibility, the object being to eventually create a confederation of states with large local powers.[89]

One is struck by the confidence the missionaries still placed first in America but also in the international system dominated by nominally Christian powers, and in a mandate system dependent on them. This utopian vision would have needed a strong League of Nations combined with a strong common political philosophy.

The report of the King-Crane Commission of August 1919 to the American delegation in Paris favored limited Armenian autonomy in parts of Asia Minor but refused Greek and Italian claims to Anatolian territory. It argued for the U.S. mandate, appealing to America's spirit of international solidarity, as did the missionaries and also the Harbord Report of October 1919. "If we refuse to assume it [a mandate], for no matter what reasons satisfactory to ourselves," Harbord argued, "we shall be considered by many millions of people as having left unfinished the task for which we entered the war, and as having betrayed their hopes."[90] Many Near Easterners who, in those decisive months, had put their hopes in the American missionaries indeed saw themselves disappointed, even betrayed, when the United States failed to assume the uncertain burden of a mandate. Leaving Asia Minor to the nationalists, however, had serious consequences. It was not liberal rulers but dictatorial ones, not pluralists but Turkists, who won the political game in Asia Minor. "Civilization" (*medeniyet*), soon to be a key Kemalist term, was not connected to democracy and human rights; recent traumatic history was not faced and clarified.

Asia Minor had been the ABCFM's biggest, most privileged field for nearly a century. Now it turned out to be a broken mirror of hope, both for missionary America and for the local people who had trusted in it. Worse, opportunistic, naive, or cynical interpretations of recent history appeared in American newspapers, such as Admiral Colby Chester's "Turkey reinterpreted" (which infuriated the experienced Harput missionary Henry H. Riggs) or the journalist Clair Price's series of articles. These contained elements of Turkish nationalist propaganda, anti-Armenian and anti-Levantine stereotypes, the euphemism that the Kemalists fundamentally differed from the CUP (most of them were old CUP and Turkish Hearth members), and the false information that "a number of Armenian Deputies" were members of the Grand National Assembly in Ankara.[91] If these and similar American statements were obviously biased, they nevertheless pointed to the painful truth that the new situation had turned out to be incompatible with the missionary hopes and some serious illusions of Protestant diplomacy. Unfortunately, Chester's and Price's fair appeals finally to give the Turk a chance was not tied to a truthful discourse. American memories of the murder of the Armenians and the related question of human rights could not be simplistically invalidated by reference to "the lasting image of the 'Terrible Turk' built up by the missionaries and relief workers," as later authors began to argue in the same vein.[92]

Even more concrete and limited missionary projects failed, such as an office of the League of Nations—so dear to the ABCFM internationalists—in Turkey, headed by a representative of the ABCFM. The League did vote to set up "an office and a 'Chief Commissioner of the League of Nations in Turkey'" in Istanbul, and the post was offered to Peet, but diplomatic pressure caused this plan to fail. Another provisionally successful project was a School of Religion, a theological school serving various Christian denominations and advocating religious dialogue. It started in Istanbul after World War I but ended when Istanbul passed under the rule of the Kemalists.[93]

The missionaries of Harput/Mamuretülaziz had cherished hopes of new interaction with the Kurds, in particular with the Alevi Dersimis after 1918. An "exile" in the United States since 1917, Tacy Atkinson wrote in 1918, "How I envy the man or woman who goes filled with the love of God, to those Dersim Kurds. How I have loved and admired them and how I have prayed that God would give them a chance."[94] But these hopes, cherished both in spiritual and political terms, broke down too. Fifteen years after the American missionaries had been forced to leave the eastern provinces for good, Dersim (Tunceli) became the theater of a destructive, almost genocidal military campaign in 1937–1938. Outside help and independent eyewitnesses were absent in that time. The modernity and the individual empowerment that American and other teachers and doctors had brought to the remotest places were nevertheless not completely lost during the twentieth century. The memory of a relatively prosperous and free, if precarious, Belle Epoque in Ottoman Anatolia in the years before 1914, and of the promoters of this modernity on the ground, was not to be forgotten.

It is true that the missionaries' internationalist and federalist hopes after 1918 of a more or less undivided Near East were illusionary. Their antinationalism, however, expressed concern about the dark sides of an exclusive ethnic nationalism, as they knew it freshly from the Balkans, and was not directed against the principle of self-determination. This attitude was also expressed by the report of the King-Crane Commission, whose members were close to the missionaries, with regard to Palestine (see "Zionism and the Critical Legacy of the Missionaries" in Chapter 4). It may be considered a historical irony that Jesus-oriented American missionaries who understood themselves from the beginning in the early nineteenth century as Zion-seekers, Zion-builders, and restorers of Israel came to be labeled, rightly or wrongly, anti-Zionists in the twentieth century.[95] After its strategic turn from Palestine and the Jews to Asia Minor and the Armenians in the 1830s, missionary America lost sight, it is true, of the restoration of Jewish Israel, focusing as it did on the reform of Ottoman Turkey. As much as American missionaries failed to understand the historical hour of European Jewish Zionism, and despite those pioneers' faith in their national project, European Zionists failed to grasp the American grassroots commitment against ethno nationalism and in favor of a pluralist, "transnational" Near Eastern society. The fact was that American Protestantism was, for plausible reasons, refused the opportunity to organize the new Near East according to its own ideas, and that political Zionism did not receive the blessing of the American missionaries, the most experienced, committed, and seminal workers for "Zion" in the Near East since the early nineteenth century.

CHAPTER 4

Oil, Palestine-Israel, and Empire of the Good

In the early twentieth century, the United States was in the Progressive Era, perhaps its most carefree period of growth, self-confidence, and mass immigration. In this period, however, fell the trauma of missionary America: the failure of its vision and the destruction of those it had most worked for, to whom it had tied its work in the Bible lands—the Anatolian Armenians. After 1918, there was no more missionary America in the sense of the century before; no more confidence and commitment for a postmillennialist mission, a Jesus-centered building up of modern institutions and civil society. Mission nevertheless took off in a new, premillennialist sense after the 1920s, and old affections for Israel were resumed in a new way in the 1940s when America began to be the globally dominating power.

The end of benevolent postmillennialism became nowhere more manifest than in the post-Ottoman world. A "shift from humanitarian-collective concerns to purely self-interested ones occurred," but the "policy of protecting the traditional Open Door was expedient and short-sighted, as most of American diplomacy was during the inter-war period," concludes a study on that inconsistent experiment in American realpolitik after 1923.[1] Loyal to the Gospel, the American missionaries of the nineteenth century had been oriented toward the poor and powerless, seen as the most promising within a millennialist economy, not toward power and material profit. The Near East Relief's impressive activism and assistance in the humanitarian emergency in the 1920s contributed in a way to suppressing the traumatic experience of the

1910s and disguising the missionaries' forced adaptation of the 1920s, permitting Americans one last time to apply sincerely the discourse of disinterested benevolence to the Near East. James Barton praised the Near East Relief (NER) as "the story of the ideals of America translated into disinterested service." President Calvin Coolidge acclaimed it as "practical Christianity," "religion in action," and "religion in terms of sacrifice and service." For him, the NER's "creed was the Golden Rule and its ritual the devotion of life and treasure to the healing of wounds." The NER for Coolidge "represented the true spirit of our country. . . . Irrespective of religion and creed, it clothed the naked, fed the starving and provided shelter." It set an example of suprareligious and supraracial humanity. "While the war was waging in Europe and Western Asia, and the contending nations were using every known engine of destruction against each other, this organization was salvaging men, women and children, not of its own race."[2] These were sublime sentences—and last goodbyes.

Those who represented "America" in the eyes of local people in the post-Ottoman world changed in the interwar period: no more the legendary missionaries but now diplomats, military advisers, and agents of companies, above all oil companies. The missionaries had partly been smiled at, sometimes detested, but most often respected as sometimes disconcerting but reliable and selfless figures, at least when compared to those who came after and to their own elites. The post-Ottoman interwar period was a passage from missionaries to businesspeople and diplomats and from post- to premillennialist mission. In Iraq and Saudi Arabia, oil companies demanded an open door from diplomacy; in Palestine, the Yishuv demanded money and support. Here, and no longer in Asia Minor, lived most (78 percent) of the American citizens in the Middle East, largely Eastern European Jews naturalized in the United States in the early twentieth century before becoming settlers in "Eretz Israel." A new factor emerged: Jewish American Zionism. The majority of American capital was concentrated in Palestine, not Asia Minor, before oil investments in Saudi Arabia prevailed at the end of the 1930s.[3]

The failure of cherished concepts and the obvious loss of profound missionary hopes were hardly debated, at least not in public. The Wilsonian Near Eastern policy as a whole had failed. Only through its struggle and victory against Nazi Germany had the United States regained confidence in its global role and found a new benchmark for good and evil in history. This also applied to the Near East, where the missionary legacy now possessed relatively little credit. World War II made the United States a superpower and endowed it with the new political role of a champion of the "free world," as well as that of a "Cyrus": a promoter and protector of Israel as a state. The United States entered a new stage but had great difficulty forming a meaningful synthesis from the old missionary "zeal for Zion," the new power politics, and the emerging U.S. Israel-centrism in the Middle East, soon to be combined with a new Christian Zionism at home.

Not Coming to Terms: The Broken Mirror of Missionary America

Inevitably, missionary America's premises centered on the Near East had to be questioned in the 1920s. The United States itself turned out to be different from the hopes of the missionary men and women on the spot. It had declined the role that Protestant diplomacy—President Wilson and its informal "missionary cabinet"—had foreseen: a mandate of the League of Nations at least for Armenia, even better for the whole of Asia Minor.

Missionary conceptions of multiethnic civil society and of federalist autonomies in the Ottoman world, particularly in Asia Minor, had proved to be wrong in "real history." From the 1920s on, the men and women of the Turkey Mission, still on the ground or back home, were left more or less alone with their traumatic memories. Eyewitnesses of a mass murder on an unprecedented scale, they faced the breakdown of the missionary work of four generations and the large-scale failure of their plans for their beloved Turkey. They were evicted from Kurdo-Armenian eastern Turkey and from many other places in the Anatolian provinces. Not only the few missionaries who stayed in the Republic of Turkey but also those who returned to the United States found themselves in a postwar society that refused to interrogate the recent past and to tackle the trauma. In Turkey itself, silence was the price the former missionary institutions paid for cooperation with the winners of the Anatolian wars of 1919–1922. Most members of the victorious Turkish elite were closely related to the CUP war regime, which had been sincerely detested by the ABCFM. The missionary community was unable to come to terms with the Christian catastrophe in Asia Minor in 1915–1923 and the shattering of its hopes. Neither could it come to terms with its attitude toward Islam, which had evolved but remained ambivalent since 1908, nor with its original, more or less suspended vision of the restoration of the Jews.

Most serious were the conflicting emotions aroused by the memory of the Armenians' destruction when, at the beginning of the 1920s, the ABCFM's Turkey Mission had to ask itself how to continue in Turkey, if at all. The shattering memory jeopardized all missionary work for the future. Henry Riggs formulated it as follows:

> During the preceding decade the Turkish people, and again especially their leaders, had been guilty, before God and man, of one of the most revolting crimes in history [1915]. The triumphant reestablishment of the Turkish sovereignty not only left that crime unpunished, but, in the mind of probably a majority of the Turks, the horrid course which they had pursued had been gloriously vindicated. In the minds of many members of the Mission were two questions which demanded an honest answer: first, could there be any hope of a regeneration of the Turkish people, and real progress toward a decent national life, without some real repentance and repudiation of that crime, in which now they glory? And second, can any missionary have any influence spiritually and permanently of value if, by keeping silence, he seemed to condone the crime?[4]

The frustration of central and eastern Anatolia missionaries went particularly deep. They had lost nearly everything. As living testimonies and indictments, moreover, they "found themselves hated and despised because of what had been done to the Christian races of Turkey," Henry Riggs wrote shortly before he died in 1943, referring to Turkey in the 1920s.[5]

The missionaries were mute but visible witnesses of times, acts, and victims the new Republic of Turkey suppressed. Most of the missionaries' clientele and brothers and sisters in faith had perished; the rest were homeless. Humanitarian help by the NER and other organizations did the best it could for the hundreds of thousands of homeless people abroad. But these were deprived of any hope of return to their homes and of any satisfying political perspective, whereas the Turks seemed to be "confirmed in the criminal position by securing their complete independence." Had all the hopes, spiritual commitment, and constructive work of nearly a hundred years been in vain? Had brute crude criminality triumphed? Or was there an undiscovered wisdom? Would the victim's memory and blessing triumph at last, the meek "inherit the land," as in the biblical story of Cain, who successfully killed his brother and built a city but witnessed the prevailing of Abel's legacy? New wisdom could be won, forgiveness could finally be given: but the innocent victims and their legacy must never be forgotten, and justice must be achieved, even if not in juridical terms. This stood in the center of biblical—in particular, Protestant—faith.[6]

The missionaries' silent agony persisted in the following decades without finding a satisfactory response either in Turkey or in established international historiography. Neither international nor new American diplomacy encouraged clarification of these matters, and even less so after the Conference of Lausanne made "exchange of population," which covered previous ethnic cleansing, internationally sanctioned policy with regard to "minority problems." The ABCFM did make one early attempt to break its silence. In its January meeting in 1923, it drew up a "statement of attitude sternly condemning the massacres and horrors of the past, and giving repentance as the one hope for a better day in Turkey." Although aware that "such a stern rebuke of the actions of the government would probably result in the summary closing up of all our work," some members submitted a motion to present the statement to the Ankara authorities, regardless of results. But the motion was voted down.[7]

In contrast to the superficial language of the new political elites in the State Department and their think tanks, the missionaries could not change their language about what had happened and what they had witnessed. Hence, they fell silent. Their testimony remained suppressed, creating an all-the-more disturbing and powerful long-term legacy. A lot of relevant recollections were set down in unpublished memoirs, of which an impressive number of relevant papers were finally published in the late twentieth and early twenty-first centuries. Both for the Indian removal of the early 1800s and the destruction of the Armenians in the early 1900s, the ABCFM archives contain accurate reports of what took place on the spot. They continue to form a crucial archival basis for the historical reconstruction of these events and their contexts today. After both the 1830s and World War I, the ABCFM itself published little and was unable to cope with its failure and loss. There was little chance of being heard in an American life that cultivated a culture of victory and success, including religious triumphalism, and that suppressed contemporary realities of suffering and injustice. The first-hand reports and some handwritten or typed retrospectives of missionaries waited in the archives for historians to come along and deal with the issue, and for editors to make relevant publications.[8]

Prewar Reflection on Islam Suspended

The end of the sultan-caliph's empire and the concomitant situation of triumphant Turkism in Kemalist Turkey and its exclusion of Islam from the political sphere did not favor reflection on, and a dynamic dialogue with, Islam in theological and historical terms. This leads us back to 1908–1923 and certain achievements of that period. In some ways, what had been gained or squandered over those years could not be repaired or surpassed in the following decades. At the beginning of the twentieth century, the missionary work among Muslims had been seriously questioned, and with it, the work among Jews—not only in pragmatic terms of success, as in the 1820s but also more fundamentally. The questioning, however, had not yet resulted in the implementation of comprehensive new attitudes, approaches, and historical-theological insights.

At the First Missionary Conference on Behalf of the Mohammedan World, held at Cairo in 1906, many discussions had gone back to the foundation periods of Islam and Christianity. It had been argued that the early church had "made a mistake in insisting on uniformity between Jewish and Greek Christians," that there "should have been a Jewish form of Christianity," that "Islam is an attempt to attain that [Judeo-Christian] position—hence they are Gentile-Jews of a Gentile-Judaizing sect," and that "in his earliest years Mohammed himself was a nominal Christian." Consequently, the Muslims should not be approached like heathens, as still was often the case. According to this historical background, mission to Muslims should focus not on conversion but on "reconversion of those who have lapsed." Hence, the dramaturgy of conversion, a particularly powerful pattern with regard to Islam and Jewry, was put into question. The evangelical model of Pauline conversion remained, however, deeply embedded in American Protestantism and would resume its prominence in the late-twentieth-century evangelical mission to Muslims.[9]

For the German pastor and director of mission Johannes Lepsius, the "reform of Islam" (he avoided the term *mission*) was part of a general movement of global spiritual and mission history that was returning from the West to the East, after the long-lasting movements of mission from the East to the West from the first to the eighteenth centuries. A kind of third—millennialist—covenant, out of the first (Hebrew) and second (Christian), was to come. Historical Islam—despite crucial imperialist and sexist flaws leading to its decline, and demands of fundamental theological and social reform—had powerfully prefigured this third covenant of the real global Kingdom of God in Jesus on earth.

There was no—or only rarely, and late[10]—question of Islamic resources to be discovered and, even if critically, taken in. But people such as ABCFM missionary George F. Herrick, who also attended the conference, and missionaries Howard Bliss, Jakob Künzler, and Johannes Awetaranian began to adopt a more respectful or even humble approach to Islam, albeit coupled with fundamental criticism of its political use and social realities. Other voices at the 1906 conference, however, and perhaps the majority of American missionaries in the 1900s and 1910s, insisted on the unyielding position that "Mohammed was really an idolater because his conception of God was really a caricature," and that his conception of God lacked love or holiness. The problem of how to approach Islam also was seen as one of practical tactics: "It would only irritate the Moslems if we deny that they worship the one true God," who was in fact an "unknown God" to them, said W. K. Eddy from the ABFMPC (American Board of Foreign Missions of the Presbyterian Church).[11]

There is no doubt that the broad missionary community held a derogatory view of Islam as a religion, culture, and history. A 1913 ABCFM book "written to make our work in Turkey interesting to the people in our churches" had an appendix for church study classes and reading circles whose suggestive questions and material—"Five minute exercises on Turkey" (e.g., "VII. the evils of Islam")—proved that more humble approaches and revised historical-theological visions were hard to find in the broad missionary community, except among some missionaries on the ground. Sharp contrasts were emphasized between conditions in Turkey and "the great evils" and the "weakness of Islam," on one hand, and the "lofty morals of the New Testament" and brilliant conditions in America on the other. Parsons's self-doubts and Evart's lesson from the Indian removal were forgotten in these circles. The aforementioned book derived hope from the change in 1908 but first drew attention to the heroic ninety-three-year-old story of the ABCFM and the "splendid results [it had] attained." In this vein, it hoped to "deepen the conviction of our Congregational churches in the sure triumph of the Kingdom of Christ in Turkey."[12] In the next decade, the reverse of all this happened; nothing "splendid" remained. How could the missionaries sincerely readjust themselves, their home base, and their understanding of history to these new facts? How to reconceive the approach toward the Muslim other?

ABCFM Foreign Secretary James Barton himself held pejorative views of Islam. He is a typical representative of missionary America's hopes, contradictions, and reversals vis-à-vis the Near East in the Progressive Era. Barton had close connections with politicians and was influential in American public life. As in the case of Clarence Ussher, his view of Islam derived, though not exclusively, from the extremely negative experience of World War I. In an article in the journal *Biblical World* in January 1913, Barton commented on "what the defeat of Turkey [in the Balkans] may mean to American Missions." The lead of the article, probably not written by Barton himself, presented the Ottoman Empire as "a brutal enemy" and "archenemy of Christianity" and compared it to the "Beast and the Harlot" in the biblical book of Revelation. Barton himself made no analysis of CUP rule and political ideology but wrongly guessed, "There is no doubt that the present war [in the Balkans] and the outcome thereof will increase the number of the Progressives as well as their progressiveness." The result, of course, was contrary:

anti-Christian resentments and the wish for thorough ethnic cleansing of Anatolia strongly increased.

For his American public, Barton showed Islam to be *the* problem in the Ottoman Near East. "Mohammedanism has maintained the cholera-center for Europe and Asia for eight hundred years, from which this dread scourge spreads to the whole Mohammedan World. Mecca, the sacred city of Islam, has been the source of cholera, and is today more dreaded than any other scourge-center in the whole world," he opined, seduced by highly devaluing metaphors and a supposed antagonism between Islam and progress. Not until toward the end of the article might a patient reader have discovered that the missionaries on the ground did not practice this kind of dichotomy and confrontationalism: "Repeatedly thoughtful Mohammedans have said to the Protestants of Turkey that there is little difference between the Mohammedans and the Protestants. . . . The position has already been reached in Turkey where Protestants and Mohammedans can calmly discuss the differences which separate them."[13]

The experience of World War I reinforced negative stances that had partly been questioned during the preceding years. In a book published in 1918, Barton concluded that "Islam is wholly inadequate to meet the needs of the [Turkish] race. It has been weighed in the balance of the centuries and has been found wanting." He argued that Muhammad's character was defective, therefore Islam was corrupt at its very source, its conception of God without love, the Muslims' worship mechanical, and its attitude toward women simply unacceptable. For Barton, the "absence of spiritual power has produced in Islam a mighty force for the destruction of spiritual impulses and religious ideals in the individual as well as in society. When it fails to save, it has become a dominant force for evil."[14] Barton was right as far as the resentful, destructive, and self-destructive Islamism of the late Ottoman period was concerned. Researches thus far suggest that a majority of Muslim clerics had disturbingly connived at the CUP's Social Darwinist mass crimes of World War I, or at least had not taken an overt stance against them.[15] Barton, however, was wrong to generalize. He overlooked the Sufi potential. He neglected the functionaries who had courageously resisted in the name of Islamic ethics. He did not mention those Alevis of Marash and Dersim who had saved thousands of Armenians.

Conversion of the ABCFM Heritage

Instead of giving up its work and its still rich infrastructure in Asia Minor, the ABCFM in 1923 decided to adapt its work to the requirements of the remaining Muslim population in the Republic of Turkey. Three institutions, however, followed the community that they had mainly served into exile. The Central Turkey College in Anteb and the Girls' College in Marash were integrated into the Aleppo College of the ABFMPC, while the Anatolia College in Marsivan, which both Hamidian and CUP and Kemalist representatives had considered a particular seat of conspiracy, was relocated to Salonika. The high schools in Istanbul, Izmir, Adana, and Marsivan (Merzifon) remained, as did colleges in Izmir and Tarsus and hospitals in Anteb and Talas (near Kayseri). Furthermore, the Robert College and the American College for Girls in Istanbul and the International College in Izmir, although independent institutions, were in close touch with the ABCFM.[16]

The new guiding principle was moral education or apolitical character formation, without any direct reference to the Gospel. Thus both civic and spiritual education, the main issues after 1908, were abandoned or strongly diluted. New key formulas were "unnamed Christianity," a "personal and sympathetic approach," "Christian radiance," "the missionary home: a social centre," "personal talks on vital subjects," "publications with a high moral tone," and "cooperation with sympathetic Turks for the uplift of their country." A considerable struggle, self-denial, and some illusions were involved in adapting to a nationalist Turkey that prohibited all religious teaching in missionary schools. What the ABCFM had been doing for a century appeared as a complete failure, any spiritual ambition as illusory, and history itself as guided by cynical logic. In Henry Riggs's view, a "century of effort with all the advantages of strong churches in Turkey had signally failed to win the Turks. . . . There was also the feeling that the Turks had proved themselves criminals in all that had passed, and had now been confirmed in the criminal position by securing their complete independence. The possibility of bringing about any spiritual regeneration among them under those conditions seemed fantastically remote."[17]

In the 1920s, the missionaries hoped that the restrictive measures against their education would soon be removed, a "hope which, it must be said, has not yet been fulfilled," Riggs wrote twenty years later. Again and again, the missionaries' unsatisfying work had to be "re-evaluated" in the interwar period.[18] Serious incidents occurred whose explosive nature lay in the simple fact that a few Turks decided to believe in Jesus Christ, a move that was interpreted as a betrayal of the national identity, unacceptable to society and its rulers; for "acceptance by a Turk of the name Christian" was "a desertion to the adversary," and "that name denotes exclusively the national groups now excluded from Turkey."[19] By contrast, a few younger missionaries seem to have been receptive to and impressed by Kemalism. William Sage

Woodworth Jr., director of the Tarsus American College, published in 1940 a hymn of praise to Mustafa Kemal Atatürk, boldly reproducing the national myths of the new Republic.[20]

Henry Riggs and his "old generation" could never go as far as Woodworth because Riggs never accepted the way in which "Turkey re-established herself on a basis excluding the Christian races," and he maintained his doubts about how the ABCFM had to adjust itself after 1923. Nevertheless, he ended his history in 1942 with the hopeful thought that the "seed so patiently planted during the earlier [Ottoman] years, nurtured by patient friendliness of Christian workers there today, is coming to manifest fruition."[21] Several missionaries and observers raised the question whether "Americanizing," instead of evangelizing, in collaboration with the Turkish nationalist elites had then become the ABCFM's real job in Turkey. This transformation also had to do with a new generation of missionaries who lacked the vocation and lifelong commitment, the familiarity with the provinces, and the contact with the people the former generations had possessed.[22]

Was the self-confident, self-determined American Near East mission of late Ottoman times finally to become, in a reduced and "adjusted" form, a servant of geopolitics, that is, of the new strategic U.S.–Turkish alliance after World War II?[23] The truth probably lies somewhere between this and Riggs's optimistic note. Contrary to what they had been, the ABCFM schools became elite-centered, and they lost much of the fundamental distance from the center of power that they had possessed. Nevertheless, despite the corset of Kemalist bureaucracy and, after 1945, the compulsion of Turko-American alliance, not a few young men and women were educated in American schools who acquired an intellectual and spiritual potential far beyond these constraints.

Zionism and the Critical Legacy of the Missionaries

Influenced by millennialist Christian Zionism, the ABCFM had possessed a strongly restorationist attitude in the early nineteenth century. Its future-oriented, eschatological roots remained alive always, but the initial vision of the restoration of the Jews, even if never formally revoked, lost much of its appeal because the first tentative steps toward Jewish restoration to Palestine and to Jesus were not successful. In discussions at the international Protestant conference in Cairo in 1906, for example, the conversion of Israel, indissolubly linked to the Jews' return to Palestine, reappeared as the last stage of a spiritual movement from West to East; this movement would take place after a reform of Islam, Johannes Lepsius postulated in his paper, presenting Islam (not derogatorily) as a "Judeo-Christian sect."[24] American, British, and continental European missionaries like Lepsius, who were members of the informal Protestant International, were highly interested in Zionism and shared a fundamental sympathy with and commitment to the "restoration of Israel."

In contrast to other groups and individuals within the powerful current of restorationism, however, the American missionaries in the Near East, the experts on the spot, maintained a remarkable distance from political Zionism, or Jewish nationalism, after it had emerged in the European fin de siècle. Their critical distance from Zionism had to do with the absence of religion in general and Jesus in particular in the Zionist articulation, as well as with ethnic nationalism, whose consequences for interethnic coexistence they feared. When, at the end of World War I, the struggle for a new order in the Near East began, the grandchildren of the restorationist pioneers were unable to harmonize Zionist concepts with their ideas of a new Near East. We see this documented by the report of the King-Crane Commission, whose members were close to the Protestant missionary establishment. This commission defended the rights of the Arab natives, as did Cleveland H. Dodge, a friend of President Wilson and pillar of the missionary community, and Howard Bliss. Bliss and James Barton pleaded for a Near Eastern federation, Arab autonomy, and a protective American lead in the area's affairs. The missionary area experts at the Paris Peace Conference looked with sympathy on a Jewish national home, but they did not endorse a nation-state. More implicitly than explicitly, they stood at odds with a second group of articulate Americans in Paris: the Zionists Felix Frankfurter, Benjamin Cohen, and Stephen Wise.[25]

A number of supplementary factors explain the distance between missionaries and Zionists. By 1830, the missionaries' interest had shifted from the Jews in Palestine to the Christians in Asia Minor. (After 1870 it was the ABFMPC, not the ABCFM, that was concerned with mission in Syria and Palestine.) The missionaries had close relationships with Arab natives and were skeptical of ambitious Eastern European newcomers, who often held their native neighbors in contempt. Exclusive Zionist self-construction violated, in the eyes of the missionaries, the basics of the Golden Rule. After 1908, the ABCFM identified with the new Ottoman order they hoped was on the way; its Ottomanist transnational orientation left less room than ever for nationalist movements. Despite innovative conceptual steps after 1908, the missionaries did not or scarcely imagine that secular socialist and nationalist forces could be working, willingly or unwillingly, for the restoration that had been one of the main reasons why the ABCFM went to the Near East in the first place (even if not chronologically first). A certain liberal Protestant blindness toward contemporary history prevailed in the early twentieth century—a lack of empathy and imagination with regard to the historical role of Eastern European socialism and Zionism. There was also a lack of confidence in Jewish self-organization and a certain contempt, shared by many American Jews, for Jews from Eastern Europe. Many *Ostjuden,* in contrast to most Western Jews, had understood half a century before the Shoah that only a radical commitment could change their own situation as *Luftmenschen,* a people with no resources, future, or project. These *Luftmenschen* felt socially excluded (like millions of non-Jewish proletarians), and they felt culturally and religiously estranged by culturally Christian surroundings (as did Muslims in Europe).

In a world where nominal Christianity was so powerful, many Christians could not imagine that—in the words of the Jewish Christian Paul—the Jews would once be "grafted again onto their own olive tree" without leading agency by a seemingly powerful West.[26] After the seminal catastrophe of World War I, post–Belle Epoque Christianity was to be haunted by the rise of bolshevism and, slightly later, fascism. Christianity in Europe was deeply disoriented. However, the historical orientation of missionary America, set solidly in the early nineteenth century, also broke down to a considerable extent. Transnational Protestantism, of which missionary America had been a factor, would need a radically self-critical reflection if not it could not liberate itself from the "cultural Protestantism" of the Belle Epoque. The German member of the Protestant International Johannes Lepsius was confused both by German defeat and the Protestant crisis, including its Near Eastern aspect. He was haunted by the specter of anti- or pseudo-Christian "messianic imperialism," which he thought to be prefigured by Great Britain. With regard to Zionism, he was much in doubt that "all peoples would founder on the Gospel and at last the Kingdom [of Jesus] would return to the Jews," as his Basel friend Johannes Heman had suggested.[27]

The ABCFM early on considered Zionism a potentially separatist ethnic nationalism like the others it had seen grow up since the mid-nineteenth century in the Balkans and the Caucasus, including the Armenian Hnchag and the ARF. Like the ARF, before 1915 the Zionists favored the reform of the Ottoman system, not autonomy, though they were less involved in Ottoman politics. American missionaries particularly disliked the instrumental use of or open contempt for religion they witnessed among protagonists of ethnic nationalism and revolutionary socialism, as well as the "necessary" violence and coercion to which these activists subscribed. By contrast, missionaries, including college professors, believed in "the fundamental place spiritual [as opposed to formalist, ritual, or ethno-national] religion must hold in the life and character of every intellectual man."[28] This, in principle, made possible deeper affinities with the cultural Zionists (*Kulturzionisten*), who also gave priority to the spiritual legacy and to intact human communications beyond ethnic boundaries, even if the *Kulturzionist* tendency toward romanticist essentialism did not fit well with pragmatism and universalism. Several ABCFM missionaries appreciated the dimension of universal solidarity but missed spirituality in socialism. They were also skeptical when ethnic nationalism was combined with socialism, as in the case of the Hnchag and the Labor Zionists. What made the missionaries greatly distrustful was the impression that Zionism speculated on the end of the Ottoman world, not on its renewal and democratization—a goal to which the ABCFM had wholeheartedly committed itself in 1908.

The editors of *The Orient* in the Bible House in prewar Istanbul had, in principle, welcomed Zionism. Their sympathy toward Zionism was also part of a general philo-Semitic attitude of Anglo-Saxon circles and the still valid eschatology of the Protestant International.[29] It did, however, show little eschatological enthusiasm. "All true friends of the Hebrew race sympathize strongly with the scheme of repatriating the Jews in their ancient home in Palestine," the editorialist of *The Orient* wrote in 1913. The same editorial, however, states in response to a letter by Israel Cohen, from the Zionist Central Office in Berlin, that Zionist literature left few doubts about the nationalist goal of a Jewish state and that this obviously must meet with bitter opposition from natives and the Ottoman government.[30] The Bible House editors read the contemporary Zionist books and papers carefully, as several references show. In good restorationist tradition, however, they considered a nationalist return to Palestine without spiritual renewal "a mockery" of the prophets.[31] The editors of *The Orient* looked with sympathy on the Ottoman Jews, be they professing Jews or *dönme* (Jews converted to Islam in the seventeenth century). They saw them as a "wideawake, progressive element, [who] may be looked to furnish future leaders of the Empire." In 1911, the editors counted not only the CUP minister of finance, Javid, but also, wrongly, the CUP minister of the interior, Talat, among the *dönme* from Salonika.[32] Concerning Arab complaints about "undue privileges given to Jews in Palestine, owing to the influence of the Jewish Deunmehs of Salonica," the editors wrote that they were "much in doubt" about this reproach, since the government "has not been nearly so much inclined to grant privileges to the Jews as their adversaries would have us believe."[33] As skepticism toward the CUP grew in 1912–1913, however, clear criticism about "certain scheming Jews from Salonica" who would manage to stay on good terms with the CUP even during World War I was not absent in *The Orient*.[34]

During the campaigns for the NER, representatives of the missionary community cooperated successfully with Rabbi Stephen Wise, a leader of American Zionism along with Louis Brandeis.[35] For these American Jewish Zionists, the Zionist project was a complement to life in the diaspora, not a substitute for it. Their American experience taught them the high value of a struggle for fulfillment of universal democracy in ethnically pluralistic, non-homogenized societies—the shadows of the American experience (e.g., the treatment of the Indians and Afro-Americans) were elegantly left aside. For Americans in the 1910s, missionaries and Jews alike, the American ideal also held good for Palestine and found its expressive codification in an American Zionist paper titled *Constitutional Foundations of the New Zion*.[36] Not to integrate the Arab natives into the project as well would have been a betrayal of one's most basic principles, as well as of the commandment "You shall love your neighbor as yourself."

The Golden Rule, however, appeared to stand in an irresolvable contradiction to the redemptive *völkisch* longing of poverty-stricken Eastern European Zionists and the strategy for which David Ben-Gurion opted in Palestine in the early 1920s. The Yishuv's proto-national institutions, including the labor union Histadruth led by Ben-Gurion, were strongly exclusivist. Nahum Goldmann, president of the Jewish World Congress, would later say that there would have been no war between Jews and Arabs if only the Zionists had spent a small part of their energy for the Arab people on the ground instead of ignoring and excluding them.[37] Native-centered missionary ideals and flagrant Zionist contradictions with ethics made many Americans critics of the political philosophy and practices of Zionism, even if they supported the establishment of a Palestinian Jewish national home. Few were so optimistic and Americanist as William Yale, expert consultant of the King-Crane Commission, believing that "a Jewish state will inevitably fall under the control of American Jews who will work out, along Jewish lines, American ideals and American civilization." Others, like the wealthy and well-established Henry Morgenthau, former U.S. ambassador in Istanbul and friend of the ABCFM, feared that successful Zionism would lead to dual loyalties and "cost the Jews of America most that they had gained of liberty, equality and fraternity." Morgenthau was nevertheless helpful to the Yishuv and the Zionists.[38]

Arrangement with British-Mandated Iraq, Kemalist Turkey, and Wahhabite Saudi Arabia

Both in Palestine and in Asia Minor, missionary America did not see its own visions implemented. A feeling of tension and lack of fulfillment resulted in both cases, most manifestly in the Republic of Turkey, which suppressed any missionary activity. In the early interwar period, leading figures such as Colby Chester, Mark L. Bristol, and Joseph Grew had begun to throw in their lot with the winners of the political game in Asia Minor. Logically, they had to silence uncomfortable truths, and they had their own reasons to do so. They preferred America to gain economic advantages in its competition with the European powers, as imperial Germany, now evicted after its defeat in World War I, had tried to do in the previous three decades, when American industrialists had failed to compete efficiently with their European rivals.[39] The Chester project had attempted to obtain the Ottoman concession for the building of railroads in eastern Anatolia as far as Mosul, including the rights of exploitation of natural resources on both sides of the railroads. A revised Chester project was signed during the Conference of Lausanne in the spring of 1923, at which the United States was only an observer. It served a successful Turkish pressing during the negotiations on economic and financial topics but was not finally implemented. In both cases, the "time of effective alliance between the State Department and American businessmen was not yet at hand." Soon after, it was.[40]

Oil began to play a central role for U.S. Middle East diplomacy in the interwar period. Oil companies penetrated territories of the post-Ottoman world such as Iraq and Saudi Arabia, where missionaries either had not been present or had ventured only in very small numbers. There, and only there, "oil companies, acting from commercial considerations, were the vanguard of U.S. penetration into the Middle East."[41] From diplomacy they demanded an "open door," which became "now the cornerstone of American policy in the Middle East," according to John DeNovo. In 1928, a U.S. consortium was able to participate in the Anglo-French Iraqi Petroleum Company, which before 1927 had been called the Turkish Petroleum Company. In Iraq, the Americans profited from the advantages of the British Mandate in terms of security, status, and communication without paying the mandate's costs. Post-Wilsonian policy, moreover, was conservative and abstained from promoting Iraqi self-determination. Not until 1930, when recognizing the state of Iraq, did U.S. policy renounce there the privileges the capitulations of the Ottoman period had continued to offer Americans.[42]

In contrast to the mandated Iraq, where the United States had remained a junior partner of the British, Saudi Arabia in the 1930s offered American companies for the first time the chance to dominate economically in a part of the post-Ottoman world. This opened a markedly new field of interaction for diplomacy-supported business in the Near East. U.S. dollars for oil began to finance a social system that obeyed Wahhabism, a fundamentalist version of Islam that, for enlightened missionaries, had to be overcome, not strengthened. In 1933, Saudi Arabia conceded the Standard Oil Company of California huge oil fields. In the same year, diplomacy concluded a treaty on diplomatic representations, legal protection, and commerce. In 1939 the Arabian-American Oil Company, a fusion of the Standard Oil Company and Texas Company, organized a huge celebration for the inauguration of a new port for tankers in Ras Tanura at the Persian Gulf. After his conquest of Mecca and Medina in 1924–1925, Ibn Saud had declared himself the ruler of a Saudi kingdom and began, in contrast to Mustafa Kemal in Turkey and Shah Reza Pahlavi in Iran, a policy of centralization, modernization, and mechanization that knew no secular connotations. He was to be largely financed by the money of American oil companies.[43]

The price of collaboration with Saudi Arabia had been the dismissal of two main concerns of missionary America: human and women's rights. The United States had no other choice if it wanted promote successful business. This was true as well for Turkey with regard to other aspects of human rights. The price the United States paid when, in 1927, it resumed normal diplomatic relations with the Republic of Turkey was the absolute dismissal of the Armenian question and, with this, the ethical imperative to address it, as well as the millennialist aspect this issue had represented in American life and minds. Domestic resistance had prevented the ratification of the Turko-American Treaty of Lausanne, established at the margins of the Lausanne Conference in 1923. Since the lack of an approved treaty jeopardized the interests of the Americans, in particular the remaining missionary institutions in Turkey, adaptive missionary leaders such as Barton supported early on America's adherence to the Turko-American Treaty. Adapting to the authoritarian nation-state, however, involved (as we have seen) a much more painful conversion of the ABCFM and its heritage, as the ever-optimistic language of this missionary strategist indicated.[44]

In 1917–1927 official relations with Turkey were interrupted, although Admiral Mark Bristol remained a semiofficial representative of the United States to the country during this time. Bristol represented the new, more secular and elitist generation of U.S. representatives in the Near East who ostentatiously set themselves apart from the missionaries before them. In a letter of March 1921 to James Barton, Bristol had appealed for "big policy" in the sense of a fair inclusion of all factors and all groups of people on the spot. But this he could no better realize than the missionaries could their vision of the Near East.[45] Bristol soon proved to be a protagonist of a narrowly calculated American *Interessenpolitik,* which did not exclude the use of the missionary legacy in the form of schools and hospitals in Anatolia.

It was finally not the Turko-American treaty of Lausanne but an exchange of notes that normalized Turko-American relations in 1927. The professional diplomat Joseph Grew, former ambassador in Bern and an observer at the Conference of Lausanne, was appointed the first U.S. Ambassador in Ankara. He negotiated and signed in 1929 a Treaty of Commerce and Navigation. A Treaty of Establishment and Sojourn (1931), a claims settlement on Turkish violations of American persons and property over 1914–1922 (1934), and an extradition agreement (1934) followed.[46] U.S. diplomacy failed to claim the property of U.S. citizens that the Republic of Turkey had expropriated because they were ex-Ottoman Christians; nor was consensus found on the nationality issue that concerned, in particular, expropriated ex-Ottoman Christians who had acquired U.S. citizenship but were not permitted to return or had no realistic opportunity to do so.

In 1939, the Republic of Turkey printed stamps marking 150 years of the American Constitution and celebrating, in stark contrast to the 1920s, Turkish–American friendship. The stamps united the flags and main icons of both countries—Mustafa Kemal Atatürk, Ismet Inönü, George Washington, Franklin Roosevelt. Post-1923 U.S. diplomacy did not dare challenge the ethno-nationalist policies of the interwar period. Kemalist Turkey's domestic agenda in terms of immigration, nationality, and expropriation of natives would in certain respects be similar to those of Israel, another post-Ottoman nation-state to which America was to be tied with old affections.[47] The exclusive internal policy of a previous military victor contradicted deeply what U.S. missionaries in the Near East had struggled for, though it mirrored *cum grano salis* the Indian removal in the United States in the nineteenth century. It was no accident that patriotic intellectuals of the defeated Germany began in those years to point (much too sweepingly) to this analogy, contending that Turkey had manifestly needed to exterminate heteroethnic rivals on its territory and "parasites" from its "social body" in order to build up a successful nation-state.[48]

The alliances with Saudi Arabia and Turkey would form, with all their inherent contradictions, a main basis of post-1945 U.S. policy in the Near East up to Iran (after the CIA-sponsored coup in 1953) and post-1967 Israel. In contrast to Saudi Arabia, the Republic of Turkey impressed the West with its Westernizing cultural and legal revolution and its largely prudent foreign policy. In 1932 it became a member of the League of Nations. It reconciled with Greece, its main adversary ten years previously, on the governmental level. In 1934, Turkey signed the Balkan Treaty with Greece, Romania, and Yugoslavia. Through the Montreux Treaty in 1936, it obtained control over the Bosporus, which hitherto had been demilitarized. In 1938–1939, it occupied and incorporated the *Sanjak* of Alexandrette, which had been a part of the French Mandate over Syria. Faced with possible war in Europe and a possible Turko-German alliance, France and Great Britain accepted. Coercive Turkification, backed by the anthropological myth of four thousand years of Turkic rule in that region, led again to a mass exodus of non-Turks.[49] The Anglo-Turkish Declaration of May 1939 had provided for mutual assistance in the case of aggressive war in the Mediterranean. In contrast to World War I, however, when Turkey had concluded a similar treaty with Germany, Turkey remained neutral during most of World War II, even if the Franco-Anglo-Turkish treaty of assistance of October 1939 reasserted the mutual assistance. After 1945, the republic turned finally to the United States (see under "Rise of an Empire" in this chapter).

Hitler, Shoah, Israel: A New Approach to the Old World

In contrast to the period following World War I, American concepts and visions succeeded during and after World War II. As in World War I, before its entrance into the war the United States discussed plans for global peace and security, beginning with the Atlantic Charter of August 1941 that called for self-determination of peoples, freedom of the seas, and disarmament, as President Wilson had done a quarter of a century before. In a leading position President Franklin Roosevelt prepared the United Nations, finally founded in San Francisco in 1945, whereas the League of Nations, a Wilsonian idea, had lacked domestic support. America's confidence in its own creative and globally leading power was now intact, in contrast to twenty-five years previously, when Europe, even if deeply damaged by war, had still continued to dominate the international game, in particular the new order in Europe and the Near East. In contrast to the Christian and Armenian catastrophe in Asia Minor, the Shoah, the Jewish catastrophe in Europe, could not be brought, wrongly or not, into any relation with American agency on the spot; therefore, the United States underwent no intimate experience of trauma such as that, of missionary America, of the 1910s (even if the United States had failed to receive persecuted Jews in a significant number). The Shoah appeared, on the contrary, to give an ultimate justification for the war against National Socialist Germany—a war that looked, like no other, to be a war of good against evil, light against darkness. World War II proved to be the act of foundation, politically and symbolically, of an "imperial America" that for the first time took leading responsibility for the Old World and the whole globe.

As I argue throughout this book, America's deep identity has nourished itself since the early nineteenth century through its interaction with the Near East qua Bible lands; this is why this book bears the title *Nearest East.* American–Near Eastern interactions were marked from the beginning by a prophetic understanding of the Bible, including the expectation of the restoration of Israel and the establishment of the global millennium, or Kingdom of Jesus, on earth. The course of these interactions was marked by the triangular dynamics of an Ottoman world in acute existential crisis, a very open future called the Oriental Question, and messengers of the Gospel coming from a young republic, the United States, which they nevertheless did not believe to be the most promising place on earth. For their part, the missionaries believed the Bible lands would be the cradle of the global Kingdom of Jesus: the place where biblical prophecy, enlightened modernity, and hunger for a better future would meet and create a new age. Americans would *lead the way to* this millennium but not *lead it* once there. During and after World War I, belief in the force of faith and the nonviolent coming of the millennium seriously suffered, and the postmillennialist American mirror of history broke. U.S. protagonists other than the missionaries took the lead in interactions that seemed now to obey a rationale of realpolitik. In deeper layers of the American soul, however, the relationship with the post-Ottoman world remained unfulfilled.

Zionism and Israel began to enter this gap in the 1940s, responding to the crucial but unfulfilled goal of prophetic restorationism. In Progressive America, many liberal Protestants had lost of sight the restoration of Israel, if they had not already begun to adhere to theologies that read metaphorically the prophecies of the Hebrew Bible and ignored the Jews' lasting particular role. Members of the missionary community themselves had, more or less, lost of sight a meaningful synergy of Gospel, history, and Israel. The cooperation between Young Turkey and Progressive America had seemed to promise a better Near East; alas, catastrophe was to come.

A generation of new Protestant theologians arose that made a sincere and intellectually powerful attempt to bridge the abyss of the *descente à l'enfer* of Belle Epoque Christianity and to understand why it had happened–without renouncing the Gospel for an existentialism devoid of the divine word. The best known of these theologians are Reinhold Niebuhr (1892–1971), an American of German parents and brother of the aforementioned Richard, and the Swiss theologian Karl Barth (1886–1968). In contrast to Niebuhr, Barth was inside the European environment where the ongoing *descente* took place. Like Barth, who was six years older, Niebuhr had turned to socialism in his youth, emancipating himself from *Kulturprotestantismus* or the false confidence, as both put it, in Protestant cultural achievements instead of faith in the living Christ and his judgment of history. This enabled both men to formulate a radically critical stance toward the political and cultural world in which they lived.

Like Niebuhr an early outspoken critic of National Socialism, who for this reason lost his professorship in Germany, but in contrast to Niebuhr a nonreconverted, though undogmatic, socialist[50] even after 1945, Karl Barth reproached his colleague, whom he had much inspired, about weakening the foundations of faith—the centrality and uniqueness of Jesus Christ in history, spiritual life, and eschatology alike—and, with this, Jesus' crucial resistance to both the deadly logic of worldly power and a religious belief allied to such power. The experience of World War I in Europe had reoriented Barth toward the church, just as it had turned the Jewish German philosopher Franz Rosenzweig to his Jewishness and post-1914 Jewish self-articulation, and away from German idealism and state-centrism.[51]

The experience of World War I, moreover, entrenched Barth once and for all in his critical stance toward the exercise of great power and its discursive backings. In contrast, the experience of World War II and the Cold War, with America judged as a force of relative but clear good, turned Niebuhr into a "Christian realist" and seminal political thinker for Washington, D.C. He strongly influenced the American liberal consensus among Christians and politicians after 1945, giving theological and intellectual backing to the American position during the Cold War, though—in contrast notably to ex-leftist neoconservatives after him—in a deeply ironic and spiritual stance. "Many in my generation of churchmen would join George Kennan, referring to the membership of the Policy Planning Staff of the State Department after the war, in calling Niebuhr 'the father of us all,'" Niebuhr admirer Franklin Littell, a Methodist minister, Holocaust scholar, and critic of cultural anti-Semitism wrote.[52]

At the beginning of American global power in the 1940s, Israel and the Near East did not shape the symbolic construction of America's exercise of this power. From the start, this exercise was a reaction: America, in reentering the Old World of World War II, was reacting against one of the most ruthless rules in human history. Franklin Roosevelt, president during the Great Depression and the New Deal, understood early on both the titanic challenge and the global chances of an active and victorious American involvement in World War II against National Socialist Germany.

German National Socialism was the movement of a radicalized cohort of racial nationalists who had been mentally and intellectually damaged by the brutal experience of World War I. Others, older than them, should have taken responsibility for this but did not do so in a society whose fundamental feeling, after the *descente,* was fear. "Fatherless," hurt in their national honor and male narcissism, shell-shocked by the Russian Revolution, and destabilized by a fragile Weimar Republic, the Nazis lost any foundation of sane self-orientation, self-respect, and faith. The generation of their fathers had implemented in 1914, as Kurt Tucholsky and Max Josef Metzger complained, the "moratorium on the Sermon on the Mount,"[53] the suspension of the very basis of the Christian covenant in the Greek New Testament—of confidence in the present, if partial, actuality and the eschatological fulfillment of a "completed humanity."

Individual faith and public confidence broke down in the fundamentally wrong "Whitsun event"[54] of August 1914, and as Metzger put it, like a flood, "Old Testament patterns" of war, expulsion, and extermination—now unbroken by divine law—became valid. This was all the more powerful as continental theologians of the early twentieth century, among them the liberal German Protestant Adolf Harnack, had put the lasting relevance of the Hebrew Bible into question. The Sermon on the Mount, *pars pro toto* of Jesus himself, had never been fully implemented in European society, but neither had it ever been so openly revoked as after August 1914. Total war between European nations; the Russian Revolution and its totalitarian repression of "class enemies"; German Nazism and its totalitarian Social Darwinist repression of "race enemies" (beginning, significantly, with Germany's own mentally ill citizens); an insane Nazi envy and the Holocaust of the biblically chosen people; and a general situation that many historians in retrospect have come to call a European civil war ending only in 1945—all this had everything, within its respective historical setting, to do with the suspension of faith in and understanding of the Christian covenant.

What triggered the U.S. entry into World War II was the serious German threat to Britain, a long-term American ally; the destructive Japanese attack at the U.S. naval base at Pearl Harbor; and a basic confidence that America's reentry onto the global scene this time would be successful politically, economically, and in terms of the Wilsonian vision. Moreover, the symbolic construction of American global power in the 1940s contained from the beginning a crucial Jewish connection, since a main target of German National Socialist hate and resentment from the early 1920s and of exclusive domestic policy from 1933 to 1941 were the Jews. Coinciding with American entry into war, in fall 1941, Nazi anti-Jewish policy radicalized and turned out to be a delirious industrial extermination of a Jewry the Nazis believed to be the global archenemy of Germany, Europe, and humankind.

Faced with a deadly situation in Europe, American Zionists along with Ben-Gurion and Chaim Weizmann convened at the Biltmore Hotel in New York in May 1942 and decided on a program for the establishment of a Jewish state in Palestine. The American Zionists and their friends had long resisted the idea of Zionism as an ethno-national liberation movement that competed for a territory still inhabited by a majority of non-Jews. They all knew that bloodshed would follow. Since the Arab uprising in 1936–1939 against both the Yishuv and the mandate power, which had allowed the Yishuv to organize itself as a proto-state, Ben-Gurion, its undisputed leader, had been preparing for war. At the same time, he planned "the transfer of millions of Jews to Palestine" in order "to solve thoroughly and completely the Jewish problem," as he wrote in a letter after the Biltmore Conference; but he remained silent on the unbearable reality that such a transfer was impossible and his "solution" valid only for a preferably young and healthy portion of the Jews.

The conference itself declared "that the new world order that will follow victory cannot be established on foundations of peace, justice and equality, unless the problem of Jewish homelessness is finally solved." A victorious outcome of World War II and the establishment of a Jewish state were therefore intrinsically linked. At the same time, two thousand years of Jewish exile were represented as an age-old wrong done by Gentiles to Jewish victims. "The Conference urges that the gates of Palestine be opened; that the Jewish Agency be vested with control of immigration into Palestine and with the necessary authority for upbuilding the country, including the development of its unoccupied and uncultivated lands; and that Palestine be established as a Jewish Commonwealth integrated in the structure of the new democratic world. Then and only then will the age old wrong to the Jewish people be righted."[55] In short, German National Socialism, the new American order, and nationalist Zionism coincided chronologically and, at least in retrospective interpretation, logically. Ben-Gurion and the American Zionists projected the Jewish nation-state as a Near Eastern pillar of an American-led democratic world, offering at the same time "a message of hope and encouragement to their fellow Jews in the Ghettos and concentration camps of Hitler-dominated Europe." The new post-Hitler age would right centuries of wrong done to the Jews. (Viewing the post–World War I order, Ben-Gurion had used identical language when he turned from a Germano-Ottoman to an Anglo-American orientation in 1915.)[56]

Hitherto, Jews and Zionists in the United States under the leadership of Rabbi Hillel Silver from Lithuania asserted themselves in a new resolute, proactive, and often vociferous way as a "Jewish lobby" that knew it must face, in the 1940s, a unique urgency. In contrast to liberal American Jewish behavior previously under Stephen Wise's leadership, the "Silver apparatus" now began systematically to use and organize for its own purposes Protestant sympathy and resources, an example of which is the American Christian Palestine Committees (which, despite their name, practiced no solidarity with Palestinian Arab Christians). For the participants of the fundamental Biltmore Conference, in particular for Ben-Gurion—alias David Grün, from the Polish town of Plonsk—Nazism figured as *pars pro toto* of a Gentile world repressive of Jews since the Roman conquest of Jerusalem.

Ben-Gurion did not take a positive view of a lasting Jewish diaspora, as did traditional American Zionists, but did all he could to obtain the maximum support for (proto-)Israel and Jewish migration there. His Eastern European Zionism was a neo-Mosaic project: those in the diaspora remained "back in Egypt" instead of liberating themselves from foreign dominion and, as he saw them, vicious Jewish diaspora traditions and degenerated Jewish ways of life in foreign surroundings.[57] It seems that Ben-Gurion did not or could not question this mental framework, based in a continental European experience, nor could he ponder the fundamental role, for his own project, of Protestant restorationism in Western history since the sixteenth century. He tended to interpret all that led to the new state as resulting from his activist European Zionism. Compared to most leaders of his times, he excels with regard to the extraordinary faith he had in the national project of Zionism, as well as to his adaptive anticipatory capacities. He developed Zionism against the backdrop both of the Hebrew Bible and modern ideology (nationalism and socialism).

Israel

The historical juxtaposition of Nazism, Shoah, emergence of imperial America, and Zionist foundation of a Jewish nation-state proved to be the strong founding framework of a world order and world understanding that would survive the global Cold War order, especially as the Cold War consolidated, or seemed to consolidate, the Biltmore vision of a democratic world, with Israel as its pillar in Palestine. For Niebuhr, the establishment of Israel in 1948 was a thrilling story, a strange and fascinating configuration of history, but nothing that possessed a particular theological quality. Niebuhr was not a restorationist or Christian Zionist in either the old postmillennialist or new premillennialist sense. Response to contemporary history was crucial in his case. His Jewish friends, the struggle against Hitler, and the Shoah made him a cofounder of the American Christian Palestine Committee and a supporter of the new state who nevertheless rejected exclusive nationalism. A main figure of American liberal Protestantism in the mid-twentieth century, Reinhold Niebuhr stood in a significant, partly skeptical liberal democrat, partly mystic-irrational, and personally colored relationship with the issue of Israel, or "his long love affair with the Jewish people."[58] Barth, by contrast, though also strongly supportive of the foundation of the state in 1948, considered it to be a testimony to God's secret lordship in history that would finally lead to Jesus' open reign. For him, however, the history of the twentieth century still stood under complete "divine reservation," that is, the "judgment of this eon."

For Barth, post-1945 Niebuhr departed to a cultural paradigm and re-endorsed American exceptionalism, sadly dismissing the crucial eschaton and its impending judgment. Barth, in turn, saw himself accused of being a quietist, a neo-orthodox biblicist, or a messianist communist who was not clear enough in condemning a perverted utopia in Russia and siding with the West. (He actually criticized both the American containment and the Russian communism as mythologies of power that misused political messianism.) Moreover, in contrast to many post-1945 theologians in Germany, the United States, and other countries, Barth continued to reject "natural theology," in this case the rewriting of the very basics of his faith after Hitler and the Shoah, according to "revelation by contemporary History" during the Cold War; to revoke Jesus' ultimate role for the Jews themselves; to insist on the religion's capacity for evil, including in the historical time of Jesus of Nazareth;[59] and to relativize or tone down the seriousness of the judgment that those who belittled Jesus or misused religion brought on themselves.[60]

Having learned from the experience of a Europe he saw staggering from a spiritually empty capitalist Belle Epoque to Hitler, Barth maintained his belief in an unconditionally transcendent God, fully revealed only by the Jew Jesus of Nazareth. In a lasting personal and intellectual, sometimes painful struggle, and in a continuous rereading of the Bible, particularly of the Greek New Testament, Barth developed a position that remained Christocentric and, in a way, "anti-Judaist," but elaborated on what he saw as the lasting unique role of the Jews and of Israel. Not personal sympathy, as in the case of Niebuhr, but intellectual theological effort brought him to approve of this role and Israel's establishment (though Barth, his family, and his friends were involved in saving Jews during the Nazi era, and he held strong Swiss sympathy for this small democratic state that was threatened but determined to survive).[61] Faced with catastrophe and intellectual failure in Europe in 1914, Barth had vehemently turned to the church and to Jesus' Kingdom, which was "not yet of this world." This orientation toward the church was also to change in his last years. Before his death in 1968, still as a resolute Christocentric, he began to rethink his hitherto traditional anti-Islamic attitude, however, leaving this previously neglected field of spiritual interaction to posterity. It was to be a further step within his own evolution from historical Eurocentrism to a global orientation. Niebuhr had little poignant to say with regard to the Muslim factor in history. In his *Irony of American History,* he compared the rise of Islam in the Middle Ages and the rise of communism in the twentieth century in civilizational terms.[62]

American cultural identity construction after 1945 changed, as Michelle Mart has recently put it, by integrating Israel and Israelis as "surrogate Americans." These identified perfectly with Judeo-Christian values, now declared fundamental, and the historical experience of a modern exodus and a modern settler republic successfully established against various odds and native resistance.[63] Arabs and Muslims in turn appeared as cultural outsiders, as had been traditional Eastern European Jewish immigrants, while Jews now became the insiders par excellence of American society. Cultural affinity and sympathy, not rational, historical, or theological conviction among the elite, was a central factor of American support to Israel during the liberal consensus from World War II until 1967–1968. In think tanks and among students and teachers at the universities, Zionism, a Christian Zionist reading of the Bible, and contemporary history of salvation were not accepted as topics worthy of intellectual consideration. The film industry, however, contributed to a quick cultural assimilation of Israel and elements of Jewish history with such broadly distributed films as *Ben-Hur, Solomon and Sheba, Exodus,* and *Cast a Giant Shadow.* In these pictures, the Bible appeared as a self-evident common cultural Judeo-Christian legacy, not the poignant challenge to humanity it had been for the pioneering missionaries.

Sympathy for the victims of Nazi persecution, biblical affections for Israel individually and in churches, and the sentimental advantages such sympathies and affections gave were therefore important instruments in gaining political impact in that period. The Baptist Church member Harry Truman, who succeeded President Roosevelt on 12 April 1945, is typical of this new kind of interaction that proved to be decisive. Whereas the State Department's assessment on the Palestine question was close to that of the well-experienced mandate power, Truman let his soul speak when he decided that the United States would vote for partition of Palestine in the UN Assembly on 27 November 1947; when ordering that "every form of pressure, direct and indirect, was brought to bear by American officials upon the countries outside of the Moslem world that were known to be either uncertain or opposed to partition";[64] and when he was one of the first to recognize the new state, founded on 14 May 1948. This is true even if domestic considerations for his reelection in 1948, the fear of Jewish mass immigration, and the beginning U.S.-Soviet competition, which offered a temporary diplomatic window of opportunity for Israel, also played their role.

Britain had abstained from voting in 1947 and recognized the new state only much later. Palestine-Israel was the sole issue in the Near East with regard to which the de facto transfer of imperial power in the Near East, from Britain to the United States, was bitter. Did Truman know what he was doing when, implicitly, he shouldered British aporia in the heart of the Near East? After the recognition in May 1948, he told Jewish dignitaries that he was Cyrus, the divine instrument of Israel's rebirth. In 1952, Israel named a new village "Truman Village" in his honor. This symbolic gift was presented to President Truman at a dinner in Washington in May 1952. "We do not have orders or decorations. . . . One thing, however, is within the power of Israel to confer. It is the gift of immortality. Those whose names are bound up with Israel's history never become forgotten. We are, therefore, now writing the name of President Truman upon the map of our country," Israeli Ambassador Abba Eben said, with a remarkable sense for the *faible* of the American president and a slight flavor of hubris (Israeli politicians offering eternal life). "Thus when the eyes of men alight on Truman Village in Israel they will pause in their successive generations to recall the strong chain which, at the middle of the 20th century, drew the strongest and the smallest democracy together with imperishable lines."

Seminally and revealingly, when entering office in April 1945, Truman had received Chaim Weizmann's compelling message that the choice for the Jews was "between statehood and extermination," that "history and providence" had placed the Jewish issue in his hands, and that Weizmann was convinced that the American president would "decide it in the spirit of the moral law." It was this same moral law that made Truman express, in 1949, his disgust toward the Israeli government with regard to its treatment of the Palestinian refugees, respectively, forced exiles. His protest nonetheless remained verbal, as did most American protests of this kind in the following decades, because hitherto the (imperial) American economy of symbols and ethics was related to Israel. President Truman stands for the new symbolic economy after the U.S. rise to superpower. He decided the dropping of two atomic bombs, a powerful anti-Soviet containment in the beginning Cold War, the backing of the nation-state Israel's foundation, and the involvement in the Korean War. American and Zionist-Israeli leadership would hopefully *lead the way to* the millennium, premillennialists concluded (see "Renewed Millennialism and Mission," below), but not *lead it* once there—just like King David, who had spread too much blood to build up and live with the temple.

U.S. agency remained powerless with regard to the "moratorium on the Sermon on the Mount" that would continue in the Near East, whereas Europe, Germany in particular, was given the chance after 1945 to rethink itself and reconsider, to a certain degree, that sermon. Mark Ethridge, Truman's emissary at the Lausanne Conference in 1949, which was the first (and failed) tentative attempt at post-1948 Near Eastern peacemaking, returned disillusioned from this conference, noting in a secret report that "Israel must accept primary responsibility. Her attitude toward refugees is morally reprehensible and politically short-sighted."[65] It was naive to expect moral behavior in what political actors understood as their national struggle, far from the Golden Rule. But Ethridge was realistic in stating that, from a long-term perspective, the absence of a moral framework in the refugee question would hamper any political peace effort, since such had to be based on both the balance of power and moral force. For ethno-national reasons, the overwhelming majority of Palestinians had not been given the chance to share in the modern project of Israel; they had not done any harm to their new Jewish neighbors but were intentionally ignored in their victimhood. The case of the Cherokees had been similar; in contrast to the United States of the 1830s, however, Israel was in danger in 1948. Independent, perspicacious, and powerful American diplomacy was needed to spare political Israel in 1949 its most painful problem: the plight of its lost, and belittled, neighbors.

Rise of an Empire

Looking back to the great wars of the twentieth century, President Dwight Eisenhower stated that "despite these holocausts" America had become "the strongest, the most influential and most productive nation in the world." To live war as a time of greatly increasing economical and political power, not first as destruction (except that deep in the souls of soldiers and their relatives), was an exclusively American experience in the first half of the twentieth century. In World War II, which cost the life of approximately 55 million military and civilians, among them roughly 5.5 million European Jews, the U.S. army did not lose more than 260,000 soldiers. The United States had been the master and rightful victor of that gigantic killing event. Even if checked by the USSR, the United States was, after World War II, the world's strongest power—politically, militarily, and, above all, economically. With Germany and Japan defeated and France and Great Britain exhausted, the rivals of the Belle Epoque had lost their dominance. Emerging victorious in this broad sense, after 1945 the United States began to build its global "empire" on the technological backwardness and the consumer needs and wishes of those depending on U.S. strength.

Moreover, after 1945 the huge "military-industrial complex" (as Eisenhower designated it) had to be abolished or take on a new role. This role emerged in Greece and Turkey at the end of the war, long before the Berlin crisis of summer 1948. "I viewed the 'cold war' that quickly developed between the USSR and the West as a continuation, in different form and focus, of World War II," wrote George McGhee, who in 1947 was a coordinator for aid to Greece and Turkey and in 1951 the U.S. ambassador in Ankara. At the beginning of 1947, Britain had informed Secretary of State George Marshall that it considered aid to Greece and Turkey to be urgently required if Soviet domination was to be prevented, but Britain was not able to provide this aid. The Soviet threat to Turkey, including territorial demands in northeastern Anatolia, was real. On 12 March 1947, Truman proclaimed the containment of Soviet communism in Greece, Turkey, and the entire Middle East.[66]

The shift of power from Britain to the United States took place in a spirit of good cooperation in the strategic region of the Near East, McGhee stated. For him, Turkey was the strategically most important country in a Middle East that, in particular for its oil, needed to be held at all costs on the side of the West. Turkey had "no hope of surviving without long-term aid from the Americans and British," he opined. U.S. aid for Turkey, a member of the North Atlantic Treaty Organization (NATO) since 1952, obeyed military priorities, including an ambitious road-building program. Further development of the existing railroads was henceforth neglected. U.S. aid for Turkey exceeded many times that for Greece, Spain, and Portugal in the same period: $700 million on average each year, added to this economic aid from Europe—in particular, on U.S. insistence, from Germany since the late 1950s. Not until the 1970s did U.S. aid for Israel begin to exceed markedly even that for Turkey.[67]

Compared to the nineteenth century, the level and quality of U.S.–Near Eastern interaction had thoroughly changed. The interactions were now dominated by elites, power centers, and strategic interests and no longer by the evangelical approach of those Near Easterners living at the margins, often in the countryside, but hoped for as the agents of a new future. This transformation concerned, to an important degree, the American schools. Looking at these changes, Ephraim K. Jernazian, a former student of the

ABCFM's Marash Theological Seminary and a friend of Jakob Künzler in Ottoman Urfa, wrote:

> I cannot help but wonder what St. Paul and the dedicated missionaries after him would say about the work of our contemporary American Board of Foreign Missions that supports schools which forbid the mention of Jesus Christ and teach the Gospel of Mammon and Materialism. What, in fact, would the early founders of the American missions say about today's Board, which joins our politicians and businessmen in defense of those who justify or deny the [Armenian] Genocide and ongoing minority persecution, lest the truth jeopardize business opportunities, covering all beneath the veil of "national security"?[68]

New academic area specialists appeared in American universities according to the exigencies of the new interactions—exigencies that included the silencing or even justification of missionary America's trauma.

> By 1918, with the definitive excision of the total Christian population from Anatolia and the Straits Area, except for a small and wholly insignificant enclave in Istanbul city, the hitherto largely peaceful processes of Turkification and Moslemization had been advanced in one surge by the use of force. . . . Had Turkification and Moslemization not been accelerated there by the use of force, there certainly would not today exist a Turkish Republic, a Republic owing its strength and stability in no small measure to the homogeneity of its population, a state which is now a valued associate of the United States.[69]

Such words, written by a Princeton professor and recalling those of German authors in the interwar period, could be spoken only by a member of a new group of players who had forgotten, had never been in touch with, or had broken with the American experience in the Near East before 1918. These players borrowed from nationalist master narratives, as did McGhee, who took Kemalist self-articulation literally because it served his purpose.

McGhee's historical knowledge was utilitarian and superficial: "As rapidly as the Turkish people adopted Western laws, dress and customs, they assimilated the principles of democracy." For him, the discriminatorily applied Turkish property tax (*varlık vergisi*), which ruined non-Muslims during World War II and forced many of them into labor camps, was just an "unpopular" measure.[70] Real human and minority rights problems, in Turkey,

Saudi Arabia, or elsewhere, he reduced to "human rights accusations" or "internal problems." As U.S. ambassador, McGhee had wanted "to convert the nationalism of the Middle East into a friendly force," but ignored America's own legacy on the ground. If nationalism did not fully conform to the mechanics of containment, it was an enemy force—as in the case of the Iran of Prime Minister Mohammad Mossadegh, a Swiss-trained lawyer overthrown by a coup in 1953. America's new secret service, the Central Intelligence Service (CIA), played a leading role in this coup that cost the lives of three hundred men and destroyed a fragile democracy.

Ambitious CIA officers, the first of whom was Near East Operations Chief Kim Roosevelt, believed the United States had achieved a brilliant success and patriotic victory in August 1953, especially as CIA operations in Eastern Europe and Korea had known many failures. In the Near Eastern long-term reality, however, the CIA contributed on 19 August 1953 to paving the way to one of America's biggest problems fifty years later. Buying off politicians, tribal chiefs, and, most important, an urban mob, or *Lumpenproletariat,* the CIA played the card of right-wing and religious antidemocrats. It released forces it would be unable to control, among them the Iranian *Ulema,* with Ayatollah Kashani and the later leader of the Islamic revolution in 1979, Khomeini. Many knew full well what was at stake. Roger Goiran, the CIA's station chief in Tehran, had questioned before the coup the alliance with the traditions of British colonialism, which he thought would be a long-term disaster for America. But Goiran was recalled by CIA chief Allan Dulles (the brother of Secretary of State John Foster Dulles). President Eisenhower himself had serious doubts; in March 1953, he still thought it might be better to stabilize Mossadegh's government by substantial loans, as in Turkey and Greece.[71]

Among the democrats on the ground, the coup of August 1953 strengthened skepticism toward the Anglo-American exercise of power in the Near East. In contrast, socialism appeared as a language of solidarity and democracy; furthermore, it responded to the (secularized) eschatological longing among a poverty-stricken youth. Against all these forces the cold warriors cold-bloodedly supported right-wing repressors, political murder, and armed networks of extreme nationalists. Even such a popular and intelligent president as John F. Kennedy was haunted by the idea that he must murder Fidel Castro, the leader of the Cuban Revolution. He was himself killed by a Castro admirer. U.S.-supported right-wing repressors believed themselves to be pleasing their sponsors even if, for example, they executed students who, in contrast to themselves or to the CIA (which had begun to use sophisticated torture techniques), had not killed or tortured anyone. The case of Deniz

Gezmiş, Yusuf Arslan, and Hüseyin İnan, all hanged in 1972, is unforgotten in Turkey, as ideologically immature as these young people may have been. This is a sad example of "fathers" who killed their sons for fear of losing power and privileged relations with the hegemon. Significantly, the youth of the remnants of Christian minorities, or missionary America's clientele, also turned to socialism as a language of hope. So did the Turko-Armenian Protestant Hrant Dink, born in Malatya in 1954 and raised in a Protestant orphanage, who was murdered in 2007, as far as is known, by a young recruit of a network of extreme nationalists supported by parts of the security apparatus.[72]

The rise of Islamism in the late twentieth century was to make evident the miscalculation of cold warriors, or "sorcerer's apprentices," who believed they could instrumentalize nationalism, conservatism, patriotism, religion, and so on in the Near East for strategic purposes. Imperial America began to lose the human credit its missionaries, who had been tied to different Near Eastern forces, had accumulated for more than hundred years previously. McGhee seems to have ignored that missionary investment, because he dates the beginning of American educational influence to 1947. Ironically, among McGhee's frequent acquaintances was the aged president Celal Bayar, a CUP hardliner in the 1910s who had wanted national Turkish sovereignty and the abrogation of the capitulations at all costs. Under Bayar and Prime Minister Adnan Menderes, however, foreign NATO personnel obtained more extraterritorial privileges and immunities than missionaries and other foreigners had ever enjoyed under the Ottoman capitulations. A total of twenty-five thousand American military personnel, one hundred times the number of missionaries around 1900, were soon stationed in Turkey. In stark contrast to the missionaries and their native collaborators, the military lived like a caste, isolated from the people around them but in touch with the players in the state and the army, the Kemalist apparatus. The latter groups profited materially and symbolically more than anyone else from the alliance and reasserted their elitist behavior. Moving in their closed circles, the cold warriors dealt with Turkey as if it was already the "guardian of civilization," "pillar of security," and "respected democratic nation" it would—as the Kemalists had well known—first have to become. The reality turned out to be, after a short prosperous period in the 1950s, a growing economic crisis, a civil war–like situation, three military coups from 1960 to 1980, and a troubled alliance with the United States.[73]

In contrast to Western Europe after 1945, where America led the way to democratic renewal and empowerment despite the constraints of the Cold War, imperial American interactions with the Near East proved to be strategic, first of all, and to destroy, not to domesticate, authentic impulses of democratic self-determination on the ground if they contradicted the mechanics of the game. It is true that the United States demanded the introduction of a multiparty system instead of the authoritarian Kemalist single-party approach when Turkey asked for an alliance after 1945. But Turkey was not forced to face history, to implement human rights, and to emancipate itself from exclusivist antiliberal nationalism, as were the Western European states. The move to a multiparty system could not change antidemocratic conditions beyond the formal system. These would be a topic of open discussion only when, with Turkey's candidature for the European Union at the end of the century, nothing short of a real and comprehensive democratization was demanded—and when a particularly detrimental Cold War legacy, a "deep state" (*derin devlet*) and its nationalist gangs, profiteers of the Cold War, would have to be decompiled.

With its missionary millennialism, a vigorous part of "the soul of America" had been present in nineteenth-century Turkey. Grassroots work, encounters in the countryside, relationships with people on the ground, and a great deal of hope for all these people had prevailed. Even if American higher education in Turkey and, above all, in the United States itself in the second half of the twentieth century greatly attracted those who could afford the costs, the "soul of America"—its democratic impulses, spiritual potential, and eschatological longing—now had little business in Turkey, though some informal missionary work continued. Military, political, and economic business prevailed. Israel instead became the focal point of America's emotions, dreams, and religious preoccupations. More than a hundred years after Fisk and Parsons, a new, premillennialist type of American missionary set foot in Palestine and many other places. This kind of American mission to the Jews began during the British Mandate, continued in Ben-Gurion's Israel, and would grow impressively after 1967. In contrast to the mission in the nineteenth century, when there was no American hard power in the Old World, the mission movement after 1945 stood in the shadow of an informal kind of American empire. If this movement wanted to be credible, and not be accused of indecent connivance with the exercise of power, it had to protect itself more sharply from such connivance than had the former missionaries, organizationally and spiritually.

In principle at least, American postmillennialism of the early nineteenth century—with regard to slavery and Indian removal, for example—and premillennialism since the late nineteenth century had shown a critical potential with regard to the American way of life, its domestic injustices, and its exercise of power abroad. After Benito Mussolini, Hitler, and Stalin, whose ideologies were easy to see through for steadfast Bible readers, much more sophisticated modern complexes of evil, power, and ideology, which explicitly and comprehensively misused the Bible itself, became conceivable.[74] It is worth thinking about the fact that under the president who cultivated the most outspoken biblical beliefs and declared "war on terror," the scale of torture and degradation inflicted on detainees suspected of terrorism reached a climax[75]—even if this case shows more the contradictions of biblicist superpower politics than a prefiguration of intentional Bible misuse.

Renewed Millennialism and Mission

The foundation of the state of Israel in the 1940s greatly reempowered the reading of prophecies in a United States as receptive as ever to eschatology. The rereading of the Bible in the light of contemporary history mostly touched Christian groups other than the liberal consensus and those Congregationalists and Presbyterians who had been the main supporters of missionary America in the Near East. In American popular religious life, a much more apocalypticist premillennialism would outweigh the more constructive and optimistic, but finally (so it seemed) defeated and illusionary, postmillennialism of pre-1914 missionary America. After the experience of the world wars, the eschatological scheme of premillennialism, of past and future catastrophes, began logically to appear more plausible for a majority of all those who continued to believe in the language of Bible prophecy. It was not constructive human agency, Jesus alone, appearing as the "global king" that would be able to illuminate the earth and establish peace after final apocalyptic catastrophes. Popular literal Bible reading found itself greatly strengthened by taking in the Zionist perspective, its nationalist reading of the Bible (Labor Zionist Ben-Gurion was a daily Bible reader), and one of the most poignant political stories of the twentieth century: the successful foundation of Israel.

To a certain extent, premillennialism had been a religious counterculture of "proletarians" in America who were materially poor and felt symbolically poor because they lacked success according to accepted patterns of construction, career, and prestige. They experienced the world as thoroughly damaged by sin, a place of injustices and hypocrisy on all levels. Together with the apocalyptic revelation of Jesus, they expected the divine judgment over their own American society. In this existential sentiment they resembled the poor Eastern European Jewry and *Luftmenschen* in the century before the Shoah, who had had nothing other than to hope in traditional terms for the coming of the Messiah and for some meager grassroots solidarity. Only a smart minority of them succeeded in emigrating, improving themselves, and establishing new patterns of life and meaning in America, Palestine, and elsewhere. Premillennalists had felt excluded in American life from both postmillennialist dynamism and secular logics of success (including everyday Social Darwinism)—in short, by the promises of all sorts of "modernists." Their doctrinary fundamentalism largely screened a primary existential longing for salvation, if not existential despair.

Although individually and socially introverted in general, premillennialists were very sensitive to world history because they looked for the signs of the coming of Jesus. The world after 1914 appeared to confirm their pessimistic assessment despite the Progressive Era, as did President Wilson's failure in Paris, economic depression at the end of the 1920s, World War II, and the atomic bombs. These all seemed strong signs of biblical tribulation. In the shadow of the liberal consensus and in contrast to its flourishing middle-class denominations, which tended toward a demythologized, individualistic eschatology, the premillennialists felt galvanized when Israel's independence was proclaimed in 1948. Against the background of partial American exception to the traditional anti-Judaism of the church, and in a significant identification with Jewry, American premillennialism quickly accommodated to the new state of Israel. It had the ability, or believed it had, to integrate the new Israel into its historiography of salvation.[76] Premillennialist Christian Zionists began pervasively to influence the post-1948 U.S. approach. Side by side with, even if separately from, the seminal group of American Jews, made up of a majority of former Eastern Europeans, they had their eyes turned to Israel. Therefore, the Middle East increasingly became America's "Nearest," pervasive and preoccupying, East in the second half of the twentieth century.

A timely premillennialist discourse, combined with social conservatism and a compelling appeal to individual conversion, led to the huge success of televangelist Billy Graham among the masses from the 1950s onward. While Reinhold Niebuhr helped convince the elites to defend American order against communist danger, Graham, one of the most important representatives of the evangelical movement of the second half of the century, functioned the same way for the broad public. He stood personally close to American presidents ranging from Dwight Eisenhower to Richard Nixon and both George Bushes. Like Niebuhr, but in more popular language, Graham questioned the existing way of life in the United States, though almost only on a moral and psychological level, not with regard to society's politics and wars. "'The American way of life' . . . has it made us happy? Has it brought us the joy and the satisfaction and the reason for living we were seeking[?] . . . Do we lose one iota of the empty feeling within us?" Graham liked to question. His largely unpolitical audience, like most premillennialist evangelicals, was clear and consistent on one point: support for the state of Israel and the vision of a Near East dominated by Israel. For example, a diagram in the 1955 book *Prophetic Light in the Present Darkness* by a professor of the influential Moody Bible Institute in Chicago allotted to the tribes of Israel the land from the Euphrates to the Nile River in geometrical strips.[77]

With new vigor, American eschatology focused on the Near East after 1948. And with the new vigor there came a new mission. The British Mandate had offered a safe haven for Christian missions and their institutions in post-Ottoman Palestine, among them the missionaries to work among the Jews of the Christian and Missionary Alliance from New York (today Colorado Springs), for whom the Jews' gathering in Palestine and their turn toward, respectively claim on, Jesus were still crucial apocalyptic events to come. These missionaries supported the establishment of a Jewish state, as did the premillennialist Karmelmission, the only German institution on the ground to do so, since most Germans (including those of the Karmelmission) enjoyed a cordial relationship with the Arabs. After 1948, everyone suddenly seemed to be "called of God" to go to Jerusalem to evangelize the new promising nation, wrote Joseph H. Cohn, son of the aforementioned Leopold Cohn and director of the American Board of Missions to the Jews. The Israeli government conserved in principle freedom of religion and mission, and, with the exception of the Germans, the property of Christian organizations. It expropriated the German owners of Talitha Kumi at King George Street in Jerusalem, as well as those of the Syrische Waisenhaus, now to be barracks. Because the government did not allow new missions to operate, bureaucratic obstacles had to be overcome by semilegal methods. Just as during the first third of the nineteenth century, openly millennialist American mission became a dominant force, both globally and, in particular, in Palestine-Israel. But its character had changed.[78]

Interestingly, Ben-Gurion and other leading Zionists resisted attempts at forbidding missionary activities in Israel. This striking difference between the Kemalists and the Zionists has to do with both the more liberal substance of Zionism and, despite its negative vision of diaspora and its Christian environment, the feeling of being supported by many Christians. Did the Zionists and the missionaries really understand each other, however? "Jewish leaders such as Ben-Gurion thought that Christians who supported Israel had an understanding of the Bible similar to their own. That the same belief that initiated support for Israel and warm feelings toward its people was the one that also inspired missionary efforts was something they often did not know or did not care to know," argues Yaakov Ariel, professor of religious studies at the University of North Carolina. Israelis tended to believe that their country was the final stage in Jewish history. Evangelicals did not, but they considered it an important stage within a broader and deeper process toward the Kingdom of Jesus. They considered Ben-Gurion's secular messianism of the 1950s a shortcut, which economized on the personal messiah, to the goal of global history: peace.

Ben-Gurion possessed a strong sense of utopian imagination and fantasy that combined pragmatism with vision. For the early twenty-first century he prophesied in 1962 "a gradual democratization of the Soviet Union," the transformation of the United States into "a welfare state with a planned economy," and a federated Europe. All would be "united in a world alliance, at whose disposal will be an international police force. All armies will be abolished, and there will be no more wars. In Jerusalem, the United Nations (a truly *United* Nations) will build a Shrine of Prophets to serve the federated union of all continents; this will be the seat of the Supreme Court of Mankind, to settle all controversies among the federated continents, as prophesied by Isaiah."[79] Ben-Gurion saw Israel and Jerusalem at the center of a secular history of salvation in accordance with his nationalist secular reading of the Bible. In the 1950s he had dismissed Zionism, which he said had fulfilled its role. He now represented a messianic vision of the state of Israel; at the same time, he openly claimed the Bible for this vision and began to pay a little more attention to the Christian contribution. Nevertheless, he still felt the emergence of Christianity in the first century to be an open wound; he still resented the Jews of that early "sect" for having refused to participate in the wars against Rome; he still condemned Paul as the "worst assimilationist the Jewish people had brought forth," because in his eyes Paul had betrayed the exclusively future-oriented, eschatological vision of "redemption of the [Jewish] people" embedded in, not to say leading to, the "redemption of the world."[80] Ben-Gurion was not ready to appreciate the role of Paul, including for the restoration of Israel, in a more holistic vision of both Jewish and global history.

For the Christian millennialists, Ben-Gurion's messianism, like his Zionism, reduced life to social and political categories. Like Billy Graham in the United States, Robert Lindsey, representative of the Southern Baptists, the largest mission in Israel during the 1950s and 1960s, spoke about a spiritual vacuum in Israeli society and the failure of Zionism with regard to the deeper needs of being human; in his eyes, Israel imitated too closely the American way of life. Not only the state but Israeli society generally tolerated missionary work, even if it liked to reproach dishonest or economic motives when Jews converted. Lindsey practiced faith healing, which attracted many needy people to him. As a translator of the Gospel into modern Hebrew, this versatile minister also became a member of the Jerusalem School of Synoptic Research, which comprised both evangelical and Orthodox Jewish scholars—among the latter, the internationally well known David Flusser. Some of these scholars were interested in minimizing the differences between Jesus and the Jewish sages of his time, while the others maintained the uniqueness of Jesus; but for missionary and historical reasons, all shared the emphasis on the Jewish origins of the church. Like many evangelicals after him, in particular after 1967, Lindsey helped promote Christian tourism to Israel. For this, he was a member of a government committee. He also served as a judge in Ben-Gurion's International Bible Contest.

Another influential missionary who made use of the Gospel's spiritual, mental, and healing power was the Canadian William L. Hull, who had started the Pentecostal Zion Apostolic Mission in Jerusalem in 1936. In 1962, he was allowed by the Israeli government to serve the former Nazi official Adolf Eichmann as a chaplain until the latter was executed as an organizer of Jewish transfer by train, and thus as jointly responsible with Reinhard Heydrich, Heinrich Himmler, and Adolf Hitler for the genocide. The crucified, resurrected King of the Jews, who had forgiven his killers, had, Hull believed, a word of truth and grace to say even to a perpetrator of mass crimes such as Eichmann. Impressive was Hull's abstention from a final judgment, his determination to accompany Eichmann as a pastor, and his insistence on looking at him until the end as a human being on whom, he, Hull, did not have the last say. Hull's book *The Struggle for a Soul* contains his talks with Eichmann and interesting observations. The book shows at the same time the limits of Hull's and his wife's fundamentalist approach: doctrinarily self-confirmatory, it attempted to perform a dramaturgy of conversion deeply embedded in evangelical tradition. Hull was impressed to see Eichmann go calmly to his execution without accepting salvation in the terms Hull proposed to him, though Eichmann appreciated his presence. Eichmann dismissed not only Hull's terms but also explicitly Jesus himself as a "Jewish tale" and a mediator he claimed not to need. Hull nevertheless noted that for Eichmann there was a crucial difference between words in the heart and those in the talk, which he considered full of lies on the basis of his own socialization in post-1914 Germany.

Like Lindsey, William L. Hull stood close to the Israeli elite. In 1954, Hull had dedicated a book to Ben-Gurion, *The Fall and Rise of Israel: The Story of the Jewish People during the Time of Their Dispersal and Regathering,* which tells the renewed millennialist story that now included the Nazi persecution and the foundation of the state of Israel. A primary reason for

Hull's accompaniment of Eichmann had been his wish to show the world that Israel had the right to judge Eichmann and that it did this decently. Hull, however, caused controversy by claiming Jesus' saving grace even for Eichmann; he declared the whole world, including the victors of World War II and the Zionist establishment (as shown, e.g., by their lies and the distortions in the Israeli press during the Lavon affair),[81] to be no more than a "rotten tree" that would also be entirely judged; and, like Hannah Arendt, he described Eichmann not as a diabolic but as a weak and impressionable person who had, instead of resisting at all costs, been the willing instrument of evil within a commanding complex of power. Despite many positive remarks on fair Israeli treatment of that former Nazi official, Hull described the trial as having been reduced to a precipitate showdown of self-righteousness that missed the question of evil.[82]

For the "Hebrew Christian" and Catholic priest Daniel (alias Oswald) Rufeisen in Haifa, Israel still was "on a fourty years journey through the desert, needing time to come to itself." Rufeisen was a Polish Jew, Holocaust survivor, and major rescuer of Jews, who himself had been saved by nuns and, in hiding, converted to Jesus in 1942. Declared Zionist (though with a difference) that he was, he understood the Shoah of his Jewish people in terms of Jesus' crucifixion and resurrection. Thus he brought together his Christian faith and the Jewish interpretation of the innocent servant's suffering in Isaiah 53. This chapter gave way to the most poignant theological reflection of the Shoah. Rabbis, including liberal rabbis such as Ignaz Maybaum (see "Embarrassed Monologue, Dialogue, and Trialogue" in Chapter 5), in contrast to Rufeisen identified the suffering servant exclusively with the Jewish people.

In the same year as the Eichmann trial took place, the Israeli high court decided on Rufeisen's appeal to be registered as a Jew according to the Law of Return, what he had been refused by the Ministry of the Interior in 1958. Gideon Hausner, the prosecutor in the Eichmann trial, represented the Ministry of the Interior against Rufeisen. As an outspoken Hebrew Christian, Rufeisen angered many nationalist or religious Jews. The court decided that "a Jew who changed his religion cannot be counted as a Jew." Nevertheless, Rufeisen was granted the Israeli citizenship. His aim, which failed, had been to establish a legal precedent, since he feared already in the 1950s that "a move into a theocratic direction might spell misfortune upon the state of Israel." For the presiding judge Moshe Silberg, Rufeisen challenged "the historical sanctified meaning of the word Jew." Rufeisen was not bitter about the verdict: "Time was not ripe." Although his expectations had been wrong, he understood that, as one of his Polish-born Jewish friends in Israel had put it, the Jewish majority had "to settle things with Christianity" and national resentments against Jesus himself. This Israeli Hebrew Christian par excellence remained nevertheless convinced that the ethno-religious definition impacted negatively on what was Israel's fundamental challenge: to open powerful moral and spiritual doors to its Arab neighbors in and outside Israel-Palestine.[83]

CHAPTER 5

American Steps and Shortcuts to "Zion" after 1967

A mix of affections, convictions, loyalties, and religious legacy had drawn, in Abba Eban's words, "the strongest and the smallest democracy together with imperishable lines." Both the United States and Israel were creations of the modern era by existentially threatened or disquieted men who were on the move and cultivated strong explicit or implicit ties to the Bible. Both countries remained in the making, fascinatingly open and unfinished projects, linked in identity to global issues. Against this background they produced particularly dynamic performances, beyond the dynamic historical settlement processes that had taken place on the ground. Nevertheless, the relationship between the two countries, and the implicit goal and vision of the Near East as shaped by this relationship, remained much more open and fragile than Eban's words indicate, even if the historical juxtaposition of Nazism, Shoah, the establishment of Israel, and Israeli–American friendship proved to be a lasting fundament of American world order after Hitler. The main focus of this order would shift increasingly from Europe to the Middle East after 1967 and definitively around 1990, when the era of Cold War ended.

The Caesura of 1967–1968

The foundation of the state of Israel had changed Christian and, in particular, American millennialism. Missionaries such as Robert Lindsey and

William Hull, in turn, had contributed to the creation of a Christian and messianic Jewish subculture in young Israel that strongly grew after 1967. With their unbroken loyalty to the founders of Israel since the 1930s, they prepared the paradoxically close interaction between Jewish Zionists and Christian premillennialists from the 1970s onward. This complex interaction could scarcely be explained alone by utilitarian factors, even if Zionists first conceived it probably in utilitarian terms. Rather, it testified to the hopes the Christians had set on the restoration of the Jews and Israel since the beginning of the modern era—but also to a spell cast by prophecy at the cost of pragmatism, human relations, and truth.

The Six-Day War of June 1967 was a watershed not only because it reshaped America's world order by giving Israel a stronger place in it but also because, after a relatively secular period in global history, it brought religious forces to the political surface: the Religious Right in the United States, Islamism in the Middle East, and religiously rooted nationalism, in particular of the settler movement, in Israel. In contrast to Muslim countries in the mid-twentieth-century Near East, Israel possessed a national consensus that integrated secular and religious forces; there were manifold tensions but no bloody confrontations and repressions as in Turkey, Syria, Iran, and Egypt. A religious renaissance swept over the Near East in the late 1960s; it was at its strongest in the Arab countries that had lost the war of June 1967, where the secular Arabism of Gamal Abdel Nasser appeared as an ideology of losers.

After 1967, both in Israel, where Ben-Gurion's Labor Zionist consensus faded away, and in the United States, where the liberal consensus broke down, Holocaust memory began to take an important place. From this "negative consensus," soon to be established throughout the West, the Muslim world felt excluded, since the public discourse, of which this memory became a meaningful part and reminder, tended in the name of Europe's rightful victims to support Israeli politics, not necessarily human rights, fairness, and coexistence—the lasting lessons of the Shoah for Europe.

The new foundation of U.S.–Near Eastern interactions, laid in the 1940s, had included problems on the ground that remained fundamentally unresolved. Democratic investments according to proclaimed American ideals, in Turkey, Pahlevi Iran, and Saudi Arabia, had been minimal or absent. The construction of Israel as a state in Palestine had been urgent in the 1940s, but the destruction of neighborhood with its Christian and Muslim fellow inhabitants and the obvious painful lack of peace were disturbing even in a skeptical assessment of Israel's opponents on the ground. Making peace in the Near East became therefore a *topos* of U.S. foreign policy; the more it was conjured up, the more it lacked substance and was a sign of a concealed helplessness. At the same time, war, "apocalypse," and Armageddon, the "final battle" in Palestine, became an increasing fascination of not only religious literature in the United States.

Believing in the metaphysical benefits of an acquaintance with Israel, President Harry Truman had begun to shoulder British aporia in the Near East. Biblical affection and emotional intelligence had made him approve of Israel's establishment in 1947–1948 against his State Department. The liberal consensus and its foremost spiritual father, Reinhold Niebuhr, had shared these affections, though with moderation and irony, without elaborating any clear-cut American vision of the Near East or attributing it a central place in history or theology. Obeying logic of the Cold War furthermore, the United States of the liberal consensus did not deal with missionary America's millennialist past, its early restorationism, or its legacy of grassroots work, educational investments, and seminal trauma in the late Ottoman world. A blatant case had been George McGhee, one of America's first cold warriors in the Near East, who almost completely ignored such historical matters. Unsurprisingly, the fragile and somewhat superficial consensus of post-1945 imperial America did not last. With regard to the Near East, it was based on particularly unsettled ground.

Open questions proved to be a gap to be filled by, among others, popular eschatological currents that political protagonists began to use. Many evangelicals and most of the post-1967/1968 Christian Right were "Christian Zionist," in the new post-1948 sense that ascribed Israel a direct divine agency. What was divine, what holy, what good? Fundamental definitions began suddenly to stand in relation to contemporary Near Eastern politics. No other topic would polarize American society as intimately and lastingly as its relationship with the Near East after 1967–1968, when the liberal consensus broke down and liberal middle-class denominations, which had grown during and after World War II, declined. Large popular groups soon to be organized as the Religious Right and a small circle of intellectuals who became known as neoconservatives reacted to a cultural revolution in 1968 that radically called into question the Cold War consensus, the foundation of imperial America, and traditional patriotism. American society's internal conventions, including class, gender, and race discrepancies, appeared to many both disturbing and un-Christian. The connection with Israel, where, since 1967, a policy of occupation, settlement, ethno-religious separation and discrimination, and administrative ethnic cleansing of Arabs had been in place, became ambivalent. The U.S. war in Vietnam and its mass violence, which obeyed the logic of Cold War, appeared to many as a cynical mass murder, the lesson of which was not, and in the existing system perhaps could not be, learned.[1]

Israel emerged after June 1967 as a vital, united, and self-confident society as never before, even if only for a short while, whereas American society was, metaphorically and literally speaking, disoriented. Conservatives were disturbed about the "disproportionate role Jews played in the anti-war movement" in the United States.[2] Both resentment of and admiration for an Israel—which acted independently but succeeded in obtaining massive U.S. aid—began to permeate the political class. The rise of the pro-Israeli neoconservatives, who tended to argue (a little too loudly) within a discourse of American interests, was an unquiet reaction against a mostly silent ambivalence among American patriots. Polarized and disoriented according to the terms of the 1967–1968 caesura, would the United States be able to gain strength from its tensions, produce creative solutions, and use its power constructively? What was its goal, or—in old American vocabulary—what was Zion, and what should it actually be? Did the United States maintain the peacefully subversive utopian potential it had, despite many flaws, been able to conserve up to mid-twentieth century?

Embarrassed Monologue, Dialogue, and Trialogue

Churches in continental Europe had not possessed the seminal postmillennialist touch of their American counterparts in the nineteenth century. Most of them had lost the prophetic power and relevance of Bible reading and had not known the dynamics of restorationism. Mainstream churches were not in a position convincingly to oppose the European catastrophe of 1914 and the criminal regime after 1933. Resistance to war after 1914 was much stronger in the United States; it took a long time for President Wilson to enter the war.[3] Members of the missionary community wrote impressive antiwar texts (one of which, by Daniel Thom, has been quoted in this book). Church representatives in continental Europe were, with a few remarkable exceptions, weak when confronted with the demons of fascism, National Socialism, and the persecution of the Jews. Christianity and Christian theology had to be radically questioned.

Most post-1945 churches in Europe were busy with their own concerns and, for good reason, deeply embarrassed and deprived of their traditional language. Many of them worked hard to cope with their anti-Judaic past, to overcome modern European anti-Semitism, and to establish sympathetic ties with Jews and a vital Israeli state. Retrospectively, they now began to understand the historical Wandering Jew not as the world's divinely condemned troublemaker, as they had before, but as the powerless one who had implicitly questioned the existing societies and who, when he had troubled, had done so because he needed to be heard and understood. They began to understand this figure as mirror of an unjust, unaccomplished world; as a willing or unwilling, conscious or unconscious sign of the Kingdom to come, of a project of Israel yet to be accomplished; as the kinship of Jesus and "chosen" despite misfortune or failure. The churches were given a chance to revisit their history and to revise their understanding of eschatology, if they wanted to have a new say on the contemporary world. Some of them began wholeheartedly to approve of Israel's reestablishment in a both new and critical reading of the Bible, though by and large they only slowly began to fathom Europe's seminal catastrophe in its significance also and in particular for the churches. Theological and church discourses were often similar to monologues in the search for a lost, divine "you": accounts of aporia, but including tenacious efforts to come to new terms. Many had lost for good the founding Christian belief in a messiah of Israel coming in might; their sense for the identity of the coming one and of Jesus of the past; and the critical and innovative sensitivity to threads that connect old and recent history. This revolution of modern Christianity required an unprejudiced faith in its chief cornerstone. It required, moreover, solid historical knowledge, the readiness to withdraw from an impressive European past, and the frank dismissal of any religious self-righteousness.

Post-1945 churches in Europe remained anxious and ambiguous and lacked the confident strength to "be salt": to redefine their historical and theological identity, to say a last goodbye to Eurocentric Christianity, to show fundamental solidarity with Israel together with fundamental solidarity with Israel's Palestinian victims, and to denounce any form of terrorism and oppression. The new crucial identification with Israel, if it took place, demanded a fresh and responsible approach to the Near East. Many early Israelis themselves were painfully conscious of the blatantly ethno-nationalist behavior and ostentatious ethnic, soon ethno-religious, pride of their society.[4] Most churches were unable to respond to the Near Eastern "moratorium on the Sermon on the Mount" because they feared falling back into old paternalist or anti-Jewish patterns, or denying the Jewish "yoke of the kingdom of God" that they had only recently begun to discover. They were, in short, afraid to see the specks in the Israelis' eyes instead of the logs in their own, but made their status worse by not insisting resolutely on their own foundation.

News of facts unmasked the naive and incorrect belief in the a priori superior ethics of the new state—beginning with Red Cross delegate Jacques de Reynier's 1948 report on the massacre by the Irgun in Deir Yassin, which triggered Palestinian mass exile, Dr. Pierre Fasel's report of the same year on the murder of UN mediator Folke Bernadotte by the Stern gang, and early thorough analyses of the refugee problem.[5] Such accounts deeply embarrassed many serious-minded Christians who were in the process of searching for a new direction. An intrepid Christian, Gertrud Kurz—the "mother of the refugees," for whom a rabbi had implored the whole blessing of Israel in the summer of 1942 and who had cofounded the Society Switzerland–Israel—was among the first public Christians in Europe ready to listen to the Palestinians and to act for them.[6] In their late and hasty effort to reappropriate Israel and its restoration into their worldview, some German theologians on the other side went so far as to speak of the "Israelwerdung Gottes," that is, to say that God had become Israel, as Bertold Klappert, a theological critic of such tendencies, has pointed out.[7]

Academic and nonacademic Christian–Jewish dialogue initiatives flourished throughout the West, both among Protestants and, since the Second Ecumenical Council of the Vatican in the 1960s, among Catholics. In its declaration *Nostra Aetate* of 1965, the Catholic Church finally dismissed its "theology of substitution," in which the church had fully taken Israel's place and left no agency to the Jews without conversion to the church. European and American Christians attempted innovative paths based on the new networks of exchange, needs of communication, and new global power relations, substantial new or old-new insights were acquired. Although in many churches a genuine post-Shoah and post-1948 consciousness took root, this failed to result in innovative, courageous theology. More often, a harmonized scholarship began to predominate; it did not hurt where necessary—when the Bible served as an ideological tool and self-righteousness or culturalism held sway—but mirrored the cultural shifts in the West and its now professed Judeo-Christian fundament.

It was now common to profess what the Jewish German thinker Franz Rosenzweig had bravely, though Eurocentrically, proclaimed in the early twentieth century, that there "was no salvation outside the church if not for Jews who remained in their religion." This theology after 1945 must come, for manifest reasons, to terms with the Shoah and its uniqueness. However, dismissing former wisdom and, for their manifest flaws, former teachers, it risked dismissing its global perspective of the unique "slain Lamb," Son of Man, coming into power: the vision with which the first Americans had begun their mission to the Near East.[8]

The new Judeo-Christian attitude toward Islam recalled in many respects a period when European pre-Shoah theology felt wrongly self-confident and superior toward Jewry, instead of developing existential empathy, spiritual humility, and historical and theological depth. The same is true for the European *Judenfrage* in the early nineteenth century, in comparison to the global "question of Islam" in the late twentieth century. Rosenzweig's "doctrine of the two roads" was now shared by Reinhold Niebuhr and many others. A few people began to revise it for a timely, more globally oriented trialogue. This could not suffice, however: instructive "heterodoxies" had to be included, static self-confirmation overcome, humble cross-border experiences ventured, and, far beyond intro- and retrospection, contemporary challenges faced.

In contrast to his mentor Rosenzweig, the liberal rabbi of London Ignaz Maybaum, who had studied in Berlin in the 1920s, in his book *Trialogue* recognized Islam as a full-grown monotheism. He postulated that all three monotheisms "must unite to combat the dark age which threatens our civilization," and that American and European civilization needed to integrate Islam. Compared to "true Jewish life," however, he showed Islam and its understanding of a "revealed law" as deficient; it was, for him, a model of antimodern, unprophetic fundamentalism and "the pattern for all forms of totalitarianism." Condescension, stereotypes, and many historical shortcomings, together with relevant, true, and lucid observations, marked Maybaum's *Trialogue* of 1973.

Among the questionable points of his piece was his naive confidence that "the Jew" (not Jesus) would "do justice to Islam and Christianity" through his "prophetic Judaism" and could unify Christianity and Islam through his "human existence." What Maybaum called "unalterable, eternal Judaism" smelled like essentialism. The main actor of Jewry's seminal revolution in the first century—without which a restoration of Israel in the modern era would scarcely have had any chance—was explicitly given "no place" in the world of Maybaum's Jew.[9] In this fundamental respect, there was no coming to terms with Jewish history in Maybaum's thought, and no modern apocalyptic opening toward a fresh and timely understanding of global human existence beyond the traditional synagogue, church, and mosque.

Which Zion?

A problem soon to be much more severe than the embarrassed dialogue or trialogue in Europe had, in the United States, to do with millennialism. After Israel's impressive victory in the Six-Day War of 1967, a number of shrill voices, inspired by Ben-Gurion's post-Zionist political messianism of the 1950s, began to declare a millennium to come, for which Jewish world saviors, a "Jewish humanist citadel in Israel and Jewish ideological outposts in the diaspora," would prepare the way.[10] This discourse of Jewish manifest destiny, ingenious agency, brilliance, superiority, and indestructibility lacked a true understanding of the Shoah and suggested dangerous illusions. In terms of own activism and justice, the Shoah had been a manifest total failure in the face of overwhelming evil; it had proved the total need for both universal solidarity and alert self-protection. At last, it urged a new self-understanding beyond activist Zionism, "unalterable Judaism," and Holocaust memory. Admiring post-1967 Christian Zionism was a religious counterpart to triumphalist Zionism. It saw Israel's "history written in advance"[11] and tended to attribute to the state of Israel a holiness and deterministic divine agency it did not and could not have, instead of loyally acting in both solidarity with and critical distance from Israel. This would have meant a tenacious yes to the new innovative state in the Near East together with a frank no to any sophistry or theology of discrimination and occupation. The lack of peace, comprehensibly innate to the European Zionist project of the second quarter of the twentieth century, called for a thoughtful questioning of certain assumptions on how Israel had been founded, how it had evolved, and what Zion should mean in both Israeli and American minds—all the more since the new state could not have evolved the way it did without the American support it increasingly received after 1967. Christians had deeply to rejoice in the refoundation of Israel; in the faith and the mutual solidarity of those involved; in the "access to power" of the most persecuted. The apocalyptic truth of the slain Lamb now in power had flashed for a moment. But it was far from being established: triumphalist discourse, ethnic and religious nationalism, reckless use of power, and a pervasive lack of humility denied it.

Israel could not escape the vicious circles related to nationalism and power politics. After June 1967, it began to administer occupied territories and slid into conflict with international law, in particular the Fourth Geneva Convention. The Israeli settler movement, the governmental connivance with it, and the reality of occupation in Gaza and the West Bank were signs of confusion in the midst of triumph. Confidence was destroyed instead of won. Immature messianism mingled with outdated theology and violence, in the case of the settler movement; nostalgia toward early Zionism combined with the nostalgic renaissance of Great Israel, now to be the "light of the Earth."[12] Israel had to carry on through paradoxes and suspenses that others did not understand or only unwillingly understood. But some elementary questions had to be answered if the modern project of Israel was to be preserved from dead ends.

Nobody knew exactly what Israel—a state without an established constitution, civil law, and boundaries—should be, and what the long-yearned-for Zion, the citadel and symbol of the coming Kingdom of God, actually meant: an American way of life, democracy, theocracy, miraculous omnipresence of Christ; or a pragmatic, prudent, but open project that did all to obey democracy and international law no less than the biblical "yoke of the Kingdom"? Was Israel to be a great Israel, an ethnonationally Jewish Israel, or a small, vibrant state that comprised those "children of Abraham" on the spot who shared in the project—even if "raised up from stones"? The post-1967 excitement among evangelicals and the added value Israel possessed as America's strategic partner did not answer these elementary questions.

Against the background of a painful lack of consensus and integrationist ethos in the United States in the late 1960s, and the fundamentally open "question of Zion," it is no accident that Holocaust memory began to play a strong and cohesive role from the 1970s onward. The greatest amount of attention was paid not to Zion and its light but to its perverted dark counterpart in the recent past and—with the eschatological notion of the "final holocaust" and the "final battle" of Armageddon—in the near future. Holocaust memory filled the need for a strong consensual symbol far beyond American Jewry. The uniqueness of the Holocaust began to serve as a safe historical and metaphysical reference. Though historically ambivalent, "uniqueness" and *Zivilisationsbruch* were true terms for a profound caesura; similar to Paul's seminal *skandalon* of the cross.[13] In the reality of Western public discourse, however, they did not always contribute to the comprehensive perception of history. While the meaning of Zion and its light—that is, a modern biblical projection of individual and global future—had become unclear, its negative opposite filled the gap. "Israel" risked being defined by Hitler; the Holocaust, the greatest catastrophe of the Jewish people after its seminal catastrophe in the first century, to become "Shoah business" (Abba Eban).

The new Holocaust consciousness had begun in Israel itself. After a period of Zionist urgency and accomplishment in the 1940s, and a period of Ben-Gurion post-Zionist state messianism in the 1950s, the Israel of Ben-Gurion ventured for the first time to look back openly at the black hole of modern Jewish experience. The disturbing opposite of the clever, successful, and strong Zionist *Muskeljude* was the weak, fragile, chosen Jew who had been tormented, targeted, and finally slaughtered in their millions by heralds of German chosenness and death in a Europe without covenant. In the context of the Eichmann trial in 1962, Ben-Gurion and others formulated for the first time a public response to the Shoah within a national discourse. A strong state of Israel, according to its message for the present and the future, took justice in its own hands, executed the evildoer, and made sure that its military strength would suffice to tackle other Eichmanns and Hitlers, thus preventing other Auschwitzes. In a similar but somewhat mystical vein, the author Elie Wiesel, winner of the highest awards in the post-1967 West, described the victory in June 1967 as the "recruitment" of two thousand years of Jewish suffering and millions of Holocaust victims who defended their heirs in that battle.[14]

Spiritualized or not, this *Muskeljude* response to the Shoah confirmed Israel as a Zionist project of Jewish hard power that moreover decided for itself what was globally right or wrong according to the interests of a legally underdefined, in reality highly ethnocentric state of Israel. The *Muskeljude* response perpetuated at the same time a political language and mental framework marked by pre-1945 Europe and transposed them to the Near East, even though Near Easterners had nothing to do with the Holocaust perpetrators. The emphasis on the Nazis fitted in well with the foundation narrative of an imperial America that, in the ideological confusion of the late 1960s, was in need of reconfirmation. But this emphasis risked causing serious analytical flaws and a weakened sense of responsibility with regard to the post-Ottoman world. Talk of Arab Hitlers, a possible Near Eastern Holocaust, appeasement traps à la Munich, and an omnipresent specter of anti-Semitism entered the repetitive discourse of political commentators. One needed to try hard in order to find a historically more careful and appropriate language and to escape the spell of Nazi Germany darkness versus its Western victors' light. The "talk of uniqueness and incomparability surrounding the Holocaust in the United States . . . promotes evasion of moral and historical responsibility," the Jewish American historian Peter Novick contended. This talk missed the Shoah's ultimate call to compassion and responsibility, not to self-confirmatory righteousness.[15]

To the problem of responsibility was added those of historical accuracy, honesty, and truth. Beginning in the 1970s, efforts were made to establish a Holocaust Museum in Washington, D.C. Its initial plans included exhibits concerning the slaughter of the Armenians in Asia Minor, who in a significant way had preceded the European Jews by twenty-five years. The Prague Jewish author Frank Werfel's *The Forty Days of Musa Dagh,* written originally in German, is a strong stand-alone testimony of this. Both slaughters were crucial events in American mental history and archives, but realpolitik and ideology, which now marked the American relationship with the Near East, caused the exclusion of the Armenian catastrophe from the museum. Leading American organizations that claimed to struggle for public honesty and truth (e.g., the Anti-Defamation League) acted analogously in their campaigns. The duplicating transfer of the setting in which the Shoah took place to the Near East, the Israeli historian Idith Zertal argues, not only perpetuated the psychology of that time and demonized Arab leaders but also distorted the historical reality of the Shoah itself.[16]

Moreover, the transfer of the vocabulary of the Shoah to the Near East gave Hitler and death omnipresence. Of this, Ben-Gurion's analysis in 1963 of Menahem Begin as an "enthusiastic Hitlerist type," a "racist eager to annihilate the Arabs," was a poignant, if exaggerated, example. While prime minister in 1978, Begin significantly provided for an official memorial stamp, with Hebrew and English inscription, for his former Irgun comrade Avraham Stern. Stern had become a leader of the terrorist Stern gang: a death-glorifying, "tragically minded" young terrorist who, in his hatred for the British, had collaborated with the Axis powers.

In 1977, the first government of the Likud, that is, of the historical rivals of Ben-Gurion's Labor Zionism, brought to the surface elements of the Zionist movement with which Israel would painfully have to come to terms. It was not an accident that modern Zionism had taken as one of its strongest symbols Masada, a place where nearly one thousand Jews had committed suicide after the fall of Jerusalem in 70 C.E. That experience of death and resentment and the whole trauma of the fall of Jerusalem after suicidal resistance had permeated the Zionist ideology. This was its dark side. It contrasted with the Zionists' faith in old and hopeful promises. It contrasted with the project of establishing a secure home for Jews without future and building up a peaceful, new society in Palestine, Eretz Israel.[17] As far as Masada was concerned, left-wing Zionism and the right-wing Zionism of Jabotinsky, of whom both Begin and Stern were disciples, did not substantially differ.

A lesser known disciple of Jabotinsky was Schalom Ben-Chorin, alias Fritz Rosenthal, who had founded in Munich circa 1930 a group of the Bethar, Jabotinsky's youth organization (named after the place Bethar, where Bar Kochba, the leader of the last and most bloody Jewish uprising against Rome, had, according to Jabotinsky, heroically committed suicide in 135 C.E.). Shortly after 1967, looking back on his life and early Zionist commitment, Ben-Chorin disarmingly confessed that in his youth he had believed that Zionism was the answer to the Jewish Question but that his certainty had disappeared during the decades. The Jewish Question remained an open one, he contended; Zionism had merely transferred it from Europe to the Near East. Triumph and success obscured the main issue that had been so clear when the Jews were at their weakest. Including the United States and post-1948 Israel itself in his skepticism, he summed up the Jewish Question with the claim that he who adores power, must curse (real) Israel.[18]

Ben-Chorin distrusted the discursive securities of the Jewish–American connection after 1967. For the German Jew Fritz Rosenthal, who had had the chance to experience a vibrant intellectual and cultural life in the Weimar Republic, left Nazi Germany and participated in the construction of the new state of Israel, and been searching since his youth for truth, life, and living faith, vital questions remained open. These questions had not been answered by Zionism, either secular or religious, or by the orthodox religion. To traditional Judaism Ben-Chorin, the son of the more or less assimilated Rosenthal family, had "converted" before becoming a revisionist Zionist—and he emancipated himself from both.[19]

In contrast to Yeshayahu Leibowitz but also a humanist critic of post-1967 Israel, Ben-Chorin did not believe in the "yoke of Torah and Mitzvoth" or self-sufficient, perpetuated religion. Nor did he frontally attack the new discourse of a "common Judeo-Christian heritage," particularly as he was a Jewish pioneer in his modern understanding of Jesus. In contrast to the revisionist Zionist Joseph Klausner, his study of Jesus was not defensive or apologetic. In significant contrast to Klausner, Maybaum, and others, moreover, Ben-Chorin was ready to cope positively with the heritage of Paul. Both Islamists and Zionists, in particular right-wing religious Zionists, shared in the twentieth century refusal of and contempt for the apostle Paul. Some did so because Paul had established among the Christians the unique historical place of the Jews by confirming the Hebrew covenant, therefore appearing to be one of the main agents of "Jewish world conspiracy"; others, because Paul had subordinated the Hebrew covenant to Jesus Christ and thus made the Jewish experience and the Torah relative.[20]

Probably more poignantly than anyone else, Paul had established the fine but sharp theological line between words of sacred scripture that give life and those that destroy oneself and others. He described the human being held captive by the logic of death.[21] For Muslim zealots, or militant Islamists, in the Near East of the late twentieth century, as for power-centered Jewish zealots two thousand years ago, Roman or Western military and cultural power usurped God's sovereignty causing the "abomination of desolation"; holy war was the sole possible answer against the ungodly intruders. Though seriously insisting on God's otherness and transcendence, zealots and their priests did not question the "holy law" (Torah, Sharia) as an instrument of deadly coercion in their society, since they used it. "Clerico-fascism" is a modern example of the pervasiveness of evil in religion.[22] The "zealots" (e.g., Qutb and those described by Flavius Josephus) detected the contradictions and opportunism of their political-religious establishment, which cooperated with the foreign power holders. They projected the future in activist, militant, even suicidal terms—all the more as they lacked a pragmatic, constructive contemporary vision. In this sense "poor in spirit" and unconsoled, but tragically minded and turned to the references of the past, one's own life should be sacrificed in a struggle against cynical evildoers. The sacrifice, at least, was a testimony against the exploiters' overwhelming force and a violent sign of longing for change in a fundamentally unjust and unconsoled world. Of this, the apocalyptical tragic mind of Masada was also a strong example.[23]

Parts of revolutionary Islam since 1979, both Sunni and Shiite, can be read in these terms. For revolutionaries and for many pious Muslims as well, Western and Israeli power deadly threatened a decent way of life in accordance with the Qu'ranic revelation; in the case of the Occupied Territories, it put into question the very basics of decent human life. Islamist terror became spectacularly visible shortly after the Islamic Revolution in Iran, when a militant group of messianist Sunni believers, who had declared *mahdi* one of their own, seized the Grand Mosque with the Kaaba in Mecca on 20 November 1979. They and their numerous sympathizers wanted religious purity in the holy territories of Islam; they opposed the opportunism of the Saudi establishment, its ostentatious, hypocritical religiosity, and its dependency on Western power. Though this event clearly exposed the fallacies of the policy of the "green belt," the American cold warriors nevertheless began to implement this policy and to support via Pakistan *jihad* fighters in Afghanistan. Here the Soviets had invaded in December 1979 to protect a secular socialist regime. Among the mujahedeen were many Saudis, last not least Osama bin Laden.[24]

Rise of Apocalypticism: Spell, Sign, or Catharsis?

The discursive certainties of the Jewish–American connection after 1967 stood historiographically on what one may call a post- and anti-Hitler fundament. Religiously, they were tied to a millennialist reading of the Bible, even more so after the liberal consensus (which had cultivated more affective than theological affinities) had ended. The millennialist reading in question, however, is striking in its highly apocalypticist tendencies, which, emotionally laden, risk lacking pragmatism and compromise, and in the end making a deadly mockery of the Sermon on the Mount.

Though the "latter days" were always present in American millennialist culture in sermons, tracts, and books, apocalyptic destruction, "final holocaust," and more generally a cultural obsession with mass death constitute a remarkable phenomenon in the late twentieth century. It is hardly an accident, even if it raises many questions, that this rise of apocalypticism coincides with the importance of the Holocaust in American life. The products of apocalypticist *imaginaire* sold and continue to sell very well on the U.S. market of books, films, and politics. Is the motor of all this an obsession with death, not to say mass death? Do fascination by, adaptation to, and expectation of death result from apocalypticist mass consumption? Or is the apocalypticist market, on the contrary, an opportunity to exorcise death, externalize fantasies of destruction, achieve catharsis, and come nearer to life?[25]

On the global religious scene, dynamic shifts and changes took place in the last third of the twentieth century, among them the emergence of a significant movement of evangelical Jews that is to a large extent the result of Jewish and American Protestant spiritual interaction.[26] No comparable downfall of a centuries-old wall took place with regard to the Muslims, who had been, together with Jews, the initial target of early missionary America on its road toward "establishing Zion." The "Islamic Renaissance" was the most visible part of the global religious renaissance in the late twentieth century. Toward the end of the twentieth century emerged large movements of much more modern and dialogue-oriented forms of Islam, especially among people in and from Turkey. There were also surprisingly strong currents of Muslim expectations of Jesus' coming rule on earth, which revitalize old Muslim eschatological traditions. These currents, however, are seen as unacceptable among teachers who claim orthodoxy in the Near East or put forward an Islamism inspired by Said Qutb and Ayatollah Khomeini, which emphasizes eschatological confrontation. More than ever, the new Muslim eschatology of the late twentieth century uses direct biblical sources. It remodels and transforms the strong input it receives from Western apocalypticism and tries to cope in its own manner with the refoundation of Israel as a sign of the end times.[27]

Popular eschatological currents in the United States barely reached the political surface before the end of the 1960s, when the liberal consensus came to its end, American society was polarized, and the "Christian Right," a movement of hitherto mostly quiet conservative Christians but henceforth with political claims, began to be organized. The rise was triggered by reception of Israel's triumph in the Six-Day War of June 1967, American self-doubts with regard to the Vietnam War, and reactions to a leftist cultural youth revolution in 1968. The Christian Right, with its vociferous connection with Israel and its apocalypticist Zionism, became a lasting and polarizing political player, as on parallel course did the intellectual circle of neoconservatives that simultaneously arose. In the case of the Christian Right, this was an apocalypticist Zionism combined with conservative domestic positions. In the case of the neoconservatives, it was American patriotism, ostentatious (but unconvincing) "realism," and a strategic American relationship with Israel that remained undisclosed in its ideological handicaps. The small network of neoconservatives was led by former Trotskyist immigrants, converted to post-1945 liberal America. They were afraid by what had happened in American life in the late 1960s and fascinated by the (seemingly) transformative geostrategic possibilities of American power politics, above all in the Near East. Both movements were born out of the post-1968 crisis; both filled the ideological gap left by the lost political and religious American consensus with a new ideological production.

More even than post-1945 premillennialism, post-1967 premillennialist Zionism entered a synergy with the Cold War by figuring the USSR as "Gog and Magog," the enemies of Israel during a final battle of history before the parousia. But it went far beyond support for Cold War. In the vein of conspiracy theories, it drew the picture of a dark world where global organizations plotted against Israel and the Bible-believers. Apocalypticist bestsellers, sold in their dozens of millions, compellingly combined Israel, the Near East, nuclear war, and evil forces such as the USSR, the emerging European community, the United Nations, and the ecumenical movement that all would be easy prey for the coming *Führer* (Antichrist).[28] The readers were compelled to loyalty toward Israel without looking at the human realities on the ground. Strikingly, though unsurprisingly, the leaders of the Christian Right movement established close relationships with Israeli leaders, in particular with those of the Likud party most vociferously committed to Israel's post-1967 frontiers, who came to power in the 1970s. After the collapse of the USSR, the apocalypticist focus turned more than ever to the Near East. Saddam Hussein was now identified as a restorer of anti-Jewish Babylon. *The Rise of Babylon: Sign of the End Times* was the title of a related book by the dean of the Moody Bible Institute; the book was fittingly supplemented in January 2003, on the eve of the U.S. invasion of Iraq, with the subheading to *Is Iraq at the Center of the Final Drama?*[29]

Has American mainstream millennialism taken on shrill overtones that cover up a game of power and greed? Has the most powerful and impressively constructive American "ideology of modernity" come to a dead end, caught up by its own shadows, the sharp fragments of its broken mirror? Has it lost its constructive course for millennium? After the Cold War ended, American apocalypticism, global politics, and mass media focused on the Middle East as never before. The huge market for apocalypticism in the United States since the late twentieth century, its products consumed by millions of people, and its secularized by-products indicate a markedly different stage of American millennialism. Is this apocalypticism a market-oriented and manipulable ideological machine? Did and does it still have to do with a prophetic reading of the Bible, radically committed to life and construction: in short, to Jesus?

Is it a sign of "discontent in civilization," of obsession by death, of rhetorical captivity, of an unhealthily overstretched, restless national ego? Or is this apocalypticism, on the contrary, still fed by human encounters, spiritual longing, and a fundamental solidarity with the project of Israel? Was and is it, at least for a number of its producers and consumers, a catharsis from apocalypticist images and sequences, preparing their mind for a less spectacular, though not less surprising, "parousia"—in whose perspective historical American millennialism and exceptionalism will be definitively laid to rest?

Conclusion

Biblically projected or not, the modern era has not led to the millennium, as hopefully anticipated by enlightened Americans in the early nineteenth century—in particular, those who set out to build up "Zion" in the Near East because they knew their young republic was not the future Zion or a prefiguration of the Kingdom of Jesus on earth. The particular modern dynamics in the United States emerged from religion and modern discoveries, from a fascinating synergy of enthusiasm for the Enlightenment, a prophetic reading of the Bible, and successful republican state building. Often smiled at by continental European theologians, restorationist Bible believers combined visionary power with energetic missionary pragmatism. Their millennialism was part of an American identity that constituted itself religiously in the interaction with and the representation of the Near East, the "cradle of Zion," the place of a better life to be won, of a modern, pious, and seminal "citadel" to be built up on earth. Palestine was Zion's geotheological place, Jesus its basic cornerstone. All this is why this book speaks of America's "Nearest East."

Millennialist manifest destiny in the early nineteenth century meant, in its deepest sense, "going Near East," not colonizing the American West, as it was usually understood. The goal was both to bring and to win peace by fulfilling old obligations toward the Jews, the old churches, and the Bible lands. This millennialist move was all the more manifest as repression and exploitation, not love, shaped the social reality of the young republic: the abolition of slavery in particular had not yet materialized, and the missionary community lost its struggle against President Andrew Jackson's politics of Indian removal in the 1830s. If the Indians "are finally ejected from their patrimonial inheritance by arbitrary and unrighteous power, the people of the United States will be impeached," ABCFM secretary Evarts had stated in 1830. Much later, the truth of Evarts's words was confirmed. "Everyone judges the westward removal of eastern Indians as one of the great injustices in United States history," a recent American textbook writes. "We accept this inheritance, this legacy of racism and inhumanity," an official of the Department of the Interior recently exclaimed.[1] During a remarkably long period, the American interaction with the Near East did not suffer from greed, strategy, or territorial conflict. For nearly a hundred years, the Bible lands were first of all a place of American missionary performance and a scene of high significance for the large missionary community at home. The interests were principally symbolic: a part of the symbolic and spiritual economy studied in this book.

Science and scholarship of the modern era contributed to liberate individuals from premodern bonds, loyalties, and ecclesiastical dependencies but did not put an end to exploitation by symbols, ideology, greed, and power. Indeed, as modern ideologies arrogated to themselves coercively the place of religion, as in the case of radical ideologies in Europe that made millions of people temporarily more unfree than had done any traditional religion, their potential for exploitation increased. The American millennialisms or "pursuits of happiness," both civil and biblical, were progressive movements. They claimed to make the American continent and the world better places than they were; subliminally, they expressed the existential feeling of men and families in motion who had left an old and, for them, unhappy world behind for the sake of a better future. In reality, the constitutional "pursuit of happiness" translated into individual and national greed that was a seminal factor of American continental and global expansion. Greed was nonetheless checked by altruism, or disinterested benevolence, of the type inherent in the evangelical millennialism in the Near East studied in this book.[2]

Politically, the Ottoman Near East of the nineteenth century had stood in stark contrast to the synergy that empowered the American experience. It was an area of political precariousness with a highly uncertain future at the southeastern end of colonialist-imperialist Europe. For most contemporary Europeans it was an annoying, not to say scandalous, thorn in the side of the flourishing, progressive Christian West, an anachronistic Muslim autocracy ruling over millions of Christians. The area itself had become the Oriental Question. This was secretly linked to another question arising in a modern

West soon to be based on assimilatory and homogenized nation-states: the so-called Jewish Question. The Oriental Question had intrigued the European diplomats since the late eighteenth century. Its core element from the late nineteenth century onward would be the Armenian Question: the question of an Ottoman future for the Armenians, the best modernizing element of Ottoman society, within a reformed egalitarian and pluralist order. Both missionary America and the globally leading British Empire were strongly concerned with the Armenian Question. Poignant elements of the modern period and the diplomatic Oriental Question, the Armenian Question and the Jewish Question were critical issues both for British diplomacy and for the millennialist "struggle for the American soul." Only in World War I did British diplomacy dare to cut the Gordian knot of the Oriental Question, which contributed to triggering the Armenian genocide, and to commit itself to establish a Jewish national home in Palestine.

As postmillennialist optimists, the members of the ABCFM had considered Ottoman precariousness promising. Talented and biblically inspired children of the rising American Republic had been sent to the Ottoman Empire in the early nineteenth century, where they were soon to be considered *the* representatives of America in the Ottoman world. The missionary community at home and on the spot believed in "apocalypse," that is, in history in the light of prophecy and revelation (*apokalypsis*). For history's progress toward a modern Kingdom of God on earth, they considered the restoration of Israel—the restoration of the Jews to Palestine and to Jesus–to be crucial. The American missionaries began to spread their message together with values of Enlightenment. Instead of Palestine, as was planned, Asia Minor became their central focus. Instead of the fall of the Ottoman Empire, the missionaries put their hopes in its reform, in its "leavening" by the Gospel and by modern education. Seminal modern institutions—schools, hospitals, factories, and printing presses—were built up. Enlightenment and prophecy, modernity and millennialism, including evangelical charity, were inseparable elements that guided the missionary activities in Asia Minor, Syria, and the Ottoman Balkans. The ABCFM was part of the "Protestant International," established in the early nineteenth century, which was at pains to evangelize the globe and to prepare the global Kingdom. Citizens of other Western countries, such as Britain and Switzerland, were also among its missionaries.

The American encounter with the Ottoman world challenged head-on an order that was based on the dominance of Sunni Islam, the submission of non-Muslim communities, and the repression or marginalization of heterodoxies. American missionaries on the ground gave Muslim spirituality, culture, and historical achievements little credit. They did not attach any value to the centuries-old imperial *pax ottomanica* covering a huge and heterogeneous area, because they viscerally believed it to be deficient in both sociopolitical and spiritual terms. As the American idea of Islam increasingly became known as derogatory, hostile, or at the least critical, the Ottoman ruling class began to see the missionary efforts as subversive of the foundations of power. This hampered a possible productive synergy of American input, the legacy of Islam, and Ottoman reform efforts. Nevertheless, America was never generally seen as an enemy. This began to change only with the new role of the United States in the second half of the twentieth century, though Sultan Abdulhamid II and Enver Pasha's anti-American attitudes had been early strong reactions to the new American soft power in the Near East.

The Americans on the spot questioned the subordination of the non-Muslim communities (*millets*) and heterodox groups to the ruling community of Sunni Muslims, which since the late eighteenth century had striven for the preservation of a threatened Ottoman Sunni domination. To effect this preservation, the ruling elite began to implement centralization, infrastructural modernization, and social homogenization. Missionaries, by contrast, strove for the establishment of self-confident, distinct identities within a modern legal framework and for equal participation of non-Sunni and non-Turkish groups, both Christians and others. In the era of Ottoman reforms, some common ground between Ottoman reform and missionary input seemed possible; the potential for synergy was particularly strong after the Reform Edict of 1856. The problem was that despite reforms the state did not recover power. The Tanzimat ended with crisis in the Balkans and a catastrophic Ottoman-Russian war. As a result, Sultan Abdulhamid began promoting Islamism, or Muslim nationalism, instead of integrative Ottomanism. In this he included the struggle against what he considered to be subversive Protestantism. Islamism was a factor in the anti-Armenian violence of the 1890s, a social earthquake that caused the ABCFM to discover, more than ever, its responsibility toward the whole Ottoman society. Reconsolidation of imperial Muslim power and empowerment of local Christians were not synergic in a Hamidian perspective, and even less so following the loss of major parts of the mainly Christian Balkans in 1878; especially as some missionary strategists, following German unification under Otto von Bismarck, began to set expansive missionary hopes on the united global power of (nominal, cultural) Protestantism.

After the Young Turk revolution in 1908, the ABCFM placed its hope in a new Turkey. The ABCFM was sympathetic to the former opposition, the Young Turks of the Committee of Union and Progress, which had partly taken power in 1908 and reinstated the constitution and deposed Abdulhamid in 1909. In response, the ABCFM began to articulate its vision of Young Turkey in a secularist language, eager to win over the Muslim educational elite. The key term *Kingdom of God* continued to be broadly used, but its vision was mostly translated into terms of responsibility, education, character building, charity, fraternity, good government, and so forth, though its fundament remained an apocalyptic history believed to progress toward the Kingdom.

The missionaries hoped that the secularist discourse would at last open the door to Muslim society, or at least to its young educational elite. But this was only in small part the case. The leading discourse of the elite became a nationalistic one that was grafted onto the old belief in the legitimate sovereignty of the Muslim ruling group. The young elite wanted to become full players again in the national and international political game, instead of reactors and victims. Such nationalism of the *millet-i hâkime,* promoted first under Abdulhamid, translated within two decades, as far as European Turkey and Asia Minor were concerned, into Turkish ethno-nationalism (Turkism). Many Young Turks and Turkists felt close to the young *Wilhelminian Kaiserreich* and its assertive, ambitious military elites, whereas missionary America repudiated German militarism. Young Turks and Wilhelminian elites believed World War I to be a window of political opportunity. It turned out to be seminal catastrophe for the Old World (Europe and the Near East). For missionary America, the criminal destruction of Christianity in Anatolia during World War I proved a poignant catastrophe.

This study has emphasized the conflictual relationship between the CUP and the ABCFM: the honeymoon period after 1908, the complete breakdown of confidence during World War I, and the failed peace, from a missionary perspective, when the Muslim resistance to the Allies, led by ex-CUP members, won the war over Anatolia and proclaimed a Turkish nation-state. Among missionaries, painful, though silenced, memories remained: first, of the catastrophe of Asia Minor's Christians; second, of the missionaries' own hopes in 1908–1914 for a peaceful Near East; and third, of the failed ideas after 1918. The close Turko-American strategic partnership after World War II can be considered a small substitute for what both parties had failed to achieve in 1908: a new Ottoman Near East coupled with a strong Turko-American friendship. Neither of the partners was really ready in 1908. The Turko-Ottoman elite was not democratic, America not congruent with the missionary avant-garde on the spot. This avant-garde, moreover, attributed too much agency to itself, giving itself an overly central role in the optimistic and self-centered process it hoped for. The great challenge would nonetheless have been to build up, as missionaries began to contend, a secular civic society fed by a common spirit beyond the boundaries of churches, mosques, synagogues, and, of course, trendy revolutionary, nationalist, or Social Darwinist ideologies.

What mainly took root instead in that time was ethnic nationalism among the educational elites and proto-fascist behavior among young imperial elites. If the late Ottoman missionaries' fears of what would result from ethnic nationalism unfortunately proved to be true during the twentieth century, the same missionaries were shown to be wrong in their visions of contemporary history before 1914. Criticism can be leveled at the missionaries' biased imagination and the expectations they awakened in the people who trusted them. And a sober conclusion is that, despite interesting departures after 1908, the turnaround toward an integrative, if critical, vision of Islam, in terms of both history and religion, was not achieved. In the United States, the period of the world wars (1914–1945), in particular the related experience of the Turkey Mission in the 1910s, gave impetus to a premillennialism whose rise had paralleled the fundamentalist movement in U.S. evangelicalism in the nineteenth century. After the crash of Young Turkey, an evangelically motivated social utopia centered on the Near East lost most of its appeal, in contrast to apocalyptical scenarios and geostrategic catastrophes. Exigencies of military and economical realpolitik, but also of the survival of some initially missionary institutions, led in the interwar period to new treaties with the Republic of Turkey, heir of the Young Turks. An oil-inspired alignment soon followed with Saudi Arabia, a conservative Islamic post-Ottoman state that contradicted most of what missionary America had striven for in the late Ottoman world.

After 1945, imperial America established globalist action for which it needed a strong vision of the evil of others and its own goodness, mostly in seminal metaphors of World War II (e.g., new Munich, new Hitler, new holocaust). As a result, it closely linked European, Near Eastern, and global history against the background of Hitler. New elites, among them recent immigrants from Germany and Eastern Europe, began to initiate policies, analyses and concepts about the Old World, including the Near East. Global interests alone were not sufficient arguments for "good wars": post-1945 war rhetoric repeated patterns comprising the concept of an enemy, the reaction against attack, and the apocalyptic vision of global peace. (Leaders invented parts of this pattern whenever war was deemed necessary.) Waging war was framed by a vision of good to be defended and evil to be crushed; even "realists" such as President Dwight Eisenhower had to use the related vocabulary of "crusades," "nation at war," "free and religious people" versus "atheists," "ruthlessness," and insidious" enemies. War and war rhetoric, however, remained checked by outspoken criticism and, as in the case of the politico-theological mentor Reinhold Niebuhr, ironic self-distance. Eisenhower himself drew attention to the "conjunction of an immense military establishment and a large arms industry" in the 1940s that was new in the American experience. He coined the seminal terms *military-industrial complex* and *scientific-technological elite* and pointed to the dangers of their "total influence." These new forces were continually to be checked, he said in his "Farewell Address," by strong and wise statesmanship and by an "alert and knowledgeable citizenry."[3]

For fifty years or so, from the 1930s to the 1980s, the United States turned much of its attention to Europe and the Soviet Union. In this time, Cold War politics in the Near East, which did not follow any serious democratizing agenda, deprived the United States of much of the symbolic capital it had enjoyed in the early post-Ottoman era. The protection and empowerment of Israel was felt to be America's major moral and religious duty in the Near East after 1948, more clearly so after 1967. For its symbolic economy, religious America began to depend on an Israel that became a strategic cornerstone of U.S. relations with the Near East. The Jews—who had not been collective political players for nearly two thousand years, and who had been victims of a comprehensive genocide in 1941–1945—became after 1948, in a poignant turn of history, important actors both in the Near East and in the United States. As a result, they were themselves for the first time exposed to the possibilities and the problems, temptations, and vicious circles of power. Israel introduced nuclear weapons to the Near East in the 1950s, began a problematic policy of occupation and settlement after 1967, and waged wars in Lebanon it could not win. With regard to Israelis, Jews, and the United States, the question of "dual loyalties" was raised, though rarely publicly. This was a reminder of the simple fact that the relationship between the peoples contained a mix of realpolitik and symbolic economy; that in terms of realpolitik there could be no complete identification of interests; that serious tensions were possible if realpolitik and symbols shifted in different directions; and that the fragile common language could be lost, so that one would feel fooled or betrayed by the other. At a deeper layer the fact was that Zionism had not received the blessing of the American pioneers of "Zion" in the Near East. In his ambivalence toward Israel and his contradictory relations with the forces in the Near East, the American "Cyrus" could not, or could only very fragmentarily, become what most U.S. presidents had aspired to be since Woodrow Wilson and Harry Truman: peacemakers in the Near East.

Despite its inexperience and shortcomings in terms of peace, Israel held on against agencies in the region that could not bear the idea of restored Jewish power in the "lands of Islam." While many continental Europeans had laughed at prospects of such a restoration in the nineteenth century and the first half of the twentieth and learned its meaning only after the *Zivilisationsbruch* of Auschwitz, the United States had begun its main mission with precisely this prospect in mind. All subsequent missionary strategies reconceived the Bible lands according to modern American millennialism. After the initial restorationism, after the long-lasting Armeno-centric axis, and after the final emphasis on civil society before the break of the world wars, the United States at last remade its attachment to Israel and "Zion," this time not with a prophetic utopia but with a state. This tie now formed the umbilical cord to an area long before reclaimed as a place of millennialist fulfillment. In a new way, as an imperial restorer of Israel like the Persian king Cyrus in the sixth century B.C.E., not first and foremost as a missionary, America had turned back to Israel remade in Palestine.

The cataclysm of World Wars I and II, the Shoah, and the foundation of Israel acquired pivotal relevance for the premillennialism that began to predominate in religious life. Premillennialist missions, which arose in the mid-twentieth century, did not pursue an independent civil agenda of a comparable size to that of the previous missionaries, since they were more pessimistic in terms of culture and history. Evangelical premillennialism did not anticipate the evolutionary coming of the millennium but rather imminent catastrophes and salvation only by faith in Jesus. In its serious-minded forms, it insisted, more than the postmillennialists or the men of the liberal consensus, on the cautious belief that the whole world, all human beings—including actors considered positive, such as the American government and Israel—still remained under Jesus' judgment. The Kingdom of God would establish a fundamentally new justice that would differ from the present justice not only in degree and quantity but in fundamental human quality. Unknown or ignored aspects of human agency and history would come to light. Even aspects of the Nazi-centric historical foundations of American power and its exercise globally and in the Near East would be carefully reassessed according to the viewpoint of the Lord of this earth of whom the Revelation wrote.

This ideal type of evangelical eschatology was exposed in the second half of the twentieth century to the reality of Cold War and the political organization of conservative Christians after 1967–1968. An organized pro-Israel Christian Right began to shape the American relationship with Israel and the Near East. The rise of this soon-to-be influential Christian Right was paralleled by the rise of the elite circle of the neoconservatives: two vastly different groups that nevertheless proved synergic in crucial moments of U.S. foreign policy. Both cultivated particular ties with Israel, while speaking different languages (religious and secular), and looked at the Near East with Israeli eyes. It is true that religious life in the United States has always cultivated eschatological images, and that much of its dynamism has been due to the prophetic reading of the Bible. Compared to European churches (and despite Jesus' warning), American latter-day preachers were, and still are, quick to provide identifications and dates; whenever proved wrong, they simply readapt their apocalyptical scenarios. Given the constraints of space in the Old World, Europeans had had to learn that certain things and words could not simply be readapted. Was evangelical premillennialism drawn into the maelstrom of power politics and corresponding needs of domestic mobilization? Did it misuse eschatology in order to limit political responsibility for change and its own duty of speaking truth to power?

However one looks at it, and however much political leaders tried to escape its impact, from 1967–1968 onward premillennialist apocalypticism was among the propelling factors of American power policy toward the Middle East, even if usually not in the direct way it was from 2001 to 2008. In January 2003, a Swiss professor of theology was contacted by French colleagues because President Jacques Chirac needed elucidation on an allusion made to him during a conversation at the beginning of 2003 with the American president (who had already decided, as the French noticed with consternation, to go to war in Iraq). President George W. Bush had told Chirac that "Gog and Magog" were threateningly in action, that prophecies were being fulfilled in the Near East, and that the French president needed to be on the right side—the side of the American president. Bush, in turn, was eager to be on the side of Israel, based on his reading of chapters 38–39 of the book of Ezekiel; these and chapter 20 of the Revelation mention Gog, a leader of enemy forces during a "final battle" against Israel.[4]

The mind of the American president manifestly anticipated this prophetic battle when deciding for the war in Iraq, but evidently without clarifying the role of his armies in contrast to those of Gog, which are the only ones described in Ezekiel. Or did he identify his armies with the heavenly hosts? Whatever Bush might have thought in early 2003, however half-baked the post-battle plans of his mostly neoconservative advisers appeared, and however deadly the war following the invasion, some wisdom still reigned. The Kurds—together with the Armenians and the Palestinians, the great losers of the twentieth century's Near East—achieved autonomy and better positions than ever. Perhaps, too, the would-be winners of the global power game learned a lesson: as sorcerer's apprentices they had misused Islam for strategy and the faith of others for their own interests, thus feeding and arming fighters who turned out to be fierce anti-American Islamists. The would-be winners were given the opportunity to learn that their actions in Iraq, combined with previous actions since 1953, led to the rise of a Near Eastern power they publicly treated as a force of evil, without taking their part of responsibility for what had politically gone wrong in that country. The representatives of this power, Iran, beginning with Ayatollah Khomeini in 1979, for their part called the United States the Great Satan. Though their own flaws are manifest—most evident, their nonacceptance of Israel—these stand in a logical relation to the shortcomings of others.

Less spectacular and more important than the clashes are successful Islamic movements of the late twentieth century that have begun to cope peacefully with the old American legacy in the Near East, especially in Asia Minor, the focal region of the ABCFM in the Ottoman world. Labeled "Islamic Calvinists," they build up industries and do global business. They have become reconciled to the secular Swiss Civil Code, introduced in Turkey in 1926. They send their "missionaries" to many countries where they found modern Islamic schools. The journalist Ahmed Şerif, who had so much missed modern Islamic agency when traveling through the late Ottoman world, would rejoice in them. Most of them, moreover, have reconciled themselves to Israel, with which they do business without sacrificing their sensitivity on the Palestinian issue. Eager to give room to suppressed potentials and "to penetrate the sources of Islam, to true humanity" (Ahmed Şerif) they are more critical of nationalism than many others, though their leaders still bother facing openly the dark sides of Turkish history. Even if not free from Ottoman nostalgia, many of them want to commit themselves to a modern global future beyond antimodern interpretations of the Sharia, the traditional Islamic law. This broad movement is one reminder among many others of the insufficiency of a solely Judeo-Christian historical-theological backbone of world order, as has been de facto the case since 1945.[5]

Since the late twentieth century, leaders and media have yielded to apocalyptically overheated religious or secular discourses and are thereby tempted to unwise vocabulary and action. Political apocalypticism provides impulsive persuasion; it feds an emotional and egocentric dialogue of confrontation. Who and which terms define the "decisive ideological struggle of our time"?[6] "Apocalypse" taken seriously, in a quiet contrast to apocalypticism, means again and again revelation in the light of parousia: "the slain Lamb, now in power." It points to the end of egocentric human relations as they had been conceived on a gradually globalizing earth. It strips history to its "true meaning"; subverts many of its heroes, who succeeded according to the all-too-often deadly logics of the globalizing eon; and implies a powerful rehabilitation of all victims of individual, familial, commercial, sexual, national, imperial, and religious egoism, coercion, and violence.

A historian's narrative may be a contribution to this quiet work that challenges established discourses, exhausts traditional symbols, questions inherited "truths"—but does not give them away easily. With hope, but without illusions about limits and breaks, it contributes to projecting avenues for the future. Not only in American missionary reading, the new order that apocalypse reveals uncovers the human being as, right from the start, not less eager to give than to take. Therefore, it redefines radically any historical "pursuit of happiness" and scheme of salvation so that at the end a frank, last goodbye can and must be said to rusted treasures of religion and collective history, as exceptional and dynamic as they may have been.

In thought, I stand up and finally leave my father's table of the early 1970s. I enjoy the benefit of hindsight. The perspective is now global, no longer Eurocentric as it was for us at that time, when it was conditioned by the world wars and the Cold War. In the not-yet-teenager's eyes, the American "white knight" of World War II had become a dark and disoriented "master of war" in Vietnam, not (much) better than the Soviet Union that invaded Czechoslovakia in 1968. That teenager learned that in a religious, national, or global polarization, neither side is completely right, at least not in the perspective of parousia and its fundamental changes. These would question and challenge both global history and each individual entirely. In this perspective alone were sides concretely to be taken.

The teenager I was admired a peaceful militant such as Martin Luther King Jr. who had spoken truth to power, the inner eye turned to the coming justice. The not-yet-teenager who identified with Israel had been impressed when, at the Zurich airport near to which he lived, militant Palestinians shot on an El Al plane in February 1969, calling on the Swiss to see them and their cause in terms of their universalized national hero William Tell.[7] Only slowly did he begin to fathom the poignant story of Israel's foundation; how much "Zion" was still a challenge in progress; how little was implemented from the potential the Sermon on the Mount, which had stood at the center of his father's teaching, had opened up. Much more could be implemented.

Even if not yet in these terms, the teenager learned that, like any powerful modern discourse, the American rhetorical synergy of millennialism, modernity, and capitalism, including its recent complex of "American Israel," could become self-righteous and deadly when it lost its breath. The teenager began to feel that, though he wanted to maintain much of his own religious and cultural socialization, he needed to go radically beyond a whole set of clashing discourses if he wanted the benefits of truth, not confusion, euphemisms, or lies. There was a road to take, and it would need time.

Notes

INTRODUCTION

1. *Tanîn* 13 June 1911 and 25 June 1910, in Ahmet Şerif, *Arnavudluk'da, Sûriye'de, Trablusgarb'de Tanîn,* ed. Mehmed Ç. Börekçi (Ankara, Turkey: TTK, 1999), 31–32, 204–205 (cf. xiii). Little is known about Ahmed Şerif's life, but he was probably a graduate of Mülkiye, the school for civil servants.

2. On political catechism, see Götz-Dietrich Opitz, *Manifest destiny im Kalten Krieg: Die Inaugurationsreden US-amerikanischer Präsidenten im Spiegel des rhetorischen Millennialismus* (Bern, Switzerland: Peter Lang, 1993), 113; cf. Sacvan Bercovitch, *The American jeremiad* (Madison: University of Wisconsin Press, 1978); Stephen D. O'Leary, *Arguing the apocalypse: A theory of millennial rhetoric* (New York: Oxford University Press, 1998). Helmut Richard Niebuhr's seminal work is *The kingdom of God in America* (Middletown, Conn.: Wesleyan University Press, 1988), xx (1st ed., 1938; in German: *Der Gedanke des Gottesreichs im amerikanischen Christentum* [New York: Church World Service, 1948]).

3. William E. Strong, *The story of the American Board: An account of the first hundred years of the American Board of Commissioners for Foreign Missions* (Boston: Pilgrim Press, 1910), xi.

4. Hans-Lukas Kieser, *Der verpasste Friede: Mission, Ethnie und Staat in den Ostprovinzen der Türkei 1839–1938* (Zurich: Chronos, 2000) (Turkish ed.: *Iskalanmış Barış* [Istanbul: Iletisim, 2005]).

5. A few bibliographical notes follow (additional citations are provided in later notes):

James L. Gordon, *American relations with Turkey, 1830–1930: An economic interpretation* (Philadelphia: University of Pennsylvania Press, 1932), and John A. DeNovo,

American interests and policies in the Middle East, 1900–1939 (Minneapolis: University of Minnesota Press, 1963), are classical and, in many respects, still useful surveys that helped give Ottoman Turkey its deserved place in U.S. history. They did not, however, use Ottoman sources or include a discussion of Near East–centered millennialism.

Working in U.S. archives, Joseph L. Grabill (*Protestant diplomacy and the Near East: Missionary influence on American policy, 1810–1927* [Minneapolis: University of Minnesota Press, 1971]) has elaborated on the seminal American missionary network in the Near East, though he did not access Near Eastern sources or study the encounters firsthand. Useful too is church historian Robert T. Handy's annotated edition of sources *The holy land in American Protestant life: A documentary history* (New York: Arno Press, 1981). A more recent study worth mentioning, which includes considerations on early American missionary Zionism, is Damascus-born scholar Fuad Sha'ban's *Islam and Arabs in early American thought* (Durham, N.C.: Acorn, 1991).

In *Power, faith, and fantasy: America in the Middle East, 1776 to the present* (New York: W. W. Norton, 2007), Michael B. Oren, an Israeli-American historian, offers multiple insights into the topic of America in the Middle East (including America's religious background), but he gives little attention to trauma and failure and their impact, and he does not elaborate on millennialism. Ussama Makdisi (*Artillery of heaven: American missionaries and the failed conversion of the Middle East* [Ithaca, N.Y.: Cornell University Press, 2008]) has analyzed the intersection of American mission with Ottoman reform in Lebanon that gave birth to innovative and conflicting routes of Lebanese Protestants. Oren and Makdisi provide little discussion of Asia Minor, the central focus of the American Protestant mission to the Near East after 1830.

On eschatology—in particular American eschatology, including the restoration of the Jews—a great deal of literature is available. A solid introduction to millennialism in America is Paul S. Boyer's *When time shall be no more: Prophecy belief in modern American culture* (Cambridge, Mass.: Harvard University Press, 1992). An insightful, sensitive study on eschatology, mission, and the Jews, based on primary sources, is Yaakov Ariel's *Evangelizing the chosen people: Missions to the Jews in America, 1880–2000* (Chapel Hill: University of North Carolina Press, 2000). Since the 1990s—and particularly during the government of George W. Bush, after the invasion in Iraq—many studies and essays on Christian Zionism were published, including Paul C. Merkley's *The politics of Christian Zionism: 1891–1948* (London: Frank Cass, 1998), on the seminal Christian support for Zionism; Stephen Sizer's *Christian Zionism: Road-map to Armageddon?* (Downers Grove, Ill.: IVP Academic, 2004), which critically analyzes premillennialist Christian Zionism; and Dan Cohn-Sherbok's *The politics of apocalypse: The history and influence of Christian Zionism* (Oxford: OneWorld, 2006), a survey based largely on secondary sources. In *An angel directs the storm: Apocalyptic religion and American empire* (London: Tauris, 2004), Michael S. Northcott, a British expert on politics and theology, offers interesting though little-consolidated reflections on apocalyptic religion and the American empire with regard to the Middle East. Moreover, many critical academic essays have appeared, including Götz Opitz's "Präsident von Gottes Gnaden," *Die Gazette,* 15 March 2004, 40–45.

Among the recent publications on Muslim apocalyptical thought are William F. Tucker's *Mahdis and millenarians: Shi'ite extremists in early Muslim Iraq* (Cambridge:

Cambridge University Press, 2008), a book on early Shiites that contains a large bibliography and, in its last section (pp. 133–141), comparative reflections up to the present; David Cook's *Contemporary Muslim apocalyptic literature* (Syracuse, N.Y.: Syracuse University Press, 2005), an important study of contemporary Muslim apocalypticism and transreligious influences; and Benjamin Lellouch and Stéphane Yérasimos's edited collection *Les traditions apocalyptiques au tournant de la chute de Constantinople* (Paris: Harmattan, 1999).

6. Anne-Laure Dupont, "Une école missionnaire et étrangère dans la tourmente de la révolution constitutionnelle ottomane," *Cahiers de la Méditerranée* 75 (2007), posted online 21 July 2008, available at http://cdlm.revues.org/index3483.htm, accessed 4 May 2009.

7. Cf. European Stability Initiative, *Islamic Calvinists: Change and conservatism in central Anatolia* (Berlin/Istanbul, 19 September 2005), available at www.esiweb.org, accessed 12 May 2009; Aylin Güney, "Anti-Americanism in Turkey: Past and present," *Middle Eastern Studies* 44, no. 3 (2008): 471–487 (this article offers insights into the film *The Valley of the Wolves—Iraq* and its reception but does not analyze its religious content). For a recent essay on American apocalypticism, published in Turkey, see C. A. Ataç and Bahar Gürsel, "Amerikan apokaliptik'inin dünü bugünü," *Doğu Batı Düşünce Dergisi* 8, no. 32 (July 2005): 73–88.

8. Quoted in Ernest Lee Tuveson, *Redeemer nation: The idea of America's millennial role* (Chicago: University of Chicago Press, 1980), 212 (1st ed., 1968).

9. Cf. Evliya Çelebi, *Im Reiche des Goldenen Apfels: Des türkischen Weltenbummlers Evliyâ Çelebi denkwürdige Reise in das Giaurenland und in die Stadt und Festung Wien anno 1665,* trans. and annot. F. Kreutel (Graz, Austria: Verlag Styria, 1987), and Hans-Lukas Kieser, "Djihad, Weltordnung, 'Goldener Apfel': Die osmanische Reichsideologie im Kontext west-östlicher Geschichte," in *Imperialismus in Geschichte und Gegenwart,* ed. Richard Faber (Würzburg, Germany: Königshausen and Neumann, 2005), 183–203, with more references.

10. *Panoplist; and Missionary Herald* 14, no. 4 (April 1818): 152–153.

11. Cf. Robert J. Allison, *The crescent obscured: The United States and the Muslim world, 1776–1815* (New York: Oxford University Press, 1995).

12. Cf. Klaus Schreiner, "Messianismus: Bedeutungs- und Funktionswandel eines heilsgeschichtlichen Denk- und Handlungsmusters," in *Zwischen Politik und Religion: Studien zur Entstehung, Existenz und Wirkung des Totalitarismus,* ed. Klaus Hildebrand (Munich: Oldenburg, 2003), 1–44.

13. Cf. Leonard L. Thompson, *The book of revelation: Apocalypse and empire* (New York: Oxford University Press, 1990); Klaus Koch, *Vor der Wende der Zeiten: Beiträge zur apokalyptischen Literatur,* ed. Uwe Glessmer and Martin Krause (Neukirchen-Vluyn, Germany: Neukirchener, 1996); Claude Tresmontant, *Enquête sur l'apocalypse: Auteur, datation, signification* (Paris: Editions F.-X. Guibert, 1994); Jens-Wilhelm Taeger, *Johanneische Perspektiven: Aufsätze zur Johannesapokalypse und zum johanneischen Kreis 1984–2003* (Göttingen, Germany: Vandenhoeck and Ruprecht, 2006); Richard J. Bauckham, *The climax of prophecy: Studies on the Book of Revelation* (Edinburgh: T. and T. Clark, 1998).

14. For a theological reflection on the "Geburt der modernen Welt aus dem Geist der messianischen Hoffnung," see Jürgen Moltmann, *Gott im Projekt der modernen*

Welt: Beiträge zur öffentlichen Relevanz der Theologie (Gütersloh, Germany: Chr. Kaiser/Gütersloher Verlagshaus, 1997), 15–30.

15. E.g., Gospel Missionary Union. Cf. Gerald H. Anderson, *Biographical dictionary of Christian missions* (Grand Rapids, Mich.: W. B. Eerdmans Publishing, 1999). Important for premillennial mission theory is Adoniram J. Gordon's *The Holy Spirit in missions* (New York: Fleming H. Revell, 1893); cf. James H. Moorhead, "The erosion of postmillennialism in American religious thought, 1865–1925," *Church History* 53 (1984): 61–77.

16. For a survey of historical Christian Zionism, see Cohn-Sherbok, *The politics of apocalypse.* Still instructive beyond Britain are Franz Kobler's *The vision was there: A history of the British movement for the restoration of the Jews to Palestine* (London: Lincolns-Prager, 1956) and Mayir Verété's "The restoration of the Jews in English Protestant thought, 1790–1840," *Middle Eastern Studies* 8, no. 1 (1972): 3–50.

17. Cf. Cook, *Contemporary Muslim apocalyptic literature; İnsanlık O'nu bekliyor: Hz. İsa* [The humanity is waiting for him], thematic issue of the Turkish Islamic journal *Aksiyon,* 8 December 2003; Tarif Khalidi, ed., *The Muslim Jesus: Sayings and stories in Islamic literature* (London: Harvard University Press, 2001) (Turkish translation: *Müslüman Hazreti İsa* [Istanbul: Kitap, 2003]); Geoffrey Parrinder, *Jesus in the Qu'ran* (London: Faber and Faber, 1965).

18. İbrahim Temo, *İttihad ve Terakki Cemiyeti'nin kurucusu ve 1/1 no'lu İbrahim Temo'nun İttihad ve Terakki Anıları* (Istanbul: Arbayay, 1987), 78 (1st ed., 1939).

19. Cf. Lellouch and Yérasimos, eds., *Les traditions apocalyptiques au tournant de la chute de Constantinople;* Barbara Flemming, "Sâhib-kırân und Mahdî: Türkische Endzeiterwartungen im ersten Jahrzehnt der Regierung Süleymâns," in *Between the Danube and the Caucasus,* ed. György Kara (Budapest: Akademiai Kiado, 1987), 41–62; Cornell H. Fleischer, "The lawgiver as Messiah: The making of the imperial image in the reign of Süleyman," in *Soliman le Magnifique et son temps,* ed. Gill Veinstein (Paris: Documentation Française, 1992), 159–177; Isaiah Tishby, "Acute apocalyptic messianism," in *Essential papers on messianic movements and personalities in Jewish history,* ed. Marc Saperstein (New York: New York University Press, 1992), 259–286; Charles Berlin, "A sixteenth-century Hebrew chronicle of the Ottoman Empire: The *Seder Eliyahu Zuta* of Elijah Capsali and its message," in *Studies in Jewish bibliography history and literature in honor of I. Edward Kiev,* ed. Charles Berlin (New York: KTAV Publishing House, 1971), 21–44.

20. Kobler, *The vision was there,* 31.

21. Mordechai Breuer, and Michael Graetz, *Deutsch-jüdische Geschichte in der Neuzeit,* vol. 1 (Munich: Verlag C. H. Beck, 1996), 219–223; Heiko Haumann, *Geschichte der Ostjuden* (Munich: Deutscher Taschenbuch Verlag, 1999), 49–53; Julius H. Schoeps, *"Du Doppelgänger, du bleicher Geselle . . .": Deutsch-jüdische Erfahrungen im Spiegel dreier Jahrhunderte 1700–2000* (Berlin: Philo), 2004, 15–19.

22. Sayyid Qutb, *Milestones* (Delhi: Markazi Maktaba Islami, 1996), 7, 11–12 (1st Arabic ed., 1964).

23. Frantz Fanon, *Les damnés de la terre* (Paris: Maspéro, 1968), esp. 9–12 and 51–52 (1st ed., 1961).

24. Cf. the discussion under the heading "Which Zion?" in Chapter 5.

25. Qutb, *Milestones,* 104, 111. The notion of primitive purity is found in a 14 January 1832 letter by William Goodell; see William Goodell, *Forty years in the Turk-*

ish Empire or, Memoirs of Rev. William Goodell, D.D., late missionary in the A. B. C. F. M. at Constantinople, ed. E.D.G. Prime, D.D. (New York: Robert Carter and Brothers, 1876), 133.

CHAPTER 1

1. As documented, e.g., in Johann Heinrich Zedler's comprehensive encyclopedia of eighteenth-century Europe; see "Tausendjähriges Reich," in Johann Heinrich Zedler, *Grosses vollständiges Universal-Lexicon aller Wissenschaften und Künste: Welche bisshero durch menschlichen Verstand und Witz erfunden und verbessert worden* (Halle, Germany: Zedler, 1732–1752), vol. 42, 444–455.

2. Surveys in Mehmed Şükrü Hanioğlu, *A brief history of the late Ottoman Empire* (Princeton, N.J.: Princeton University Press, 2008), and Erik Jan Zürcher, *Turkey: A modern history* (London: I. B. Tauris, 2004).

3. Rev. Richard Beere, quoted in Mayir Verété, "The restoration of the Jews in English Protestant thought, 1790–1840," *Middle Eastern Studies* 8, no. 1 (1972): 31.

4. Michael B. Oren, *Power, faith, and fantasy, 1776 to the present* (New York: W. W. Norton, 2007), xv.

5. Cf. James E. Force and Richard P. Popkin, eds., *The millenarian turn: Millenarian contexts of science, politics, and everyday Anglo-American life in the seventeenth and eighteenth centuries* (Dordrecht, Netherlands: Kluwer, 2001), 95–118; Brian Stanley, "Christianity and civilization in English evangelical thought," in *Christian missions and the enlightenment,* ed. Brian Stanley (Grand Rapids, Mich.: W. B. Eerdmans Publishing, 2001), 169–197.

6. Henry Laurens, *La question de Palestine,* vol. 1: *L'invention de la terre sainte, 1799–1922* (Paris: Fayard, 1999), 14–15; Simon Schwarzfuchs, *Napoleon, the Jews and the Sanhedrin* (London: Routledge and Kegan Paul, 1979), 24–25.

7. Cf. the monumental (24 vols.) and seminal *Description de l'Egypte, ou, Recueil des observations et des recherches qui ont été faites en Egypte pendant l'expédition de l'armée française,* published according to the orders of His Majesty the Emperor Napoléon the Great (Paris: Imprimérie impériale, 1809–1828).

8. Cf. Henry Laurens, *L'expédition d'Egypte, 1798–1801* (Paris: Editions du Seuil, 1997); Juan Cole, *Napoleon's Egypt: Invading the Middle East* (New York: Palgrave Macmillan, 2007).

9. Joseph Priestly, *A comparison of the institutions of Moses with those of the Hindoos and other ancient nations* (1799), quoted in Franz Kobler, *The vision was there: A History of the British movement for the restoration of the Jews to Palestine* (London: Lincolns-Prager, 1956), 45.

10. Cf. Dominique Trimbur, ed., *Europäer in der Levante: Zwischen Politik, Wissenschaft und Religion (19.–20. Jahrhundert)/ Des Européens au Levant: Entre politique, science et religion (XIXe–XXe siècles)* (Munich: Oldenbourg, 2004).

11. Cotton Mather, *The great works of Christ in America: Magnalia Christi Americana,* vol. 2 (Edinburgh: Banner of Truth Trust, 1979), 555 (1st ed., 1702).

12. Ibid., 25.

13. Cotton Mather, *The present state of New England* (New York: Haskell House, 1972), 35–36 (1st ed., 1690).

14. Quoted in Ernest Lee Tuveson, *Redeemer nation: The idea of America's millennial role* (Chicago: University of Chicago Press, 1980), 25 (1st ed., 1968).

15. Helmut Richard Niebuhr, *The kingdom of God in America* (Middletown, Conn.: Wesleyan University Press, 1988), 174 and 179 (1st ed., 1938; in German: *Der Gedanke des Gottesreichs im amerikanischen Christentum* [New York: Church World Service, 1948]).

16. In his sermon *The Church's flight into the wilderness: An address on the times, containing some very interesting and important observations on Scripture prophecies* (New York: S. Loudon, 1776), 20, 33, 43; available at http://digitalcommons.unl.edu, accessed 28 August 2007. Cf. Reiner Smolinski, ed., *The kingdom, the power, and the glory: The millennial impulse in early American literature* (Dubuque: Kendall/Hunt Publishers, 1998).

17. Nathan O. Hatch, *The sacred cause of liberty: Republican thought and the millennium in revolutionary New England* (New Haven, Conn.: Yale University Press, 1977). Cf. Richard Connors and Andrew Gow, eds., *Anglo-American millennialism, from Milton to the Millerites* (Leiden, Netherlands: Brill, 2004), in particular Stephen A. Marini's chapter "Millennialism and political theology in revolutionary America," 159–176.

18. Henry Finch, *The world's resurrection or the calling of the Jewes. A present to Judah and the children of Israel that ioyned with him, and to Ioseph (that valiant tribe of Ephraim) and all the House of Israel that ioyned with him* (London: Edward Griffin for William Bladen, 1621), quoted in Douglas J. Culver, *Albion and Ariel: British puritanism and the birth of political Zionism* (Bern, Switzerland: Peter Lang, 1995), 109. Cf. Wilfrid Prest, "Finch, Sir Henry (c. 1558–1625)," *Oxford Dictionary of National Biography* (Oxford: Oxford University Press, 2004); available at http://www.oxforddnb.com/view/article/9436, accessed 28 August 2007.

19. English clergyman Andrew Burnaby, quoted in Tuveson, *Redeemer nation,* 101.

20. See President Barack H. Obama's inaugural address of 20 January 2009.

21. Cf. Elena Astafieva, "Imaginäre und wirkliche Präsenz Russlands im Nahen Osten in der zweiten Hälfte des 19. Jahrhunderts," in Trimbur, *Europäer,* 161–186.

22. Verété, "Restoration," 36–41.

23. *A sermon, preached in the audience of His Excellency Caleb Strong, esq., governor, the other members of the Executive, and the Honorable Legislature of the Commonwealth of Massachusetts, on the anniversary election,* May 29, 1805 (Boston: Young and Minns, 1805), 36–37.

24. 22 January 1820, *Memoir of Reverend Levi Parsons* (Hartford, Conn.: Cooke and Co. and Packard and Butler, 1830), 280 (1st ed., 1824).

25. Joseph Harvey, *A sermon before the Foreign Mission Society of Litchfield County* (New Haven, Conn., 1815), 9, quoted in Clifton J. Phillips, *Protestant America and the pagan world: The first half century of the American Board of Commissioners for Foreign Missions, 1810–1860* (Cambridge, Mass.: Harvard University Press, 1969), 8.

26. Rufus Anderson, *Memorial volume of the first fifty years of the American Board of Commissioners for Foreign Missions* (Boston: The Board, 1861), 62.

27. Timothy Dwight, *A sermon, delivered in Boston, September 16, 1813, before the American Board of Commissioners for Foreign Missions at their fourth annual meeting*

(Boston: Samuel T. Armstrong, 1813), quoted in Charles L. Chaney, *The birth of missions in America* (South Pasadena, Calif.: William Carey Library 1976), 283–284.

28. Goodell continued, "Long before the expiration of that period we may have done with steam, have found something much more useful. . . . Who can tell but we may yet tame the volcano, or hitch on to the lightning, or ride above the clouds!" (William Goodell, letter of 14 February 1842, in *Forty years in the Turkish Empire or, Memoirs of Rev. William Goodell, D.D., late missionary in the A. B. C. F. M. at Constantinople,* ed. E.D.G. Prime, D.D. [New York: Robert Carter and Brothers, 1876], 274). Ten years earlier, in a letter of 17 October 1832 to a friend in New York, Goodell wrote, "[We rejoice] at the unexampled prosperity which God has given to our country, and especially at the numberless spiritual blessings which He has graciously bestowed upon it,—blessings which have scarcely a parallel in the whole history of the church. There is but little in this part of the Old world that looks like the industry, virtue, thrift, enterprise, rising, greatness, and moral dignity of your part of the New" (154).

29. In Samuel Hopkins *The system of doctrines: Contained in divine revelation, explained and defended* (Boston: Lincoln and Edmands, 1811), 410–538, here 523.

30. Verété, "Restoration," 38–39; Martin Brecht and Johannes van den Berg, eds., *Geschichte des Pietismus,* for the Historische Kommission zur Erforschung des Pietismus (Göttingen, Germany: Vandenhoeck and Ruprecht, 1993), vol. 1.

31. Paul Jenkins, "The church missionary society and the Basel mission: An early experiment in inter-European co-operation," in *The church missionary society and world Christianity 1799–1999,* ed. Kevin Ward and Brian Stanley (Grand Rapids, Mich.: W. B. Eerdmans Publishing, 2000), 42–63. An impressive overview of that "International" may be seen by the *Missionary Register,* published by the Church Missionary Society (e.g., London: Seeley, Jackson, and Halliday, 1823 and 1828).

32. Hannah Adams, *The history of the Jews: From the destruction of Jerusalem to the present time* (London: London Society, 1840), 543, 549–554 (1st ed., 1812).

33. Victor Shepherd wrote: "His [Calvin's] theology, [was] written for a pursued people permitted no rest on account of Counter Reformation persecution. . . . For homeless, stateless, hapless refugees, God's hand—never to relax and drop them into that 'abyss' that Calvin did not doubt—remained the sole, saving solace. In the same vein Oberman brings to light the role of social location in the well-known fact that the Jewish people have fared much better in Reformed lands than elsewhere. Before Calvin, Luther and Zwingli had adopted the Augustinian notion, pregnant with horrors for Jewish people throughout the Middle Ages, that Jews wandered refuge-less inasmuch as God had consigned them to misery on account of their non-recognition of Jesus. It was only when Calvin and those he sustained found themselves forever wandering just because of their recognition of Jesus that they began to re-read scripture and to find in it the promise that no human violation of the covenant induces God to abandon us" (review of Heiko A. Oberman, *The two Reformations: The journey from the last days to the New World* [New Haven, Conn. : Yale University Press, 2003], in *Toronto Journal of Theology* (Spring 2004), available at http://www.victorshepherd.on.ca/Other%20Writings/book_review97.htm, accessed 5 September 2007; for the relevant self-understanding of a French Protestant (*huguenot*), see Armand Laferrere, "The Huguenots, the Jews, and me: A tale of French philo-Semitism," *Azure* 11, no. 26 (Autumn 2006): 63–82.

34. It is probably in this sense that "the most forceful expression of early American ambivalence toward Jews is to be found in the writings of Hannah Adams" (Arthur Hertzberg, *The Jews in America: Four centuries of an uneasy encounter: A history* [New York: Simon and Schuster, 1989], 88).

35. Adams, *History of the Jews,* 554; Gary D. Schmidt, *A passionate usefulness: The life and literary labors of Hannah Adams* (Charlottesville: University of Virginia Press, 2004), 302 and 358.

36. William R. Hutchison, *Errand to the world: American Protestant thought and foreign missions* (Chicago: University of Chicago Press, 1987), 43–46. Quotation in Oren, *Power, faith, and fantasy,* 87–88.

37. Parsons, *Memoir,* 42.

38. Among many studies and retrospectives, see Chaney, *Birth of missions in America;* Hutchison, *Errand to the world;* Niebuhr, *Kingdom;* Abdul Latif Tibawi, *American interests in Syria 1800–1901: A study of educational, literary and religious work* (London: Oxford University Press, 1966), 10–11; Rufus Anderson, *Foreign missions: Their relations and claims* (New York: Charles Scribner, 1869), 24–27; Rufus Anderson, *Memorial volume of the first fifty years of the American Board of Commissioners for Foreign Missions* (Boston: The Board, 1861).

39. George Bush, *Treatise on the millennium, in which the prevailing theories on that subject are carefully examined and the true scriptural doctrine attempted to be elicited and established* (New York: J. and J. Harper, 1832), xii.

40. See John A. Andrew III, *From revival to removal: Jeremiah Evarts, the Cherokee nation, and the search for the soul of America* (Athens: University of Georgia Press, 1992); David S. Heidler and Jeanne T. Heidler, *Indian removal* (New York: W. W. Norton, 2007); see also Angie Debo's classic work *And still the waters run: The betrayal of the five civilized tribes* (Princeton, N.J.: Princeton University Press, 1940).

41. David M. Wishart, "Evidence of surplus production in the Cherokee nation prior to removal," *Journal of Economic History* 55, no. 1 (March 1995): 120–138, esp. 134.

42. Andrew, *From revival to removal,* 153.

43. James Mooney, *Myths of the Cherokee* (Mineola, N.Y.: Dover, 1996), 118 (1st ed., 1897–1898).

44. Sean Wilentz, *Andrew Jackson* (New York: Times Books, 2005), 68–69. Historian Harold Bradley considers an "indelible stain" on Jackson's record that he failed to support the Supreme Court by implementing federal authority in Georgia in favor of the Cherokees. The Supreme Court had ruled against Georgia in this issue, but Jackson sympathized with Georgia's local government and enforced finally, after years of anti-Indian harassment, the Indian Removal Act of 1830. Total destruction did not occur. "However tragic the removal of the southern tribes war, the tribes moved west under treaties that recognized them lands in the West in fee simple," historian Francis P. Prucha concludes (in Jeremiah Evarts, *Cherokee removal: The "William Penn" essays and other writings,* ed. and intro. Francis Paul Prucha [Knoxville: University of Tennessee, 1981], 40; see also Harold Bradley, "Jackson, Andrew," *Encyclopædia Britannica,* available at http://search.eb.com/eb/article-9043159, accessed 9 January 2008).

45. Phillips, *Protestant America and the pagan world,* 70.

46. Evarts, *Cherokee removal,* 3–40.

47. Ibid., 282.

48. Phillips, *Protestant America and the pagan world,* 72.

49. Sarah H. Hill, "Cherokee removal: Forts along the Georgia Trail of Tears," draft report, National Park Service and the Georgia Department of Natural Resources/Historic Preservation Division, 2008, 27, available at http://www.nps.gov/archive/trte/TRTE/Georgias%20Trail%20of%20Tears%20Report%20ONLY.pdf, accessed 10 January 2008.

50. Ussama Makdisi, *Artillery of heaven: American missionaries and the failed conversion of the Middle East* (Ithaca, N.Y.: Cornell University Press, 2008), 145.

51. Quoted in Kurt R. Spillmann, *Amerikas Ideologie des Friedens: Ursprünge, Formwandlungen und geschichtliche Auswirkungen des amerikanischen Glaubens an den Mythos von einer friedlichen Weltordnung* (Bern, Switzerland: Peter Lang, 1984), 173.

CHAPTER 2

1. Referred to in *Missionary Herald* (July 1909): 281.

2. Cf. remarks on the Golden Apple in the introduction of this book; and Hans-Lukas Kieser, "Djihad, Weltordnung, 'Goldener Apfel': Die osmanische Reichsideologie im Kontext west-östlicher Geschichte," in *Imperialismus in Geschichte und Gegenwart,* ed. Richard Faber (Würzburg, Germany: Königshausen and Neumann, 2005), 183–203.

3. Orhan F. Köprülü, "Tarihte Türk-Amerikan Münasebetleri," *Belleten* 51 (August 1987): 927–947, esp. 928–929; James L. Gordon, *American relations with Turkey, 1830–1930: An economic interpretation* (Philadelphia: University of Pennsylvania Press, 1932), 43.

4. Cf. Mehmed Şükrü Hanioğlu, *A brief history of the late Ottoman Empire* (Princeton, N.J.: Princeton University Press, 2008), 58–60; Tobias Heinzelmann, *Heiliger Kampf oder Landesverteidigung? Die Diskussion um die Einführung der allgemeinen Militärpflicht im Osmanischen Reich 1826–1856* (Frankfurt am Main: Peter Lang, 2004), 47–66.

5. In English and Ottoman in Fahir Armaoğlu, *Belgelerle Türk-Amerikan münasebetleri* (Ankara, Turkey: TTK, 1991), 1–6.

6. William Goodell, *Forty years in the Turkish Empire or, Memoirs of Rev. William Goodell, D.D., late missionary in the A. B. C. F. M. at Constantinople,* ed. E.D.G. Prime, D.D. (New York: Robert Carter and Brothers, 1876), 121–122, 164, 285.

7. Ibid., 480–482. For an English translation of the Rescript of Gülhane, see http://www.anayasa.gen.tr/gulhane.htm, accessed 14 May 2009.

8. Armaoğlu, *Belgelerle,* 7–13; and Gordon, *American relations with Turkey,* 41–55.

9. Joseph L. Grabill, *Protestant diplomacy and the Near East: Missionary influence on American policy, 1810–1927* (Minneapolis: University of Minnesota Press, 1971), 5.

10. Levi Parsons, *Memoir of Reverend Levi Parsons* ((Hartford, Conn.: Cooke and Co. and Packard and Butler, 1830), 155 (1st ed., 1824).

11. Ibid., 181–182, 213.

12. Cf. ABCFM missionary Asahel Grant's *The Nestorians or the lost tribes: Con-*

taining evidence of their identity (New York: Harper and Brothers, 1841); Hans-Lukas Kieser, *Der verpasste Friede: Mission, Ethnie und Staat in den Ostprovinzen der Türkei 1839–1938* (Zurich: Chronos, 2000), 63–68 (Turkish ed.: *Iskalanmış Barış* [Istanbul: Iletisim, 2005]).

13. Parsons, *Memoir,* 183, 196, 206; cf. Ulrike Brunotte, *Puritanismus und Pioniergeist: Die Faszination der Wildnis im frühen Neu-England* (Berlin: Walter de Gruyter, 2001).

14. *Sermon, preached in the Park-Street Church Boston, Sabbath evening, Oct. 31, 1819, just before the departure of the Palestine mission, by Levi Parsons, A. M.* (Boston: Samuel T. Armstrong, 1819), 12–13.

15. Ibid., 7.

16. Ibid., 14.

17. Instructions from the Prudential Committee of the American Board of Commissioners for Foreign Missions (ABCFM) to the Reverend Levi Parsons and the Reverend Pliny Fisk, missionaries designated for Palestine, in *Sermon, preached in Park-Street Church Boston,* 51–52.

18. *Sermon, preached in Park-Street Church Boston,* 26–27.

19. Timothy Dwight, sermon delivered in Boston, 16 September 1813, before the ABCFM at their Fourth Annual Meeting (Boston 1813), 26, quoted in Clifton J. Phillips, *Protestant America and the pagan world: The first half century of the American Board of Commissioners for Foreign Missions, 1810–1860* (Cambridge, Mass.: Harvard University Press, 1969), 11.

20. Ignace de Mouradja d'Ohsson, *Tableau général de l'Empire Othoman, divisé en deux parties, dont l'une comprend la législation mahométane, l'autre l'histoire de l'empire othoman,* vol. 1 (Paris: Impr. de Monsieur, 1788), 427.

21. Parsons, *Memoir,* 214.

22. Thomas W. Marshall, *Christian missions: Their agents and their results,* vols. 2–3 (London: Longman, 1863; 1st ed., 1862).

23. Parsons, *Memoir,* 230 and 247.

24. Ibid., 252 and 257.

25. Ibid., 246.

26. Ibid., 295.

27. Parsons, *Sermon, preached in Park-Street Church Boston,* 30.

28. Parsons, *Memoir,* 304.

29. Ibid., 343.

30. Ibid., 222, 231.

31. Ibid., 366, 368.

32. Quoted in ibid., 382.

33. "He [Parsons] needed only to know their [his parents'] will, and it was obeyed," wrote the contemporary editor of Parsons's memoir, Daniel Morton (ibid., 7).

34. Ibid., 336.

35. Goodell, *Forty Years,* 64.

36. Henry G. O. Dwight and Eli Smith, *Researches of the Rev. E. Smith and Rev. H.G.O. Dwight in Armenia: Including a journey through Asia Minor, and into Georgia and Persia, with a visit to the Nestorian and Chaldean Christians of Oormiah and Salmas* (Boston: Crocker and Brewster, 1833).

37. Cf. H.G.O. Dwight, *Christianity revived in the East; or, A narrative of the work of God among the Armenians of Turkey* (New York: Baker and Scribner, 1850).

38. Goodell, *Forty Years,* 185.

39. Draft of letter of British Foreign Ministry to Vice Consul William Young, 31 January 1839, quoted in Yaron Perry, *British mission to the Jews in nineteenth-century Palestine* (London: Frank Cass, 2003), 29.

40. Perry, *British mission,* 71–80.

41. Yaron Perry, "John Steinbeck's roots in nineteenth-century Palestine," *Steinbeck Studies* 15, no. 11 (Spring 2004): 47–72, esp. 48, quoted from a letter of a settler from Elberfeld of 28 November 1850.

42. "Wenn man dann die gläubigen Israeliten Priester des Herrn heißen und Diener unsers Gottes nennen wird, so achten wir es für hohe Ehre, wenn wir ihre Ackerleute und Weingärtner sein dürfen" (letter of Friedrich Grosssteinbeck to his parents in Germany, Jerusalem, April 1850, quoted in Jakob Eisler, ed., *Deutsche Kolonisten im Heiligen Land: Die Familie John Steinbeck in Briefen aus Palästina und USA* (Stuttgart: Verlag S. Hirzel, 2001), 31–32.

43. Samuel Gobat, *Samuel Gobat: Evangelischer Bischof in Jerusalem: Sein Leben und Wirken, meist nach seinen eigenen Aufzeichnungen* (Basel: C. F. Spitteler, 1884), 265 and 279.

44. Cf. Hilton Obenzinger, *American Palestine: Melville, Twain, and the Holy Land mania* (Princeton, N.J.: Princeton University Press, 1999); Hannah Arendt, *Elemente und Ursprünge totaler Herrschaft* (Munich: Piper, 1998), 169–190.

45. William Goodell, *The old and the new; or The changes of thirty years in the East, with some allusions to oriental customs as elucidating scripture* (New York: M. W. Dodd, 1853), v.

46. Goodell, *Forty years,* 443; cf. 39–42, where Goodell explains his redirection from Jerusalem, where he never went, to Istanbul.

47. Goodell, *The old and the new,* 47.

48. Joseph K. Greene, *Leavening the Levant* (Boston: Pilgrim Press, 1916), 140. For the particular importance of missionary agency in eastern Anatolia, see Kieser, *Der verpasste Friede.*

49. Cf., e.g., the statistics in Abdul Latif Tibawi, *American interests in Syria 1800–1901: A study of educational, literary and religious work* (London: Oxford University Press, 1966), 228, with those in Kieser, *Der verpasste Friede,* 565–568.

50. For this draft, did they collaborate in a spirit of partnership with their Armenian friends in Istanbul? This and many other questions in relation with the Protestant dynamics of the 1850s need further research.

51. Leon Arpee, *The Armenian awakening* (Chicago: University of Chicago Press, 1909), 194.

52. M.O.H. Ursinus, "Millet," *Encyclopaedia of Islam,* 2nd ed. (Leiden, Netherlands: Brill Online, 2009), available at http://www.brillonline.nl/subscriber/entry?entry=islam_COM-0741, accessed 22 April 2009.

53. Arpee, *Armenian awakening,* 184–185.

54. Cf. Maurus Reinkowski, *Die Dinge der Ordnung: Eine vergleichende Untersuchung über die osmanische Reformpolitik im 19. Jahrhundert* (Munich: R. Oldenbourg Verlag, 2005), 257.

55. In an unpublished paper read during the workshop "Was hält ein Imperium zusammen? Das Osmanische Reich aus translokaler Perspektive," held at the University of Zurich, 22–23 February 2008.

56. On this topic relevant Ottoman sources, translated and introduced, can be found in Charles Kurzman, ed., *Modernist Islam, 1840–1940: A sourcebook* (Oxford: Oxford University Press, 2002).

57. Arpee, *Armenian awakening,* 184–194; Macit Kenanoğlu, *Osmanlı millet sistemi: Mit ve gerçek* (Istanbul: Klasik, 2004), 129–130. Quotation in Roderic H. Davison, "The *Millets* as agents of change in the nineteenth-century Ottoman Empire," in *Christians and Jews in the Ottoman Empire: The functioning of a plural society,* vol. 1: *The Central Lands,* ed. Benjamin Braude and Bernard Lewis (New York: Holmes and Meier 1982), 319–337, esp. 329.

58. Manoog B. Dzeron, *Village of Parchanj: General history (1600–1937)* (Boston: Baikar Press, 1984), 150.

59. For a discussion of this dynamic, see Roderic H. Davison, "The advent of the principle of representation in the government of the Ottoman Empire," in *Essays in Ottoman and Turkish History, 1774–1923: The impact of the West* (Austin: University of Texas Press, 1990), 96–109. Moreover, Davison points to the local religiously mixed councils established in the 1840s as the "true start of representative government" in the Ottoman Empire (100) and to the administrative council (*meclis-i idare*), the local courts, and the general assembly (*meclis-i umumî*) established according to the province (*vilayet*) reform of 1864 (103–104). For more details on local councils and assemblies, see İlber Ortaylı, *Tanzimat devrinde Osmanlı mahallî idareleri (1840–1880)* (Ankara, Turkey: TTK, 2000).

60. Armenian constitution reproduced in English in H.F.B. Lynch, *Armenia: Travels and studies,* vol. 2: *The Turkish provinces* (London: Longmans, Green, 1901), 445–467.

61. Arpee, *Armenian awakening,* 193.

62. Ussama Makdisi, *Artillery of heaven: American missionaries and the failed conversion of the Middle East* (Ithaca, N.Y.: Cornell University Press, 2008), 180–213.

63. Davison, *Essays in Ottoman and Turkish History,* 96–109.

64. Cf. Engin Deniz Akarlı, *The long peace: Ottoman Lebanon, 1861–1920* (London: I. B. Tauris, 1993).

65. Quoted in André N. Mandelstam, *Le sort de l'empire ottoman* (Lausanne, Switzerland: Payot, 1917), 284.

66. Selim Deringil, "'There is no compulsion in religion': On conversion and apostasy in the late Ottoman Empire, 1839–1856," *Comparative Studies in Society and History* 42, no. 3 (2000): 547–575, esp. 566.

67. Goodell, *Forty years,* 387; Leon Arpee, *A history of Armenian Christianity from the beginning to our own time* (New York: Armenian Missionary Association, 1946), 290.

68. Cf. Hans-Lukas Kieser, "L'Alévisme kurde," *Peuples Méditerranéens* no. 68–69 (Paris: Anthropos, 1994), 57–76.

69. Henry H. Riggs, "The religion of the Dersim Kurds," *Missionary Review of the World* 23 (October 1911): 741–742.

70. The first letter dealing with the Kizilbash was probably that of George Nutting,

Arabkir, 24 October 1854. He wrote to Rufus Anderson, the secretary of the ABCFM in Boston: "There [in Tchemishgezek] is a sect of nominal Moslems scattered through this region of whom I think you have not heard. They bear the name Kuzulbash, which means literally 'redhead.' . . . They never or almost never go through the Muslim forms of prayer; nor do they keep their fast. They are a people by themselves. A peculiar people and open to the Gospel. . . . The Turks seem to regard them very much as they do the Koords, as worthless heretics, and not worth caring for" (ABC 16.7.1, Archives of the ABCFM, Houghton Library, Harvard University, Cambridge, Massachusetts).

71. Cf. ABCFM missionary Stephen van Rensselaer Trowbridge's article "The Alevis, or deifiers of Ali," *Harvard Theological Review,* no. 2 (1909): 340–353; for a missionary reflection on the notion of *insan-i kâmil,* see R. Siraj ud-Din, "The vital forces of Christianity and Islam," in *International Review of Mission* 3 (London: Oxford University Press, 1913), 113–114.

72. Cf. *Missionary Herald* (1855): 338–340; (1856): 295–298; (1857): 83–85, 220, and 395; (1858): 23–24 and 112–115; (1860): 45; (1861): 72; (1863): 116–118 and 309–312; (1866): 67–69; and (1872): 315–317. The *Missionary Herald* reproduces excerpts of letters and station reports. The originals are in the ABCFM archives.

73. "The oppressions which they suffer from the dominant race are more severe than those endured by any class of the Christian subjects. In this respect they are the most abused people in Turkey. They are industrious and frugal, and with protection would become rich and prosperous; but as it is now, they are eaten up by greedy pashas and other exorbitant officials," Sanford Richardson wrote 1856 from Arabkir (*Missionary Herald* [1856]: 295–298).

74. "The Moslems do not consider them as Moslems, and the only reason why they should oppose their evangelization is that now they have often opportunity to oppress them in various ways, in respect to taxes, etc., and they fear that when they become Protestants we shall inform the powers above them of their oppressions, and bring them to punishment, or prevent such wrongs," George Nutting wrote in the *Missionary Herald* (1860): 347. Cf. *Missionary Herald* (1857): 144–145; (1858): 110; (1861): 71–73 and 100–102.

75. For more on this topic, see Hans-Lukas Kieser, "Muslim heterodoxy and Protestant utopia: The Interactions between Alevis and missionaries in Ottoman Anatolia," *Die Welt des Islams* 41, no. 1 (2001): 89–111; and idem, "Some Remarks on Alevi Responses to the Missionaries in Eastern Anatolia (19th–20th cc.)," in Eleanor H. Tejirian and Reeva Spector Simon, eds., *Altruism and imperialism: Western cultural and religious missions to the Middle East (19th–20th cc.)* (New York: Columbia University Press, 2002), 120–142.

76. *Annual Report of the ABCFM* (Boston, 1878), xxvi–xxvii. Cf. the articles Arthur T. Pierson, "The world evangelized in twenty years," *Missionary Herald* (1881): 277–278; and William H. Ward, "American influence in Turkey," *Missionary Herald* (1885): 120–122; Kieser, *Der verpasste Friede,* 117–127.

77. Kemal H. Karpat, *The politicization of Islam: Reconstructing identity, state, faith, and community in the late Ottoman state* (Oxford: Oxford University Press, 2001), 182.

78. Cf. Selim Deringil, *The well-protected domains: Ideology and the legitimation of power in the Ottoman Empire. 1876–1909* (London: I. B. Tauris, 1998), 68–111;

Bayram Kodaman, *Sultan II. Abdulhamid devri doğu Anadolu politikası* (Ankara, Turkey: Türk Kültürünü Araştırma Enstitüsü zayınları, 1987); Selçuk A. Somel, *The modernization of public education in the Ottoman Empire, 1839–1908: Islamization, autocracy, and discipline* (Leiden, Netherlands: Brill, 2001); Karpat, *Politicization of Islam,* 155–240.

79. In 1913 a *dede* of the region of Koçgiri, east of Sivas, denied in a conversation with the young Ottoman official Hasan Reşid (Tankut) any important difference between Armenians and Alevis: "The distance between Alevis and Armenians is not more thick than the membrane of an onion" (Hasan R. Tankut, "Zazalar hakkinda sosyolojik tetkiler," in M. Bayrak, *Açık-gizli/resmi-gayriresmi Kürdoloji belgeleri* (Ankara, Turkey: Özge, 1994), 470–473 (1st ed., 1935). Cf. the reports sent to Abdulhamid speaking of the "terrible" political dangers and loyalty problems Alevis's "wrong faith" represented. Its adherents were, according to the Vali of Ankara, completely outside of Islam" and Muslims "only by name" (Baki Öz, *Alevilik ile ilgili Osmanlı belgeleri* (Istanbul: Can, 1997), 148. George E. White of the ABCFM wrote shortly before the Young Turk revolution of July 1908, "Yet in the stronghold of Turkish power, the fair provinces of Asia Minor, about one-forth of the people are not Mohammedan at all but Eastern Christians, and of the Mohammedan population about one-fourth—some propose one-third—are not Sunnitic at all but are schismatic Shias [Alevis]. For the present this line of cleavage is kept very much out of sight, but circumstances might easily take such shape that this internal breach would come to the surface as a deadly wound" ("The Shia Turks," in *Transactions of the Victoria Institute,* vol. 40 [London, 1908], 225–239, here 225–226.

80. Arpee, *History of Armenian Christianity,* 280–281; quotation in A. N. Andrus, letter to James Barton, Mardin, 8 August 1914, ABC 16.9.3, Archives of the ABCFM.

81. Kieser, *Der verpasste Friede,* 137–138 and 173–174. Cf. Deringil, *Well-protected domains;* Ali Karaca, *Anadolu ıslahâtı ve Ahmet Şâkir Paşa (1838–1899)* (Istanbul: Eren, 1993).

82. Cyrus Hamlin, "A dangerous movement among the Armenians," *The Congregationalist* (28 December 1893): 992. Letter reproduced in Ali Söylemezoğlu, *Die andere Seite der Medaille. Hintergründe der Tragödie von 1915 in Kleinasien. Materialien aus europaäischen, amerikanischen und armenischen Quellen* (Cologne: Önel, 2005), 248–249.

83. Kieser, *Der verpasste Friede,* 230–234, Corinna Shattuck, Urfa, 24 January 1896, 540–543 (a handwritten copy of the letter is in the Archives of the ABCFM, ABC Indiv. Biogr. 54:21).

84. See Jelle Verheij, "Die armenischen Massaker von 1894–1896: Anatomie und Hintergründe einer Krise," in *Die armenische Frage und die Schweiz/La question arménienne et la Suisse (1896–1923),* ed. Hans-Lukas Kieser (Zurich: Chronos, 1999), 69–129; cf. Kieser, *Der verpasste Friede,* 154–234.

85. Kieser, *Der verpasste Friede,* 159–162; Samir Boulos, "Wahrnehmung von Juden und Arabern durch die Karmelmission in Palästina 1908–1939" (unpublished master's thesis, University of Zurich, 2006); Yaakov Ariel, *Evangelizing the chosen people: Missions to the Jews in America, 1880–2000* (Chapel Hill: University of North Carolina Press, 2000), 22–37; official Web site of the Christian and Missionary Al-

liance, available at http://www.cmalliance.org/whoweare/whoweare-past.jsp; official Web site of the Chosen People Ministries, available at http://www.chosenpeople.com/main/page/our_history.html, accessed 30 June 2008.

86. Quoted in Ernest R. May, *Imperial democracy: The emergence of America as a great power* (New York: Harcourt, Brace and World, 1961), 59–60.

87. "But thou, my country, though no fault be thine / For that red horror far across the sea. / Though not a tortured wretch can point to thee, / And charge thee for the selfishness supine / Of those great Powers that cowardly combine / To shield the Turk in his iniquity, / Yet, since thy hand is innocent and free, / Arise, and show the world the way divine. / Thou canst not break the oppressor's iron rod, / But thou canst minister to the oppressed. / Thou canst not loose the captive's heavy chain, / But thou canst bind his wounds and ease his pain. / Armenia calls thee, Empire of the West, / To play the Good Samaritan for God" (Henry van Dyke, "A call to America" [1896], in Greene, *Leavening*, iv).

88. George C. Raynolds to Henry O. Dwight, Bible House, 6 July 1896, cited in Kieser, *Der verpasste Friede*, 220.

89. ABC 16.9.7, vol. 17, Archives of the ABCFM.

90. ABC, Pers. Papers J. Barton 11:2, Archives of the ABCFM; quoted in Kieser, *Der verpasste Friede*, 221; cf. 219–220.

91. Kieser, *Der verpasste Friede*, 456; Theophil Waldmeier, *Aufruf zur Gründung der ersten Irrenanstalt im Orient* (Bern, Switzerland: n.p., 1896); Archives of the Lebanon Hospital for Mental and Nervous Disorders, available at http://www.mundus.ac.uk/cats/4/1065.htm, accessed 25 August 2009.

CHAPTER 3

1. Erik Jan Zürcher, *The Unionist factor: The rôle of the Committee of Union and Progress in the Turkish national movement 1905–1926* (Leiden, Netherlands: Brill, 1984).

2. On the Young Turks, see Mehmed Şükrü Hanioğlu, *The Young Turks in opposition* (New York: Oxford University Press, 1995); Mehmed Şükrü Hanioğlu,, *Preparation for a revolution: The Young Turks, 1902–1908* (New York: Oxford University Press, 2001). On Turkish nationalism, see François Georgeon, *Aux origines du nationalisme turc: Yusuf Akçura (1876–1935)* (Paris: Editions ADPF, 1980). For a recent sophisticated approach to the Russian Turks in late Ottoman Istanbul, see Volker Adam, *Russlandmuslime in Istanbul am Vorabend des Ersten Weltkriegs* (Frankfurt am Main, Germany: Peter Lang, 2002); for an analysis of propaganda literature, see Erol Köroğlu, *Ottoman propaganda and Turkish identity: Literature in Turkey during World War I* (London: I. B. Tauris, 2007).

3. A letter by Bahaeddin Şakir and Nazım of 1906 says that "our party is a purely Turkish party [*halis bir Türk cemiyeti*] that will never admit opinions of people hostile to Islam and Turkdom [*İslamlik ve Türklük*]" (Yusuf Hikmet Bayur, *Türk inkılâbı tarihi* [Ankara, Turkey: Türk Tarih Kurumu Basımevi, 1991], vol. 2, part 4, 115). Cf. Hanioğlu, *Young Turks in opposition*, 213–216; and Hanioğlu, *Preparation for a revolution*, 173–178.

4. Cf. Hans-Lukas Kieser, *Vorkämpfer der "neuen Türkei": Revolutionäre Bildungseliten am Genfersee (1870–1939)* (Zurich: Chronos, 2005), 11–12.

5. Hanioğlu, *Preparation for a revolution,* 313.

6. Cf. Anne-Laure Dupont, "Une école missionnaire et étrangère dans la tourmente de la révolution constitutionnelle ottomane," *Cahiers de la Méditerranée* 75 (2007): para. 12, with bibliographical references.

7. Yusuf Akçura, "Hüseyinzâde Ali Bey," *Türk Yurdu* 5, no. 81 (15 April 1915; new ed., Ankara, Turkey: Tutibay, 1998), vol. 4, 104–106; Adam, *Russlandmuslime,* 137.

8. *Yurdcular Yasası. İsviçre'de Cenevre şehrine yakın Petit-Lancy Köyünde Pension Racine'de kurulan İkinci Yurdcular Derneği'nin muzakerat ve mukerreratı* (Istanbul: Yeni Turan Matbaası, 1914), 69–70, translated in Kieser, *Vorkämpfer,* 149.

9. In this "anticomprador" perspective, the Young Turks read, e.g., the seminal articles on economic exploitation by Alexander Parvus-Helphand, a revolutionary socialist from Germany (originally from White Russia) who advocated world war, including anti-Russian Ottoman participation, as a means for salutary world revolution. Together with Leon Trotsky, Parvus-Helphand was among the leaders of the 1905 revolution in St. Petersburg. Cf. his "İş işten geçmeden gözlerinizi açınınz!" in *Türk Yurdu,* 23 March 1329 (3 April 1913) (Istanbul: Matbaat-i Hayriye ve Şürekâsı; transliterated ed., Ankara, Turkey: Tutibay, 1999), 200–203; "İktisat—Köylüler," in *Türk Yurdu,* 9 March 1327 (22 March 1912), 145–148; and "Meine Stellungnahme zum Krieg," *Die Glocke* no. 3 (Berlin: Verlag für Sozialwissenschaft, 1 October 1915), 148–162.

10. Cf. *Missionary Herald* (October 1908): 455–458.

11. Halide Edip Adıvar, *Memoirs* (London: Murray, 1926), 259.

12. *World Missionary Conference: Reports of commissions,* 9 vols. (Edinburgh: Oliphant, Anderson and Ferrier, 1910).

13. James L. Barton, "What the changes mean to us," *Missionary Herald* (1908): 467–469, esp. 468.

14. James L. Barton, *Daybreak in Turkey* (Boston: The Pilgrim Press, 1908).

15. "We, and we alone, as a mission board are upon the ground. . . . Our duty is inevitable; our privilege is unsurpassed. . . . The field is ours; we occupy the great centers of influence and population; ours are the missions and colleges, schools, printing presses, hospitals, and Christian institutions. Shall we use all these to the limit of their capacity for the purpose for which they were established, and for the advancement of the kingdom of God in Turkey?" (*Missionary Herald* [1908]: 469).

16. Raymond H. Kévorkian, *Le génocide des Arméniens* (Paris: Odile Jacob, 2006), 97–150; Dikran Mesrop Kaligian, *The Armenian Revolutionary Federation under Ottoman constitutional rule, 1908–1914* (Ph.D. diss., Boston College, 2003), 214.

17. Howard S. Bliss, "The Balkan War and Christian work among Moslems," in *International Review of Mission* 3 (London: Oxford University Press, 1913), 643–656, esp. 648.

18. Charles T. Riggs, "Editorial," *The Orient* 4, no. 21 (21 May 1913): 5.

19. *World Missionary Conference,* vol. 3, 223.

20. "Personally, I have always been particularly interested, for instance, in the extraordinary work done by the American schools and colleges in the Turkish Empire . . . ; and this, although among the Mohammedans there has been no effort to convert them, simply an effort to make them good citizens, to make them vie with their fellow-citizens who are Christians in showing those qualities which it should be the pride of every creed to develop. And the present movement to introduce far-

reaching reforms, political and social, in Turkey, an effort with which we all keenly sympathize, is one in which these young Moslems, educated at the American schools and colleges, are especially fitted to take part." (Theodore Roosevelt, from an address in the Metropolitan Memorial Methodist Episcopal Church, Washington, D.C., in *Missionary Herald* [March 1909]: 130).

21. Dupont, "Une école missionnaire."

22. *World Missionary Conference,* vol. 1, 21–34 and 184–187.

23. Bliss, "Balkan War and Christian work," 643–656, esp. 652–655.

24. One occasion was when the United States under President Howard Taft was unwilling to submit an international case to the Hague Tribunal (i.e., the claim, or open "blunder," as the men in the Bible House in Istanbul wrote) to exempt some U.S. ships from duties when passing through the Panama Canal. See "Editorial" in *The Orient* 4, no. 3 (15 January 1913): 5.

25. Edward B. Haskell, "A plan for social work in the foreign mission field," *The Orient* 2, no. 35 (13 December 1911): 2–3.

26. Arthur C. Ryan, "A club that reaches Turks," *Missionary Herald* (October 1912): 445–446; Hans-Lukas Kieser, *Der verpasste Friede: Mission, Ethnie und Staat in den Ostprovinzen der Türkei 1839–1938* (Zurich: Chronos, 2000), 303–304.

27. *World Missionary Conference,* vol. 1, 27, 33, 35.

28. Edward Riggs, "The Ottoman liberty club," *Missionary Herald* (January 1909): 33–34; Herman Barnum, "Field notes—Seven months after," *Missionary Herald* (May 1909): 211–212.

29. James L. Fowle, "The birth of an Ottoman nation," *Missionary Herald* (December 1908): 568–569.

30. For a comparison, see Kieser, *Der verpasste Friede,* 281–286.

31. Thomas D. Christie from Tarsus wrote in a letter to William W. Peet on 19 April 1909: "The Armenian young men of Adana are nearly all revolutionists—different from here. . . . The Armenians [of Adana] were incited by a very bad man, their bishop [Musheg], now safe in Egypt. If he and a few others had been put in prison last fall this thing would not have happened." Red Goodsell from Aintab wrote in a letter of 13 May 1909 to Peet: "You will be interested to know the testimony of a prominent Turk in Aintab as to the connection of the college difficulty with the present situation. He said to one of the professors very openly: 'We have worked hard to prevent an outbreak in Aintab because we knew that there were a great many Armenians here who thoroughly discountenanced the Armenian revolutionary propaganda. We have come to understand very clearly that the College is thoroughly opposed to that sort of thing from its recent action with regard to the sixty students who were not permitted to return'" (cited in Kieser, *Der verpasste Friede,* 288–292, esp. 288–289 and 454).

32. Fowle, "Birth of an Ottoman nation," 569.

33. Ahmet Şerif, *Tanîn* (18 April 1910); transliterated ed., Ahmet Şerif, *Tanîn,* ed. Mehmed Ç. Börekçi (Ankara, Turkey: TTK, 1999), vol. 1, 186–187; "A Turkish Correspondent's Views" in *The Orient* 1 (27 April 1910): 2.

34. Şerif, *Tanîn* (27 July 1911), in Şerif, *Tanîn,* vol. 1, 257–258.

35. Şerif, *Tanîn* (25 June 1910), in Şerif, *Tanîn,* vol. 2, 33–34.

36. Şerif, *Tanîn* (28 April 1911), in Şerif, *Tanîn,* vol. 2, 155–156.

37. Şerif, *Tanîn* (13 June 1911), in Şerif, *Tanîn,* vol. 2, 204–206.

38. Cf. Şerif, *Tanîn* (15 March 1910), in Şerif, *Tanîn,* vol. 1, 160; Şerif, *Tanîn* (28 April 1911), in Şerif, *Tanîn,* vol. 2, 155.

39. "Islam is linking itself up with the atheism and deism of western lands, and is securing much protection and also added prestige by the support it receives at the hands of officials from the West who have broken with Christianity. These men carry over to the Moslem camp all the armoury of the deistic and atheistic school" ("The opportunity and the urgency of carrying the gospel to all the non-Christian world," *World Missionary Conference,* vol. 1, 19).

40. Concerning the CUP's annual meeting in Salonika in September 1911, *The Orient* wrote: "We are told that the sessions of the Committee are to be behind closed doors. . . . If the Committee is worthy of the confidence of the country, certainly the country should be deemed worthy of the confidence of the Committee" ("Committee of Union and Progress to meet," *The Orient* 2, no. 24 [27 September 1911]: 2).

41. Cf. Bliss, "Balkan War and Christian work"; *Études* (Paris: Dumoulin, 1913), vol. 184, 175–180; Richard Schäfer, *Geschichte der Deutschen Orient-Mission* (Potsdam, Germany: Tempel-Verlag, 1932), 78.

42. "The refugees of Asia Minor," *The Orient* 4, no. 1 (1 January 1913): 6; cf. Wilfred Post, "Christian relief for Moslem refugees," *The Orient* 4, no. 7 (12 February 1913): 3–4.

43. Greene, *Leavening,* 163; Mary M. Patrick, "Among the educated women of Turkey," in *Daylight in the harem: A new era for Moslem women. Papers on present-day reform movements, conditions and methods of work among Moslem women read at the Lucknow Conference 1911,* ed. Annie van Sommer and Samuel M. Zwemer (Edinburgh: Oliphant, Anderson and Ferrier, 1911), 89.

44. "Are we dreaming?" *The Orient* 4, no. 50 (10 December 1913), 3–4; Serpil Çakır, *Osmanlı Kadın Hareketi* (Istanbul: Metis, 1994), 257.

45. "His Majesty Rıza Bey, senator," *The Orient* 3, no. 5 (31 January 1912), 1. Rıza had left the Central Committee of the CUP in 1910 after political murders against journalists; after the putsch in January 1913, he kept his distance from the Central Committee.

46. "The parliamentary elections," *The Orient* 3, no. 6 (7 February 1912): 1.

47. "Trying to come to terms" and "Editorial" in *The Orient* 4, no. 1 (8 January 1913): 1 and 5.

48. "It becomes us to speak circumspectly regarding the events of the past week, lest censorial wrath be upon us. But an administration founded on violence and murder is seldom a success; and no one can approve of the method by which the present ministry has come into power" (Charles Riggs, "Editorial," *The Orient* 4, no. 5 [29 January 1913]: 5).

49. Charles Riggs, "Editorial," *The Orient* 4, no. 1 (1 January 1913): 5.

50. Cf. Charles C. Tracy, president of the Anatolia College, Marsivan, in *World Missionary Conference,* vol. 3, 231.

51. Fahreddin, *Sırat-ı Müstakîm,* 11 July 1910, cited in Johannes Awetaranian, *Geschichte eines Mohammedaners, der Christ wurde, Von ihm selbst erzählt* (Potsdam, Germany: Missionshandlung und Verlag, 1930), 147–148 (1st ed., 1905).

52. Cf. Hans-Lukas Kieser, ed., *Aspects of the political language in Turkey (19th–20th centuries)* (Istanbul: ISIS, 2002), 78–82.

53. Roderic H. Davison, *Essays in Ottoman and Turkish History, 1774–1923: The impact of the West* (Austin: University of Texas Press, 1990), 196. Cf. Kévorkian,

Génocide, 194–211; *Journal de Genève* (18 April 1914); Davison, *Essays in Ottoman and Turkish history,* 1.

54. Ahmed Djemal (Pascha), *Erinnerungen eines türkischen Staatsmannes* (Munich: Drei Masken Verlag, 1922), 337–354, esp. 353–354; Talât (Paşa), *Talât Paşa'nın hâtıraları,* ed. A. Kabacalı (Istanbul: Iletişim, 1994), 58–71 (1st ed., 1946).

55. Cf. Hasan R. Tankut, "Zazalar hakkında sosyolojik tetkiler," in Mehmet Bayrak, *Açık-gizli/resmi-gayriresmi Kürdoloji belgeleri* (Ankara: Özge, 1994), 472 (1st ed., 1935); Riza Nur, *Hayat ve Hatıratım. Rıza Nur-Atatürk Kavgası* (Istanbul: Işaret, 1992), vol. 3, 112 (1st ed., 1967–1968).

56. Charles T. Riggs, "Editorial," *The Orient* 4, no. 4 (22 January 1913): 5.

57. Cf. Henry H. Riggs, *Days of tragedy in Armenia: Personal experiences in Harpoot, 1915–1917* (Michigan: Gomidas Institute, 1997), 45–46.

58. Hüseyin Cahit's article was translated under the title "Are the Armenians justly treated" in the *The Orient* 4, no. 2 (8 January 1913): 6.

59. Köroğlu, *Ottoman propaganda.*

60. Charles Riggs, "Editorial," *The Orient* 4, no. 29 (16 July 1913): 5.

61. Fully cited in Kieser, *Der verpasste Friede,* 336.

62. T. C. Genelkurmay Başkanlığı, *Arşiv belgeleriyle Ermeni faaliyetleri 1914–1918/ Armenian activities in the archive documents 1914–1918,* vols. 1–2 (Ankara, Turkey: Genelkurmay Basım Evi, 2005). Cf. the review by Hans-Lukas Kieser, "Urkatastrophe am Bosporus: Der Armeniermord im Ersten Weltkrieg als Dauerthema internationaler (Zeit-)Geschichte," *Neue Politische Literatur* 2 (2005): 217–234, esp. 229–231.

63. The Turkish Republic Prime Ministry General Directorate of the State Archives, Directorate of Ottoman Archives (ed.), *Armenians in Ottoman documents (1915–1920)* (Ankara, Turkey: n.p. , 1995), 26.

64. Cf. Hans-Lukas Kieser, "Der Völkermord an den Armeniern 1915/16: Neueste Publikationen," in *Sehepunkte* 7, no. 3 (15 March 2007), available at http://www.sehepunkte.de/2007/03/10400.html; Hans-Lukas Kieser, "Armenians, Turks, and Europe in the shadow of World War I: Recent historiographical developments," in *Der Genozid an den Armeniern, die Türkei und Europa/The Armenian Genocide, Turkey and Europa,* ed. Hans-Lukas Kieser and Elmar Plozza (Zurich: Chronos, 2006), 52–53.

65. Cf. André N. Mandelstam, *Le sort de l'empire ottoman* (Lausanne, Switzerland: Payot, 1917), 284.

66. Kévorkian, *Génocide,* 913–919; Kieser, *Der verpasste Friede,* 396–398; Refik Ahmet, *İki komite, iki kitâl* (Ankara, Turkey: Kebikeç, 1994), 47–82 (1st ed., 1919); Hamit Bozarslan, "L'extermination des Arméniens et des juifs: Quelques éléments de comparaison," in *Der Völkermord an den Armeniern und die Shoah/The Armenian Genocide and the Shoah,* ed. Hans-Lukas Kieser and Dominik Schaller (Zurich: Chronos, 2002), 317–345, esp. 322–323.

67. *World Missionary Conference,* vol. 7, 47–49.

68. "I hope to meet [him] some day in the kingdom of Heaven" (Tacy W. Atkinson, *Account of the events in Turkey during the past three years as I have seen them and as they have had an effect upon our work in the Annie Tracy Hospital* [1917], ABC 16.9.7, 12–13, Archives of the ABCFM, Houghton Library, Harvard University, Cambridge, Massachusetts).

69. Cf. Kieser, *Der verpasste Friede,* 355, 434–435, 422–425, 449–450; and Hans-Lukas Kieser, "Dr Mehmed Reshid (1873–1919): A political doctor," in *Der Völkermord,* ed. Kieser and Schaller, 245–280, esp. 264–265.

70. "A decoration from Enver Pahsa," *Missionary Herald* (January 1917): 28.

71. Kieser, *Der verpasste Friede,* 430.

72. On Graffam, see Susan Billington Harper, "Marie Louise Graffam: Witness to genocide," in *America and the Armenian genocide of 1915,* ed. Jay Winter (Cambridge: Cambridge University Press, 2003), 214–239; for Künzler, see Jakob Künzler, *In the land of the blood and tears: Experiences in Mesopotamia during the World War (1914–1918)* (Arlington, Mass.: Armenian Cultural Foundation, 2007).

73. Cf. Kieser, *Der verpasste Friede,* 476.

74. Reproduced in Kieser, *Der verpasste Friede,* 434–435.

75. Riggs, *Days of tragedy,* 140.

76. A selection of records of those interrogations in Diyarbekir has recently been published: Başkanlığı, *Arşiv belgeleriyle Ermeni,* vol. 1, 287–291.

77. Kieser, "Dr Mehmed Reshid," 264–265.

78. On 26 May 1915, when Armenian removal began, Peet wrote to U.S. Ambassador Henry Morgenthau in the same city, "I also enclose the document which you kindly handed me yesterday in regard to refugee Armenians who have been expelled from the Zeitoun region. I had a call this morning from Consul Mordtmann from the German Embassy, who came to deliver a message received through the German Consul at Erzroom from our missionaries at Erzroom asking for relief funds to aid the [Armenian] Christians who are now being expelled from Erzroom in pursuance of orders lately given. I am today telegraphing Lt. 150.00 for this purpose" (quoted in Kieser, *Der verpasste Friede,* 339).

79. Kieser, *Der verpasste Friede,* 348–353; James L. Barton, *Story of Near East Relief (1915–1930)* (New York: Macmillan, 1930); Kieser, *Der verpasste Friede,* 348–353.

80. Beatrice Rohner, "Pfade in grossen Wassern," in *Sonnenaufgang* 36 (Frankfurt am Main, Germany: Deutscher Hülfsbund für Christliches Liebeswerk im Orient, 1934), 14–15, 21, 30–31, 38–39, 45–46, 54–56.

81. Cf. Hilmar Kaiser, in collaboration with Luther Eskijian and Nancy Eskijian, *At the crossroads of Der Zor: Death, survival, and humanitarian resistance in Aleppo, 1915–1917* (Princeton, N.J.: Gomidas, 2001), 69–71; Hans-Lukas Kieser, "La missionnaire Beatrice Rohner face au génocide des Arméniens," in *La résistance aux génocides. De la diversité des actes de sauvetage,* ed. Jacques Semelin (Paris: Presses de Sciences Po, 2008), 383–98.

82. Enver, "Misyoner tehlikesine karşı," *Sebîlürreşad* 15, no. 366 (August 1334 [1918]): 36–37; transliteration and translation in Kieser, *Der verpasste Friede,* 561–564. On Hasan Enver see *NTV Tarih Dergisi* (May 2009): 80–81.

83. Against Joseph L. Grabill, *The Protestant diplomacy and the Near East* (Minneapolis: University of Minnesota Press, 1971), 247–268.

84. Robert L. Daniel, "The Armenian Question and American-Turkish Relations, 1914–1927," *Mississippi Valley Historical Review* 46, no. 2 (1959): 252–275, esp. 259.

85. Quoted in Grabill, *Protestant diplomacy,* 174; cf. 102–104 and 124.

86. ABC Charles Ussher Personal Papers, Archives of the ABCFM. Transliteration and translation, in German, of the whole letter in Hans-Lukas Kieser, ed., *Kurdistan*

und Europa. Beiträge zur kurdischen Geschichte des 19. und 20. Jahrhunderts/Regards sur l'histoire kurde (19–20e siècles) (Zurich: Chronos, 1997), 138 and 147–148.

87. From *Plan for the peaceful repatriation of the Armenians and Kurds,* ABC Ussher Personal Papers. Cf. Richard G. Hovannisian, *The Republic of Armenia,* vol. 2: *From Versailles to London, 1919–20* (Berkeley: University of California Press, 1982), 44–48; and Kieser, *Der verpasste Friede,* 364–369.

88. "The Turk has forfeited his right to rule even himself & Islam has demonstrated that it cannot justly govern other races, nor wisely govern its co-religionists. The Kurd, a nation with fine possibilities, has been held back by Islam and cannot claim even a written language in which to make his communications, but the Turk and Kurd are human beings, and as such are entitled to our consideration. In fact, for our own sake that consideration is necessary. Islam because of its fatalism and clannishness is retrogressive and unproductive. . . . The Armenians have been oppressed and held back for centuries and now need years of tutelage before they can be fit to govern themselves. . . . To place anyone of the component elements of the Turkish Empire in control of the others would be a mistake and to break up the empire would be inexpedient" (ABC Ussher Personal Papers).

89. ABC Ussher Personal Papers.

90. James G. Harbord, "The chief of the military mission to Armenia (Harbord) to the secretary of state" (report of 16 October 1919), in *Papers relating to the foreign relations of the United States 1919* (Washington, D.C.: Government Printing Office, 1934), 840–889, esp. 874.

91. Colby Chester, "Turkey reinterpreted," *Current History* 16 (September 1922): 939–947; Clair Price, "A defense of Young Turkey," *New York Times,* 3 July 1921; Grabill, *Protestant diplomacy,* 265–266.

92. Daniel, "Armenian Question and American-Turkish Relations," 273.

93. Henry H. Riggs, *A. B. C. F. M. History 1910–1942: Section on the Turkey Missions,* 1942, ABC Ms. Hist. 31, chap. 4: "Beginning again in the Turkey Missions," 18–22, citation 18, in the Archives of the ABCFM.

94. Tacy Atkinson, letter to James Barton of 28 January 1918, ABC 16.9.7.

95. Stuart E. Knee, *The concept of Zionist dissent in the American mind 1917–1941* (New York: Robert Speller and Sons, 1979), 180–197.

CHAPTER 4

1. Stuart E. Knee, "Anglo-American relations in Palestine 1919–1925: An experiment in *realpolitik,*" *Journal of American Studies of Turkey* 5 (1997): 3–18, available at http://www.bilkent.edu.tr/~jast/Number5/Knee.html, accessed 27 June 2008.

2. James L. Barton, *Story of Near East Relief (1915–1930)* (New York: Macmillan, 1930), xi; Coolidge in the *Introduction* to Barton, *Story of Near East Relief,* viii–x.

3. Peter Grose, *Israel in the mind of America: The untold story of America's 150-year fascination with the idea of a Jewish state, and of the complex role played by this country and its leaders in the creation of modern Israel* (New York: Alfred A. Knopf, 1984), 100–101.

4. Henry H. Riggs, *A. B. C. F. M. History 1910–1942: Section on the Turkey Missions,* 1942, ABC Ms. Hist. 31, chap. 4: "Beginning again in the Turkey Missions," 13,

in the Archives of the ABCFM, Houghton Library, Harvard University, Cambridge, Massachusetts.

5. Ibid., chap. 4, 13.

6. For a later poignant article on the crucial perspective, memory, and legacy of victims, see the Protestant theologian Lukas Vischer's "Gewalt und Gewaltlosigkeit," in *". . . und Friede auf Erden": Beiträge zur Friedensverantwortung von Kirche und Israel,* ed. Rüdiger Lux (Berlin: Institut Kirche und Judentum, 1988), 98–108.

7. Riggs, *Turkey Missions,* chap. 4, 20–21.

8. Cf. various recent editions by Ara Sarafian, Hilmar Kaiser, and others.

9. Cf. "Renewed Millennialism and Mission" in this chapter; and Thomas S. Kidd, *American Christians and Islam: Evangelical culture and Muslims from the colonial period to the age of terrorism* (Princeton, N.J.: Princeton University Press, 2009), 75–143.

10. Cf. R. Siraj ud-Din, "The vital forces of Christianity and Islam," in *International Review of Mission* 3 (London: Oxford University Press, 1913), 96–117. Siraj ud-Din was an Indian convert from Islam and resident of Lahore.

11. *Methods of mission work among Moslems: Being those papers read at the First Missionary Conference on behalf of the Mohammedan World held at Cairo April 4th–9th, 1906, and the discussions thereon, which by order of the conference were not to be issued to the public, but were to be privately printed for the use of missionaries and the friends of missions* (London: Fleming H. Revell, n.d. [1906]), 23–26. Cf. also Jane I. Smith, "Christian missionary views of Islam in the nineteenth and twentieth centuries," *Islam and Christian–Muslim Relations* 3, no. 9 (1998): 357–373, esp. 360–363; and Shamir Khalaf, "Protestant images of Islam: Disparaging stereotypes reconfirmed," *Islam and Christian–Muslim Relations* 2, no. 8 (1997): 211–229. For Johannes Lepsius and his missionary approach, see Andreas Baumann, *Der Orient für Christus: Johannes Lepsius. Biographie und Missiologie* (Giessen, Germany: Brunnen, 2007); Hans-Lukas Kieser, "Zion—Armenien—Deutschland: Johannes Lepsius und die protestantische Internationale," *Armenisch-Deutsche Korrespondenz* 1 (2009): 15–21.

12. David Brewer Eddy, *What next in Turkey?* (Boston: The American Board, 1913), ix–x, 185–191.

13. James L. Barton, "What the defeat of Turkey may mean to American missions," *Biblical World* 41, no. 1 (January 1913): 3–8.

14. James L. Barton, *The Christian approach to Islam* (Boston: Pilgrim Press 1918), 167–177, available at http://www.answering-islam.org/Books/Barton/11.htm, accessed 10 September 2007.

15. In this the Muslim clerics are similar to the Christian churches during the Shoah, despite some strong Christian voices in Europe against the persecutions of the Jews. For researches on rescue of Armenians by Muslims during the Armenian genocide, see the chapters by Fatma M. Göçek, Hasmik Tevosyan, Raymond Kévorkian, and Ugur Ü. Üngör in *La résistance aux génocides: De la diversité des actes de sauvetage,* ed. Jacques Sémelin, Claire Andrieu, and Sarah Gensburger (Paris: Presses de Sciences Po, 2008).

16. Hans-Lukas Kieser, *Der verpasste Friede: Mission, Ethnie und Staat in den Ostprovinzen der Türkei 1839–1938* (Zurich: Chronos, 2000), 373–374.

17. Riggs, *Turkey Missions,* chap. 4, 13.

18. Ibid., chap. 4, 14. "Reevaluation" then became "one of the watchwords of the Mission."

19. Ibid., chap. 4, 33; cf. Kieser, *Der verpasste Friede,* 374.

20. Some lines of this hymn are as follows: "Mustafa Kemaldir, devlet banisi, / Kemal Atatürktür, Türk sevgilisi. / Zafer, istiklâli emanet etti, / Türklerçin yarattı Cumhuriyeti. / İnönü, Sakarya, sonradan Lozan / Türkün Zaferidir, İdmete [İsmete] şükran!" (William Sage Woodworth, "Ne Mutlu Ben Türküm diyene," *İÇEL, Mersin Halkevi Aylık Dergisi* [April 1940]), 14.

21. Riggs, *Turkey Missions,* chap. 4, 8, and chap. 5, 5–6. For some thoughts on the "old generation" of missionaries, see Riggs, *Turkey Missions,* chap. 4, 28–29.

22. Cf. Kieser, *Der verpasste Friede,* 376–377.

23. Cf. James E. Dittes, "The Christian mission and Turkish Islam," *Muslim World* 45 (1955): 141–142; Roger R. Trask, "'Unnamed Christianity' in Turkey during the Atatürk era," *Muslim World* 55 (1965): 101–108, esp. 109–111; Joseph L. Grabill, *The Protestant diplomacy and the Near East* (Minneapolis: University of Minnesota Press, 1971), 296–298.

24. *Methods of mission,* 25–26.

25. Cf. Hertzel Fishman, *American Protestantism and a Jewish state* (Detroit: Wayne State University Press, 1973), 23–29; Eleanor H. Tejirian, "Faith of our fathers: Near East Relief and the Near East Foundation—From mission to NGO," in *Altruism and imperialism: Western cultural and religious missions to the Middle East (19th–20th cc.),* ed. Eleanor H. Tejirian and Reeva S. Simon (New York: Middle East Institute of Columbia University, 2002), 301; Grose, *Israel in the mind,* 85.

26. New (Greek) Testament, Letter to the Romans 11:24.

27. Letter to Albert Weckesser of 2 December 1922, Dr. Johannes-Lepsius-Archiv, LAH 1555.

28. W. B. A., "Syrian Protestant College," *The Orient* 3, no. 5 (31 January 1912): 3.

29. Cf. Hope Moulton, "A Missionary Survey of the Year 1912," in *International Review of Mission* 3 (London: Oxford University Press, 1913), 1–95, esp. 64.

30. Charles T. Riggs, "Editorial," *The Orient* 4, no. 1 (1 January 1913): 5.

31. "The one disappointing feature of the Zionist program is the lack of adequate emphasis on the religious side of the Return of the Diaspora. The mere physical return to the land of their forefathers without a return to Jehovah, and insistence on a life in accord with the teachings of the prophets of the Lord, is a mockery. The only real and solid ground for a successful Zionist movement is on the basis of a return to the Lord, as urged by Isaiah, Jeremiah and Malachi" ("Zionist Work in Palestine," in *The Orient* 4, no. 16 [16 April 1913] 4). For information on later liberal Protestant attitudes toward Zionism, see Paul Charles Merkley, *Christian attitudes towards the state of Israel* (Montreal: McGill-Queen's University Press, 2001, 21–50).

32. "Jews and deunmehs," *The Orient* 2, no. 30 (30 August 1911): 3.

33. Charles T. Riggs, "Editorial," *The Orient* 4, no. 6 (5 February 1913): 5.

34. Charles T. Riggs, "Editorial," *The Orient* 4, no. 1 (1 January 1913): 5.

35. Cf. Kieser, *Der verpasste Friede,* 351.

36. Horace M. Kallen, *Constitutional foundations of the New Zion* (New York: Federation of American Zionists, May 1918). Cf. Allon Gal, "The enigma of Louis Brandei's 'Zionization': His first public Jewish address," in *American public life and the historical imagination,* ed. Wendy Gamber, Nichael Grossberg, and Hen-

drik Hartog (Notre Dame, Ind.: University of Notre Dame Press, 2003), 139–162, esp.156.

37. Nahum Goldmann, *Das jüdische Paradox* (Cologne: Europäische Verlagsanstalt, 1978), 278. For the notion of *völkisch* (mystically and mythically ethno-nationalist) and redemption, see, e.g., Chaim Weizmann, *Memoiren: Das Werden des Staates Israel* (Hamburg: J. P. Toth, 1951), 106, 109, 138.

38. Morgenthau and Yale quoted in Grose, *Israel in the mind,* 72 and 90; for Felix M. Warburg, a non-Zionist sponsor of the Yishuv, see 103–104. On a revealing episode with Morgenthau, see Jehuda Reinharz, "His Majesty's Zionist emissary: Chaim Weizmann's mission to Gibraltar in 1917," *Journal of Contemporary History* 27, no. 2 (April 1992): 259–277.

39. Cf. Donald Bloxham, *The great game of genocide: The destruction of the Ottoman Armenians in international history and politics* (Oxford: Oxford University Press, 2005), 185–206, esp. 198–199.

40. John A. DeNovo, "A railroad for Turkey: The Chester project, 1908–1913," *Business History Review* 33, no. 3 (Autumn 1959): 300–329, esp. 300.

41. Not in general, as Stivers suggests: William Stivers, *Supremacy and oil: Iraq, Turkey and the Anglo-American world order, 1918–1930* (Ithaca, N.Y.: Cornell University Press, 1982), 110.

42. Stivers, *Supremacy and oil,* 134; John A. DeNovo, *American interests and policies in the Middle East: 1900–1939* (Minneapolis: University of Minnesota Press, 1963), 196 and 202.

43. DeNovo, *American interests,* 167.

44. Cf. Roger R. Trask, *The United States response to Turkish nationalism and reform: 1914–1939* (Minneapolis: University of Minnesota Press, 1971), 37–64; Jacob C. Hurewitz, "Türk-Amerikan ilişkileri ve Atatürk," in *Çağdaş düşüncenin ışığında Atatürk* (Istanbul: D. Nejat F. Eczacıbaşı Vakfı, 2004), 483–514, esp. 507–508 (1st ed., 1983); Suzanne E. Moranian, "The American missionaries and the Armenian question: 1915–1927" (Ph.D. diss., University of Wisconsin, Madison, 1994), 549–580. James Barton began in Harput in the bloody fin de siècle, hoped enthusiastically for Young Turkey after 1908, and became a missionary strategist, political adviser, and humanitarian diplomat in the 1910s and 1920s. Scholarly biographical approaches to him and other important Turkey missionaries such as Henry H. Riggs, Charles T. Riggs, and Tacy Atkinson are still lacking.

45. Letter quoted in full on http://www.ataa.org/reference/bristol_letter.html, accessed 13 June 2008.

46. DeNovo, *American interests,* 236–240; Fahir Armaoğlu, *Belgelerle Türk-Amerikan münasebetleri* (Ankara: Türk Tarih Kurumu, 1991), 110–116.

47. Kemal Kirişci, "National identity, asylum and immigration: The EU as a vehicle of post-national transformation in Turkey," in *Turkey beyond nationalism: Towards post-nationalist identities,* ed. Hans-Lukas Kieser (London: I. B. Tauris, 2006), 184.

48. "If we abstract from the human aspect, the exclusion of the Armenians from the body of their [Turkish] state was no less a constraining necessity than . . . was the extermination of the Indians for the new state of the white people in America" (Dagobert von Mikusch, *Gasi Mustafa Kemal zwischen Europa und Asien: Eine Lebensgeschichte* [Leipzig: Paul List, 1929], 83). Cf. Dominik J. Schaller, "Die Rezeption des

Völkermordes an den Armeniern in Deutschland, 1915–1945," in *Der Völkermord an den Armeniern und die Shoah/The Armenian Genocide and the Shoah,* ed. Hans-Lukas Kieser and Dominik J. Schaller (Zurich: Chronos, 2002), 517–555; Hans-Lukas Kieser, "Deplorable, unavoidable, functional, salutary: Some remarks on the acceptance of mass violence by Turkish and German élites in the context of the Armenian genocide," *Bridges* 12, no. 1/2 (2005): 189–227.

49. Cf. Berna Pekesen, "The exodus of Armenians from the Sanjak of Alexandretta in the 1930s," in Kieser, *Turkey beyond nationalism,* 57–66.

50. Of the particular group of *religiöse Sozialisten* (religious socialists) that formed around 1900, the South German pastor and socialist member of the regional parliament Christoph Friedrich Blumhardt was a spiritual father, and Switzerland, an early center. Cf. Leonhard Ragaz, *Der Kampf um das Reich Gottes in Blumhardt, Vater und Sohn—und so weiter!* (Erlenbach, Switzerland: Rotapfel, 1922); Eduard Buess and Markus Mattmüller, *Prophetischer Sozialismus: Blumhardt, Ragaz, Barth* (Freiburg, Switzerland: Edition Exodus, 1986); Arnold Pfeiffer, ed., *Religiöse Sozialisten* (Olten, Switzerland: Walter, 1976). Religious socialism and its "socialist millennialism," which longed for a global "prophetic kingdom of justice and peace," exerted on the Swiss left a lasting influence (beyond the churches) that began to take its own path in the early twentieth century. Especially during and after World War I, the majority of the Swiss left distinguished itself from the revolutionary socialists from Russia in Swiss exile, among them Vladimir Lenin, whom they knew closely. Cf. Alfred E. Senn, *The Russian revolution in Switzerland 1914–1917* (Madison: University of Wisconsin Press, 1971).

51. See Franz Rosenzweig, *Der Stern der Erlösung* (Frankfurt am Main, Germany: Kauffmann, 1921).

52. Franklin Littell, "Reinhold Niebuhr and the Jewish people," *Holocaust and Genocide Studies* 6, no. 1 (1991): 45–61, esp. 46, 50; cf. Yehuda Bauer, "An interview with Prof. Rev. Franklin H. Littell," 23 July 1998, Yad Vashem, Jerusalem, available at http://www1.yadvashem.org/odot_pdf/Microsoft%20Word%20-%203725.pdf, accessed 23 June 2008. For Barth's criticism of *Kulturprotestantismus,* see his *Die protestantische Theologie im 19. Jahrhundert. Ihre Vorgeschichte und ihre Geschichte* (Zollikon, Switzerland: Evangelischer Verlag, 1946). The book goes back to lectures Barth gave in Germany before 1933. For a recent intervention on Reinhold Niebuhr and the liberal consensus, see Jason Stevens, "Should we forget Reinhold Niebuhr?" *Boundary 2* 34, no. 2 (Summer 2007): 135–148; cf. Eyal Naveh, *Reinhold Niebuhr and non-utopian liberalism: Beyond illusion and despair* (Brighton, England: Sussex Academic Press, 2002).

53. Available at http://www.schwabenmedia.de/St-wolfgang/Dr-metzger/Friedensarbeit.htm, accessed 23 June 2008.

54. *Pfingsterlebnis;* for this notion with regard to 1914 and 1933 in Germany, see Manfred Gailus, *Protestantismus und Nationalsozialismus: Studien zur nationalsozialistischen Durchdringung des protestantischen Sozialmilieus in Berlin* (Berlin: Böhlau Verlag, 2001), 637–666.

55. The Biltmore Program, 11 May 1942, available at http://www.mideastweb.org/biltmore_program.htm, accessed 19 June 2008; Ben-Gurion's letter quoted in Michael Bar-Zohar, *David Ben Gurion. 40 Jahre Israel. Die Biographie des Staatsgründers* (Bergisch Gladbach, Germany: Bastei Lübbe, 1988), 198.

56. Grose, *Israel in the mind,* 170–176. For Ben-Gurion's language, cf. "Catastrophe and redemption," New York, September 1915, in David Ben Gurion, *De la classe au peuple* (Tel Aviv: Arn Oved, 1956), 9–11, quoted in *Sionismes: Textes fondamentaux,* ed. Denis Charbit (Paris: Albin Michel, 1998), 180–183.

57. Rudolf C. Nothdurft, *David Ben Gurion: Seine gesellschaftlichen, religiösen und politischen Anschauungen und ihr Einfluss auf seine Haltung gegenüber der Bundesrepublik Deutschland* (n.p., 1983), 185.

58. Naveh, *Reinhold Niebuhr,* 83–86.

59. He said Jesus abolished "religion" once and for all—including "christianism," understood as religion and not actual revelation in Jesus. Cf. Karl Barth, *Kirchliche Dogmatik,* vol. 1.2 (Zollikon, Switzerland: Evangelischer Verlag, 1948), 324—356.

60. Against these points of Barth's theology and historical understanding, criticism was raised in particular by those engaged after 1945 in the Christian–Jewish dialogue, even by those who did not reinterpret the whole Bible under the impression of the Shoah. See, e.g., Bertold Klappert, *Miterben der Verheissung: Beiträge zum jüdisch-christlichen Dialog* (Neukirchen-Vluyn, Germany: Neukirchener, 2000), 170–182.

61. For Barth's attitude to Israel, see his huge *Kirchliche Dogmatik,* easily accessible by its detailed index; see in particular vol. 3.3 ; and Mark R. Lindsay, *Barth, Israel, and Jesus: Karl Barth's theology of Israel* (Aldershot, England: Ashgate, 2007). On Barth and Islam, see Werner Schatz, *"Kommt zu einem Wort, das uns und euch gemeinsam ist": Beiträge zum christlich-muslimischen Dialog* (Neukirchen-Vluyn, Germany: Neukirchener Verlagshaus, 2007), 68–69.

62. Reinhold Niebuhr, *The irony of American history* (New York: Charles Scribner, 1952), 128. On Niebuhr and Israel, see Littell, "Reinhold Niebuhr and the Jewish people"; and Paul C. Merkley, *The politics of Christian Zionism: 1891–1948* (London: Frank Cass, 1981), 141–142. On Niebuhr and Barth, see, among others, Thomas McCollough, "Reinhold Niebuhr and Karl Barth on the relevance of theology," *Journal of Religion* 43, no. 1 (January 1963): 49–55, and Paul Merkley, *Reinhold Niebuhr: A political account* (London: McGill-Queen's University Press, 1975), 70–81; Naveh, *Reinhold Niebuhr,* 33–34 (on Niebuhr and Cold War, 101–107).

63. Michelle Mart, *Eye on Israel: How America came to view the Jewish state as an ally* (Albany: State University of New York Press, 2006), ix.

64. Sumner Welles, quoted in Paul Charles Merkley, *American presidents, religion, and Israel: The heirs of Cyrus* (Westport, Conn.: Praeger, 2004), 9.

65. "We do not have orders" quoted in Paul Charles Merkley, *The politics of Christian Zionism: 1891–1948* (London: Frank Cass, 1998), 190–192; Weizmann's message quoted in Merkley, *American presidents,* 8, 20. For the Lausanne Conference, see Neil Caplan, *The Lausanne Conference, 1949* (Tel Aviv: The Moshe Dayan Center for Middle Eastern and African Studies, 1993); Ilan Pappé, *The making of the Arab-Israeli conflict 1947–1951* (London: I. B. Tauris, 1994), 203–243. Ethridge quoted in Donald Neff, "1949 Lausanne Conference seals fate of Palestine," *Washington Report on Middle East Affairs* (April 1996): 37–38.

66. George C. McGhee, *The US-Turkish-NATO Middle East connection: How the Truman doctrine and Turkey's NATO entry contained the Soviets* (London: Macmillan Press, 1990), xiii; Herfried Münkler, *Imperien: Die Logik der Weltherrschaft—vom Alten Rom bis zu den Vereinigten Staaten* (Berlin: Rowohlt, 2005), 241; Eisenhower

in "Farewell address to the American people," 17 January 1961, available at http://www.yale.edu/lawweb/avalon/presiden/speeches/eisenhower001.htm, accessed 14 July 2008.

67. McGhee, *US-Turkish-NATO,* 6, 18, 68; Eugen Krieger, "Turkey's fragile EU perspectives since the 1960s," in Kieser, *Turkey beyond nationalisms,* 167–174; Jeremy M. Sharp, *U.S. foreign aid to Israel,* CRS Report for Congress, 2 January 2008, available at http://www.fas.org/sgp/crs/mideast/RL33222.pdf, accessed 17 June 2008.

68. Ephraim Jernazian, *Judgment unto truth: Witnessing the Armenian genocide* (New Brunswick, N.J.: Transaction Publishers, 1990), 121–122.

69. Lewis V. Thomas and Richard N. Frye, *The United States and Turkey and Iran* (Cambridge, Mass.: Harvard University Press, 1951), 61–62.

70. This tax was imposed in an arbitrary and unprecedented manner on the fixed assets belonging to non-Muslim inhabitants, even if formally the *varlık vergisi* concerned also Muslim property. Those Greeks, Jews, and Armenians who were unable to pay the enormous sum demanded were arrested and removed to forced labor camps, where many of them died. Cf. Corry Guttstadt, *Die Türkei, die Juden und der Holocaust* (Berlin: Assoziation A, 2008), 202–210; Rıfat N. Balı, *Cumhuriyet yıllarında Türkiye Yahudileri: Bir Türkleştirme serüveni (1923–1945)* (Istanbul: Iletisim, 1999), 424–495; Ayhan Aktar, *Varlık vergisi ve "Türkleştirme" politikaları* (Istanbul: Iletisim, 2000).

71. Tim Weiner, *Legacy of ashes: The history of the CIA* (New York: Anchor Books, 2008), , 92–105 (1st ed., 2007); Hamit Bozarslan, *Une histoire de la violence au Moyen-Orient: De la fin de l'Empire Ottoman à Al-Qaida* (Paris: La Découverte, 2008), 75–76.

72. McGhee, *US-Turkish-NATO,* 14, 64, 167. Cf. *Modern Türkiye'de siyasî düşünce,* vol. 8 (Istanbul: Iletisim, 2007), index of names; Bozarslan, *Une histoire de la violence,* 92–93.

73. McGhee, *US-Turkish-NATO,* 8, 92, 139, 154, 173, 179. Cf. George S. Harris, *Troubled alliance: Turkish–American problems in historical perspective, 1945–1971* (Washington, D.C.: American Enterprise Institute–Hoover Institution, 1972), 9–30 and 54–57; Hamit Bozarslan, *Histoire de la Turquie contemporaine* (Paris: La Découverte, 2004), 50–67; Rıfat N. Bali, *Turkish students' movements and the Turkish left in the 1950's–1960's,* U.S. diplomatic documents presented and annotated by R. N. Bali (Istanbul: Isis Press, 2006).

74. E.g., Gottlob Schrenk in his *Die Erwartung des Weltendes* (Basel, Switzerland: Heinrich Majer, 1950), 20–25.

75. Cf. Jane Mayer, *The dark side: The inside story of how the War on Terror turned into a war on American ideals* (New York: Doubleday, 2008).

76. Cf. Paul S. Boyer, *When time shall be no more: Prophecy belief in modern American culture* (Cambridge, Mass.: Harvard University Press, 2000), parts 1 and 2 (1st ed., 1992).

77. "Empty feeling within us" quoted in Stevens, "Should we forget." See Kenneth S. Wuest, *Prophetic light in the present darkness* (Grand Rapids Mich.: Eerdmans, 1956; 1st ed., 1955), scheme reproduced in Boyer, *When time shall be no more,* 280–281.

78. Yaakov Ariel, *Evangelizing the chosen people: Missions to the Jews in America,*

1880–2000 (Chapel Hill: University of North Carolina Press, 2000), 144; Samir Boulos, "Wahrnehmung von Juden und Arabern durch die Karmelmission in Palästina 1908–1939" (unpublished master's thesis, University of Zurich, 2006), 115; Roland Löffler, "Die langsame Metamorphose einer Missions- und Bildungseinrichtung zu einem sozialen Dienstleistungsbetrieb. Zur Geschichte des Syrischen Waisenhauses der Familie Schneller in Jerusalem 1960–1945," in Dominique Trimbur, *Europäer in der Levante: Zwischen Politik, Wissenschaft und Religion (19.–20. Jahrhundert)/Des Européens au Levant: Entre politique, science et religion (XIXe–XXe siècles)* (Munich: Oldenbourg, 2004), 77–106, esp. 103.

79. Quoted in Michael Keren, *Ben-Gurion and the intellectuals: Power, knowledge, and charisma* (De Kalb: Northern Illinois University Press, 1983), 23–24; Ariel, *Evangelizing the chosen,* 158–158.

80. David Ben Gurion, *Israel: Der Staatsgründer erinnert sich* (Frankfurt: Fischer Verlag, 2004), 12 (1st Hebrew ed., 1969); cf. Anita Shapira, "Ben-Gurion and the Bible: The forging of an historical narrative?" *Middle Eastern Studies* 33, no. 4 (October 1997): 645–667.

81. Probably in order to prevent the withdrawal of the British, as encouraged by a relatively Nasser-friendly U.S. policy, Israeli military intelligence used young Egyptian Jews of a Zionist club in Cairo to plant bombs in Egyptian, American, and British institutions in the summer of 1954. The covert action failed and the activists were arrested; one or two of them committed suicide, while two others were executed. Instead of facing the scandal and Israeli guilt in this precise event, major parts of the Israeli press vociferously accused Egypt of Nazi-like anti-Semitism. Pinhas Lavon, the defense minister, and Binyamin Gibli, the head of Israeli military intelligence, had finally to resign. Cf. Joel Beinin, *The dispersion of Egyptian Jewry: Culture, politics, and the formation of a modern diaspora* (Berkeley: University of California Press, 1998), 19–20 and 90–119.

82. William Lovell Hull, *The struggle for a soul* (New York: Doubleday, 1963; in German, with Eichmann's original letters, *Kampf um eine Seele: Gespräche mit Eichmann in der Todeszelle* [Wuppertal, Germany: Verlag Sonne, 1964]); Hannah Arendt, *Eichmann in Jerusalem: A report on the banality of evil* (London: Faber and Faber, 1963); Ariel, *Evangelizing the chosen,* 150–156; the official Web site of the Jerusalem School of Synoptic Research, available at http://www.js.org, accessed 30 June 2008; June 2003 newsletter of the Jerusalem Cornerstone Foundation (the former Zion Apostolic Mission), available at http://www.jerusalemcornerstone.org, accessed 30 June 2008.

83. Cf. Nechama Tec, *In the lion's den: The life of Oswald Rufeisen* (New York: Oxford University Press, 1990), 225–231; Michael Krupp, "Ein Symposium zu einem umstrittenen Thema: Kann ein Christ auch Jude sein?" *Materialdienst. Evangelischer Arbeitskreis Kirche und Israel in Hessen und Nassau,* no. 6 (December 2007), available at http://www.lomdim.de/md2007/06/info.htm, accessed on 5 May 2009; "In Memoriam Daniel Rufeisen (1922–1998): Zionist, Karmelit und Seelsorger," *Freiburger Rundbrief. Zeitschrift für christlich-jüdische Begegnung* 6 (1999): 62; Hans-Christoph Gossmann, *". . . denn das Heil kommt von den Juden" (Joh 4, 22): Christliche Zugänge zum Judentum und zum christlich-jüdischen Dialog* (Münster: Waxmann, 2005), 56–59.

CHAPTER 5

1. This, despite former defense secretary Robert McNamara's late tearful *mea culpa* in the 1990s; see Robert McNamara, *In Retrospect: The tragedy and the lessons of Vietnam* (New York: Times Books, 1995); Bernd Greiner, *Krieg ohne Fronten: Die USA in Vietnam* (Hamburg: Hamburger Edition, 2007).

2. Michael B. Oren, *Six days of war: June 1967 and the making of the modern Middle East* (Oxford: Oxford University Press, 2002), 112.

3. Ernest A. MacKay, *Against Wilson and war, 1914–1917* (Malabar, Fla.: Krieger Publishing Company, 1996).

4. As testify, for example, the novels of Yizhar Smilansky, an early and longtime Knesset member. Cf. Stefana Sabin, "Die Landschaft der Seele. Ein Gründungsvater der israelischen Literatur: zum Tod des Schriftstellers S. Yishar," *Neue Zürcher Zeitung* (22 August 2006): 139; Gershom Gorenberg, "The war to begin all wars," *New York Review of Books* 9, no. 56 (28 May 2009), available at http://www.nybooks.com/articles/22701, accessed 21 August 2009.

5. Jacques de Reynier, *1948 à Jérusalem* (Geneva: Georg, 2002), 52–63 (1st ed., 1950); Rony F. Gabbay, *A political study of the Arab-Jewish conflict: The Arab refugee problem. A case study* (Geneva: Droz, 1959).

6. On the importance of Kurz for the young Palestinian student in Germany Sumaya Farhat-Nasr in the 1960s, see Sumaya Farhat-Nasr, *Thymian und Steine: Eine palästinensische Lebensgeschichte* (Basel, Switzerland: Lenos, 1995), 55. For Kurz, the rabbi, and other reminiscences, see Gertrud Kurz, *Unterwegs für den Frieden: Erlebnisse und Erfahrungen* (Basel, Switzerland: Friedrich Reinhardt, 1977). Kurz established also Jewish-Christian working groups and was a cofounder of the Society Switzerland–Israel in 1957. Cf. Hermann Kocher "'Flüchtlingsmutter' Gertrud Kurz Hohl (1890–1972), in *FrauenLeben Appenzell: Beiträge zur Geschichte der Frauen im Appenzellerland, 19. und 20. Jahrhundert,* ed. Renate Bräuniger (Herisau, Switzerland: Appenzeller Verlag, 1999), 706–722.

7. Bertold Klappert, *Miterben der Verheissung: Beiträge zum jüdisch-christlichen Dialog* (Neukirchen-Vluyn, Germany: Neukirchener, 2000), 153. Cf. Herman Ruether and Rosemary Ruether, *The wrath of Jonah: The crisis of religious nationalism in the Israeli-Palestinian conflict* (Minneapolis: Fortress Press, 2002), pt. 3 (1st ed. 1989).

8. Rosenzweig's dictum is quoted in Friedrich Georg Friedmann, and Christian Wiese, *Heimkehr ins Exil: Jüdische Existenz in der Begegnung mit dem Christentum* (Munich: C. H. Beck, 2001), 187. For an instructive theological autobiography by a Jewish Protestant pastor who had studied in the 1930s in Germany and the United States, see Ellen Flesseman–van Leer, "Christsein als Jude—aus autobiographischer Sicht," in "*. . . und Friede auf Erden": Beiträge zur Friedensverantwortung von Kirche und Israel,* ed. Rüdiger Lux (Berlin: Institut Kirche und Judentum, 1988), 51–66. For the experience of Christian indifference and prejudice toward Palestinians in Germany in the 1960s and 1970s, see Farhat-Nasr, *Thymian und Steine,* 46–55. For a Basel experience in beginning Islamic–Christian dialogue, see Werner Schatz,*"Kommt zu einem Wort, das uns und euch gemeinsam ist": Beiträge zum christlich-muslimischen Dialog* (Neukirchen-Vluyn, Germany: Neukirchener, 2007). The declaration *Nostra Aetate* is available at http://www.vatican.va/archive/hist_councils/ii_vatican_council/

index.htm, accessed 7 May 2009. Cf. also Manfred Vogel, "Some reflections on the Jewish-Christian dialogue in the light of the Six-Day War," *Annals of the American Academy of Political and Social Science* 387 (January 1970): 96–108.

9. Ignaz Maybaum, *Trialogue between Jew, Christian and Muslim* (London: Routledge and Kegan Paul, 1973), esp. 5, 44, 47–48, 54–55, 85–86, 154, 163. Maybaum claimed, as had Barth for Christ, a situation beyond religion for "the Jew": he was "himself the belief," "at home in his Father's house" (80–81 and 85–86, with references to Rosenzweig). Cf. Jacques Waardenburg, *Muslims and others: Relations in context* (Berlin: Walter de Gruyter, 2003), 52–53; Norman Solomon, Richard Harries, and Tim Winter, eds., *Abraham's children: Jews, Christians, and Muslims in conversation* (New York: Continuum, 2006), 187–188.

10. Max I. Dimont, *The indestructible Jews: Is there a manifest destiny in Jewish history?* (New York: New American Library, 1971), 329–330.

11. Quoted in Paul S. Boyer, *When time shall be no more: Prophecy belief in modern American culture* (Cambridge, Mass.: Harvard University Press, 1992), 189.

12. Cf. the writings of Avraham Y. H. Kook, spiritual father of Gush Emunim ("Block of Fidels"), an Israeli politico-religious movement that encouraged Jewish settlement in the occupied territories beginning in 1968. Extracts of his writings in Denis Charbit, ed., *Sionismes textes fondamentaux* (Paris: Albin Michel, 1998), 477–498.

13. Letter to the Galatians 5:11.

14. Idith Zertal, *Nation und Tod: Der Holocaust in der israelischen Öffentlichkeit,* translated from the Hebrew by Markus Lemke (Göttingen, Germany: Wallstein, 2003), 184.

15. Cf. Peter Novick, *The Holocaust in American life* (Boston: Houghton Mifflin, 1999), 15. On the question on how to build (not only critically decompile) Holocaust memory, cf. Alan Mintz, *Popular culture and the shaping of Holocaust memory in America* (Seattle: University of Washington Press, 2001).

16. Edward T. Linenthal, *Preserving memory: The struggle to create America's Holocaust Museum* (New York: Viking, 1995); Hans-Lukas Kieser and Dominik Schaller, eds., *Der Völkermord an den Armeniern und die Shoah/The Armenian Genocide and the Shoah* (Zurich: Chronos, 2002); Zertal, *Nation und Tod,* 162.

17. On Stern and death, see Joseph Heller, "The failure of fascism in Jewish Palestine, 1925–1948," in *Fascism outside Europe: The European impulse against domestic conditions in the diffusion of global fascism,* ed. Stein Ugelvik Larsen (Boulder, Colo.: Social Science Monographs, 2001), 362–392, esp. 384–385. The stamp is available at http://en.wikipedia.org/wiki/Image:Stern-stamp.jpg, accessed 1 July 2008. Ben-Gurion quoted in Rudolf C. Nothdurft, *David Ben Gurion: Seine gesellschaftlichen, religiösen und politischen Anschauungen und ihr Einfluss auf seine Haltung gegenüber der Bundesrepublik Deutschland* (n.p., 1983), 111–112. For a critical approach to the Israeli uses of Masada together with the Shoah, see Zertal, *Nation und Tod,* 13 and 286–287. For the notion of "tragic mind" in relation to an eschatological "tragic vision" of the world in the case of Near Eastern "terrorists" up to now, see Hamit Bozarslan, *Violence in the Middle East: From political struggle to self-sacrifice* (Princeton, N.J.: Markus Wiener, 2004).

18. Schalom Ben-Chorin, *Jugend an der Isar* (Gütersloh, Germany: Gütersloher Verlagshaus, 2001), 63, 134 (1st ed., 1974); Wladimir Jabotinsky, *Die jüdische Legion im Weltkrieg* (Berlin: Jüdischer Verlag, 1930), 126.

19. Ben-Chorin, *Jugend an der Isar,* 37.

20. Schalom Ben-Chorin, *Jesus im Judentum* (Wuppertal, Germany: Theologischer Verlag Rolf Brockhaus, 1970); Schalom Ben-Chorin, *Paulus: Der Völkerapostel aus jüdischer Sicht* (Munich: Paul List Verlag, 1970); Yeshayahu Leibowitz, *Judaism, human values, and the Jewish state,* ed. Eliezer Goldman (Cambridge Mass.: Harvard University Press, 1992), 256–262; David Cook, *Contemporary Muslim apocalyptic literature* (Syracuse, N.Y.: Syracuse University Press, 2005), 21, 39, 46, 198; Joseph Klausner, *Von Jesus zu Paulus* (Jerusalem: Jewish Publishing House, 1950).

21. Letter of Paul to the Romans and Second Letter of Paul to the Corinthians in the New Testament.

22. The first time I heard this term used publicly was not with regard to the well-known collaboration of the Catholic Church with European fascists or as the trendy, but inaccurate, neoconservative notion of "Islamofascism" but during a speech by Aron Bodenheimer from Jerusalem, a former psychiatrist in Zurich, at the University of Basel on 16 August 2003. He used the term to designate influential constellations in contemporary Israeli political culture. Cf. his essay *Rabins Tod* (Zurich: Chronos, 1996).

23. Martin Hengel, *Die Zeloten: Untersuchungen zur jüdischen Freiheitsbewegung in der Zeit von Herodes I. bis 70 n. Chr.* (Leiden, Netherlands: Brill, 1961), 261–296; Flavius Josephus, *Geschichte des Jüdischen Krieges,* trans. and annotated by Heinrich Clementz (Halle: Hendel, 1900), 393–429 (book 4, chaps. 3–6).

24. Hamit Bozarslan, *Une histoire de la violence au Moyen-Orient: De la fin de l'Empire Ottoman à Al-Qaida* (Paris: La Découverte, 2008), 106–107; Guido Steinberg, *Der nahe und der ferne Feind: Die Netzwerke des islamistischen Terrorismus* (Munich: C. H. Beck, 2005), 145–147.

25. The most recent and most successful product of this market is the *Left Behind* series that counts more than a dozen novels and comprises related comics, films, computer games, and the like. Tim LaHaye and Jerry B. Jenkins, *Left behind: A novel of the earth's last days* (Left Behind series; Wheaton, Ill.: Tyndale, 1995–). The coauthor Tim LaHaye has been one of the main organizers of the Christian Right since the 1970s.

26. Yaakov Ariel, *Evangelizing the chosen people: Missions to the Jews in America, 1880–2000* (Chapel Hill: University of North Carolina Press, 2000), 220–251.

27. Cook, *Contemporary Muslim apocalyptic literature,* 13–58.

28. E.g., Hal Lindsay and Carole C. Carlson, *The late great planet Earth* (Grand Rapids: Zondervan, 1970); Tim F. LaHaye, *The beginning of the end. Amazing fulfillment of prophecy tells earth's future* (Wheaton, Ill.: Tyndale, 1972).

29. Charles H. Dyer, *The Rise of Babylon: Is Iraq at the center of the final drama?* (Chicago: Moody Publishers, 2003; 1st ed., 1991).

CONCLUSION

1. Jeremiah Evarts, *Cherokee removal: The "William Penn" essays and other writings* (Knoxville: University of Tennessee Press, 1981), 282; David S. Heidler and Jeanne T. Heidler, *Indian Removal* (New York: W. W. Norton, 2007), 1; Kevin Gover, Assistant Secretary-Indian Affairs, Department of the Interior, speech of 8 September 2000, quoted in Richard E. Ellis, *Andrew Jackson* (Washington, D.C.: CQ Press 2003), 246–247.

2. Cf. the meaningful title of the instructive volume of essays edited by Eleanor H. Tejirian and Reeva S. Simon, *Altruism and imperialism: Western cultural and religious missions in the Middle East* (New York: Middle East Institute of Columbia University, 2002).

3. Dwight D. Eisenhower's "I shall go to Korea" speech, 25 October 1952, available at http://tucnak.fsv.cuni.cz/~calda/Documents/1950s/Ike_Korea_52.html, accessed 27 June 2008; and his "Farewell address to the American people," 17 January 1961, available at http://www.yale.edu/lawweb/avalon/presiden/speeches/eisenhower001.htm, accessed 14 July 2008.

4. Jocelyn Rochat, "George W. Bush et le code Ezéchiel," *Allez savoir!* no. 39 (September 2007): 34–41. My thanks to Professor Pierre Bühler of the University of Zurich, who drew my attention to this article and sent me copies of it.

5. Cf. European Stability Initiative, *Islamic Calvinists: Change and conservatism in central Anatolia* (Berlin and Istanbul, 19 September 2005), available at www.esiweb.org, accessed 12 May 2009. This movement has to do with the *Nurculuk:* its founder, the Kurdish Sheyk Said Nursi (ca. 1876–1960), had found exemplary the ABCFM schools in his native eastern Anatolia. Influential today in particular is the movement of Fethullah Güven (b. 1941), a Turkish imam close to the *Nurcu,* who influenced a whole religious youth in Turkey and its global diaspora in the late twentieth century; since 1999, he has lived in the United States. Cf. Hakan Yavuz and John L. Esposito, eds., *Turkish Islam and the secular state: The Gülen Movement* (Syracuse, N.Y.: Syracuse University Press, 2003); Şükran Vahide, *Bediuzzaman Said Nursi: The author of the Risale-i Nur* (Istanbul: Sözler, 2004; 1st ed., 1992). For the acceptance of the secular civil law, see Hans-Lukas Kieser, Astrid Meier, and Walter Stoffel, eds., *Revolution islamischen Rechts:Das Schweizerische ZGB in der Türkei* (Zurich: Chronos, 2008).

6. Words used by George W. Bush in his speech on Iraq of 10 January 2007.

7. Alfred, Berchtold, *Guillaume Tell: Résistant et citoyen du monde* (Geneva: Editions Zoé, 2004), 245.

Selected Bibliography

For a complete listing of archival and bibliographical references, see the Notes section.

Adams, Hannah. *The history of the Jews: From the destruction of Jerusalem to the present time.* 2 vols. Boston: John Eliot, 1812.

Anderson, Rufus. *Memorial volume of the first fifty years of the American Board of Commissioners for Foreign Missions.* Boston: The Board, 1861.

Andrew, John A., III. *From revival to removal: Jeremiah Evarts, the Cherokee nation, and the search for the soul of America.* Athens: University of Georgia Press, 1992.

Ariel, Yaakov. *Evangelizing the chosen people: Missions to the Jews in America, 1880–2000.* Chapel Hill: University of North Carolina Press, 2000.

Armaoğlu, Fahir. *Belgelerle Türk-Amerikan münasebetleri.* Ankara, Turkey: Türk Tarih Kurumu, 1991.

Arpee, Leon. *The Armenian awakening.* Chicago: University of Chicago Press, 1909.

Barth, Karl. *Protestant theology in the nineteenth century: Its background and history.* Grand Rapids, Mich.: W. B. Eerdmans Publishing, 2002 (1st German ed., 1946).

Barton, James L. *Daybreak in Turkey.* Boston: Pilgrim Press, 1908.

Bauer, Yehuda. *Rethinking the Holocaust.* New Haven, Conn.: Yale University Press, 2001.

Bayrak, Mehmet. *Açık-gizli/resmi-gayriresmi Kürdoloji belgeleri.* Ankara, Turkey: Özge, 1994.

Bliss, Howard S. "The Balkan War and Christian work among Moslems." In *International Review of Mission.* Vol. 3. London: Oxford University Press, 1913, 643–656.

Boyer, Paul S. *When time shall be no more: Prophecy belief in modern American culture.* Cambridge, Mass.: Harvard University Press, 1992.

Bozarslan, Hamit. *Une histoire de la violence au Moyen-Orient: De la fin de l'Empire Ottoman à Al-Qaida.* Paris: La Découverte, 2008.

Charbit, Denis, ed. *Sionismes: Textes fondamentaux.* Paris: Albin Michel, 1998.

Connors, Richard, and Andrew Gow. *Anglo-American millennialism, from Milton to the Millerites.* Leiden, Netherlands: Brill, 2004.

Cook, David. *Contemporary Muslim apocalyptic literature.* Syracuse, N.Y.: Syracuse University Press, 2005.

Culver, Douglas J. *Albion and Ariel: British puritanism and the birth of political Zionism.* Bern, Switzerland: Peter Lang, 1995.

Davison, Roderic H. *Essays in Ottoman and Turkish history, 1774–1923: The impact of the West.* Austin: University of Texas Press, 1990.

——. "The *millets* as agents of change in the nineteenth-century Ottoman Empire." In *Christians and Jews in the Ottoman Empire: The functioning of a plural society.* Vol. 1: *The Central Lands.* Ed. Benjamin Braude and Bernard Lewis. New York, Holmes and Meier, 1982, 319–337.

DeNovo, John A.. *American interests and policies in the Middle East: 1900–1939.* Minneapolis: University of Minnesota Press, 1963.

Deringil, Selim. "'There is no compulsion in religion': On conversion and apostasy in the late Ottoman Empire: 1839–1856." *Comparative Studies in Society and History* 42–43 (2000): 547–575.

d'Ohsson, Ignace de Mouradja. *Tableau général de l'empire othoman, divisé en deux parties, dont l'une comprend la législation mahométane, l'autre l'histoire de l'empire othoman.* 7 vols. Paris: Impr. de Monsieur, 1788–1824.

Dupont, Anne-Laure. "Une école missionnaire et étrangère dans la tourmente de la révolution constitutionnelle ottomane." *Cahiers de la Méditerranée* 75 (2007). Posted online 21 July 2008. Available at http://cdlm.revues.org/index3483.htm.

Dwight, H.G.O. *Christianity revived in the East; or, A narrative of the work of God among the Armenians of Turkey.* New York: Baker and Scribner, 1850.

Dwight, H.G.O., and Eli Smith. *Researches of the Rev. E. Smith and Rev. H. G. O. Dwight in Armenia: Including a journey through Asia Minor, and into Georgia and Persia, with a visit to the Nestorian and Chaldean Christians of Oormiah and Salmas.* Boston: Crocker and Brewster, 1833.

Farhat-Naser, Sumaya. *Thymian und Steine: Eine palästinensische Lebensgeschichte.* Basel, Switzerland: Lenos, 1995.

Farschid, Olaf, Manfred Kropp, and Stephan Dähne eds. *The First World War as remembered in the countries of the Eastern Mediterranean.* Würzburg, Germany: Ergon, 2006.

Force, James E., and Richard P. Popkin, eds. *The millenarian turn: Millenarian contexts of science, politics, and everyday Anglo-American life in the seventeenth and eighteenth centuries.* Dordrecht, Netherlands: Kluwer, 2001.

Gaunt, David. *Massacres, resistance, protectors: Muslim-Christian relations in Eastern Anatolia during World War I.* Piscataway, N.J.: Gorgias Press, 2006.

Goodell, William. *Forty years in the Turkish Empire or, Memoirs of Rev. William Goodell, D.D., late missionary in the A. B. C. F. M. at Constantinople.* Ed. E.D.G. Prime, D.D. New York: Robert Carter and Brothers, 1876.

Grabill, Joseph L. *Protestant diplomacy and the Near East: Missionary influence on American policy, 1810–1927.* Minneapolis: University of Minnesota Press, 1971.

Greene, Joseph K. *Leavening the Levant.* Boston: Pilgrim Press, 1916.

Grose, Peter. *Israel in the mind of America: The untold story of America's 150-year fascination with the idea of a Jewish state, and of the complex role played by this country and its leaders in the creation of modern Israel.* New York: Alfred A. Knopf, 1984.

Hanioğlu, Mehmed Şükrü. *A brief history of the late Ottoman Empire.* Princeton, N.J.: Princeton University Press, 2008.

Harris, George S. *Troubled Alliance: Turkish-American problems in historical perspective, 1945–1971.* Washington, D.C.: American Enterprise Institute for Public Policy Research, 1972.

Haumann, Heiko, ed. *Der Traum von Israel: Die Ursprünge des modernen Zionismus.* Weinheim, Germany: Beltz Athenäum, 1998.

Hutchison, William R. *Errand to the world: American Protestant thought and foreign missions.* Chicago: University of Chicago Press, 1987.

Karpat, Kemal H. *The politicization of Islam: Reconstructing identity, state, faith, and community in the late Ottoman state.* Oxford: Oxford University Press, 2001.

Kévorkian, Raymond H. *Le génocide des Arméniens.* Paris: Odile Jacob, 2006.

Kieser, Hans-Lukas. *Der verpasste Friede: Mission, Ethnie und Staat in den Ostprovinzen der Türkei 1839–1938.* Zurich: Chronos, 2000 (Turkish ed.: *Iskalanmış Barış.* Istanbul: Iletisim, 2005).

——, ed. *Turkey beyond nationalism: Towards post-nationalist identities.* London: I. B. Tauris, 2006.

Kieser, Hans-Lukas, and Dominik J. Schaller, eds. *Der Völkermord an den Armeniern und die Shoah /The Armenian Genocide and the Shoah.* Zurich: Chronos, 2002.

Klappert, Bertold. *Miterben der Verheissung: Beiträge zum jüdisch-christlichen Dialog.* Neukirchen-Vluyn, Germany: Neukirchener, 2000.

Köroğlu, Erol. *Ottoman propaganda and Turkish identity: Literature in Turkey during World War I.* London: I. B. Tauris, 2007.

Krämer, Gudrun. *A history of Palestine: From the Ottoman conquest to the founding of the State of Israel.* Princeton, N.J.: Princeton University Press, 2008 (1st German ed., 2002).

Künzler, Jakob. *In the land of blood and tears: Experiences in Mesopotamia during the World War (1914–1918).* Arlington, Mass.: Armenian Cultural Foundation, 2007 (1st German ed., 1921).

Kurzman, Charles, ed. *Modernist Islam 1840–1940: A sourcebook.* Oxford : Oxford University Press, 2002.

Lellouch, Benjamin, and Stéphane Yérasimos, eds. *Les traditions apocalyptiques au tournant de la chute de Constantinople.* Paris: Harmattan, 1999.

Makdisi, Ussama. *Artillery of heaven: American missionaries and the failed conversion of the Middle East.* Ithaca, N.Y.: Cornell University Press, 2008.

Mart, Michelle. *Eye on Israel: How America came to view the Jewish state as an ally.* Albany: State University of New York Press, 2006.

McGhee, George C. *The US-Turkish-NATO Middle East connection: How the Truman doctrine and Turkey's NATO entry contained the Soviets.* London: Macmillan, 1990.

Merkley, Paul C. *The politics of Christian Zionism: 1891–1948.* London: Frank Cass, 1998.

Niebuhr, Helmut Richard. *The kingdom of God in America.* Middletown, Conn.: Wesleyan University Press, 1988 (1st ed., 1938).

Novick, Peter. *The Holocaust in American life.* Boston: Houghton Mifflin, 1999.

Obenzinger, Hilton. *American Palestine—Melville, Twain, and the Holy Land mania.* Princeton, N.J.: Princeton University Press, 1999.

Oren, Michael B. *Power, faith, and fantasy: America in the Middle East, 1776 to the present.* New York: W. W. Norton, 2007.

Perry, Yaron. *British mission to the Jews in nineteenth-century Palestine.* London: Frank Cass, 2003.

Philips, Clifton J. *Protestant America and the pagan world: The first half century of the American Board of Commissioners for Foreign Missions, 1810–1860.* Cambridge, Mass.: Harvard University Press, 1969.

Qutb, Sayyid. *Milestones.* Delhi: Markazi Maktaba Islami, 1996 (1st Arabic ed., 1964).

Riggs, Henry H. *Days of tragedy in Armenia: Personal experiences in Harpoot, 1915–1917.* Ann Arbor, Mich.: Gomidas Institute, 1997 (1918 manuscript).

Şerif, Ahmet. *Arnavudluk'da, Sûriye'de, Trablusgarb'de Tanîn.* Ed. Mehmed Ç. Börekçi. Ankara, Turkey: TTK, 1999.

Shapira, Anita, "Ben-Gurion and the Bible: The forging of an historical narrative?" *Middle Eastern Studies* 33, no. 4 (October 1997): 645–674.

Tejirian, Eleanor H., and Reeva S. Simon, eds. *Altruism and imperialism: Western cultural and religious missions in the Middle East.* New York: Middle East Institute of Columbia University, 2002.

Trask, Roger R. *The United States response to Turkish nationalism and reform: 1914–1939.* Minneapolis: University of Minnesota Press, 1971.

Winter, Jay, ed. *America and the Armenian genocide of 1915.* Cambridge: Cambridge University Press, 2003.

World Missionary Conference: Reports of commissions. 9 vols. Edinburgh: Oliphant, Anderson and Ferrier, 1910.

Zertal, Idith. *Israel's holocaust and the politics of nationhood.* Cambridge: Cambridge University Press, 2005.

Index

ABCFM (American Board of Commissioners for Foreign Missions); and Abdulhamid, 55–57, 62, 83; and Alevis, 51–55, 96 (*see also* Alevi [*Kızılbaş*]); archives of (*see* missionary archives); and Armenians, 34, 44–51, 57–62 (*see also* Armenians); and civil disobedience, 87; and CUP, 74–80, 87–90, 100, 104, 110–111, 156–157; Eastern Turkey Mission, 61; foundation of, 2, 24–27; grassroots commitment of, 97, 129, 139; and Indians, 10, 27–33, 38; and Iroquian language, 29; and Islam, 40, 71–74, 102–105, 158 (*see also* Islam); and Jews, 38; and Kemalist Turkey, 100–102, 105–107; and Kurds, 56–57; main focus of, on Asia Minor, 5, 34, 46, 96–97, 108, 155, 166n5; Palestine Mission, 38–43; and penetration of eastern Anatolia, 46; Prudential Committee, 39; and slavery, 27, 29, 53, 129, 154; and socialism (*see* America: and socialism); strategists for, 55; visions of, after 1918, 93; and Young Turk Revolution, 67–76; and Zionism (*see* America: and Zionism)

Abdulhamid II, Sultan, 35, 37, 51–52, 55–67, 77, 82–83, 156–157

Abdülkadir, Seyid, 93

Abdulmejid, Sultan, 32, 35, 37, 46

Abel, 101

ABFMPC. *See* ABCFM

Abraham, children of, 145

Adams, Hannah, 25–26, 40

Adams, John B., 20

Adams, William, 46

Adana, 106; massacres of, 69, 75–76

Adiyaman, 54

Afghanistan, 149

Afro-Americans, 111

Ahmed Jemal Pasha, 76, 82, 86, 90

Ahmed Rıza, 79

Ahmed Şerif, 1, 4, 76–78, 81, 83, 162, 165n1

Akçura, Yusuf, 66

Alabama, 28

Albania, 77

Aleppo, 86, 90

Aleppo College, 106

Alevi (*Kızılbaş*), 34–35, 51–56, 82, 86–87, 105; Alevi-Armenian "alliance," 56; and Christians, 56. *See also* ABCFM

Alexander, Michael S., 45

Alexandrette, *Sanjak* of, 115

Alexandria, 41, 43

Ali (ibn Abî Tâlib), 52–53

Ali Bey Hüseyinzâde (Turan), 66

Ali Fuad (governor), 86

Ali Gako (Kurdish chief), 54

Ali Kemal (Ottoman Minister), 93

Allyn, John, 23

altruism, American, 154

America: imperial, 116, 120, 123, 128, 139, 146, 158; missionary, 5, 9, 15–16, 25–27, 45, 55, 58, 62–64, 80–81, 92–93, 96, 98, 109, 112, 115, 130, 150, 155, 157; as new Canaan, 2, 19; and socialism, 84, 109–110; and Zionism, 97, 108–111; soul of (*see* soul of America). *See also* United States
American altruism, 154
American Anti-Slavery Society, 27
American Bible Society, 24
American Board of Commissioners for Foreign Missions. *See* ABCFM
American Board of Foreign Missions of the Presbyterian Church (ABFMPC), 46, 104, 106, 108
American Board of Missions to the Jews, 60, 132
American Christian Palestine Committee, 120–121
American Civil War, 10
American cold warriors, 127–128, 149 (*see also* Cold War)
American College in Marsivan, 75
American College for Girls in Scutari, 79, 106
American empire, idea of, 22
American exceptionalism, 8, 53, 121, 152
American "home-feeling," 46
American ideals, 138
American Indians. *See under* ABCFM
Americanism, 77
American mandate, 93, 95
American-Ottoman (American-Turkish) Treaty. *See* Treaty, American-Ottoman (American-Turkish)
American patriotism, 151
American project, 28, 30, 33, 137
American Red Cross, 79
American Revolution, 21, 29
American University of Beirut, 1, 4, 66, 70–72
amira, oligarchy of the, 50
Anatolia: eastern Anatolia, 81–82, 84, 86, 93, 100; home of the Turks, 67; "promised land," 66. *See also* Asia Minor
Anatolia College in Marsivan, 77, 88, 106
Andover Theological Seminary, 19–20, 27, 38
Anglo-Turkish Declaration, 115; treaty of assistance, 115
Ankara, 96, 102, 114, 125
Anteb, 106
Antichrist, 151
Anti-Defamation League, 146
anti-Judaism, 12, 26, 121, 131
anti-Semitism, 12, 140, 146, 192n81
apocalypse: in contrast to apocalypticism, 162; revelation, 155, 162–163; Social Darwinist, 64–65, 68, 74, 84, 90, 118; term, 8
Apocalypse, Book of. *See* Revelation (Book of)
apocalyptic history, 15, 157
apocalypticism, 2, 10, 12–13, 149–152, 161–162; turn to Near East, 151
apocalyptic truth, 2, 22, 144
apocalyptic war, 67, 84; compared to "just war," 20–21
Arabism, 138
Arabs, 4, 108, 111, 122, 132, 136, 147. *See also* Palestine
Ararat, 46
Arendt, Hannah, 45, 135
ARF (Armenian Revolutionary Federation), 58, 78, 109; and church, 75; CUP-ARF alliance, 58, 68–69, 85
Ariel, Yaakov, 132
Armageddon, battle of, 139, 143. *See also* apocalyptic war
Armenakan party, 57
Armenia, 44, 61, 93; Eastern (Russian), 85, 93; mandate for, 100; mission to (*see* ABCFM); Republic of, 87; socialist, 58
Armenian Apostolic (Gregorian) Church, 47, 49, 54, 58–59, 75
Armenian genocide, 86, 90, 126, 155, 186n15
Armenianism, 49, 93
Armenian *millet,* 49–51
Armenian Question, 113, 155
Armenian reforms. *See* reforms of the Ottoman eastern provinces
Armenian revolutionaries, 57–58
Armenian Revolutionary Federation. *See* ARF
Armenians, 5, 34, 44–51, 57–62, 146; and Young Turkey, 75–77; "revive," 5 (*see also* ABCFM)
Arpee, Leon, 47, 50, 52
Arslan, Yusuf, 128
Asfuriya hospital, 62
Asia Minor, 16, 46, 50–51, 60, 64, 81, 90, 95, 99–100, 105, 112, 115, 157, 162, 178n79; American citizens in, 99; American mandate for, 93, 100; Christian catastrophe in, 100, 115, 146, 157; missionary orientation to (*see* ABCFM). *See also* Anatolia
Aşiret Süvari Alayları, 82
Atatürk, Mustafa Kemal, 107, 113–114
atheism, 78
Atkinson, Tacy, and ABCFM, 88, 96
Atkinson, Henry H., and ABCFM, 88
Atlantic Charter, 115

atomic bombs, 123, 131
Auschwitz, 146, 160
Auspicious Event (*Vak'a-i Hayriye*), 36
Austria-Hungary, 37, 85–86, 147
Avedaper, 46
Awakening, Great, 27
Awakening, Second, 27
Awetaranian, Johannes, 103

Babylon: anti-Jewish, 151; appeal of ancient, 21; exile in, 25
Bahaeddin Şakir, 65, 86
Baku, 66
Balkans, 1, 16, 55, 57, 79, 97, 104, 109, 155, 156
Balkan Wars (1912–1913), 67, 69–70, 80
Barbary piracy, 6
Bar Kochba, 147
Barnum, Herman, and ABCFM, 74
Barth, Karl, 84, 117, 121–122, 189n52, 190nn60–61
Barton, James, and ABCFM, 68, 93, 99, 104–105, 108, 114
Basel, 90, 109; Missionary Society, 25
Bayar, Celal, 128
Beast and Harlot, 104
Beecher, Lyman, 20
Begin, Menahem, 146
Beirut, 1, 46, 66, 78. *See also* Syrian Protestant College
Bektashis, 36
Belle Epoque, 60, 68, 76, 109, 121, 125; in Anatolia, 97; Christianity, 116
Ben-Chorin, Schalom (alias Fritz Rosenthal), 147–148
Ben-Gurion, David (alias David Grün), 111, 119–120, 129–130, 132, 138, 147; messianism of, 133, 143, 145
Ben Hur, 122
Berlin, 110; crisis, 125
Berlin Congress, 55, 82; ABCFM lobbying at, 55. *See also* Treaty of Berlin
Bern, 114
Bernadotte, Folke, 142
Bethar, 147
Bible: "Bible lands," 2, 9, 16, 43, 59, 64, 98, 116, 153–154, 160; Bible women, 49; distribution of, 42, 44; Hebrew, 116; International Bible Contest, 134; literal reading, 39, 130; New Testament, 41, 43, 104, 118, 121; prophetic reading, 116, 130, 153; Zionist reading, 130
Bible House Istanbul, 70, 73, 78, 90, 110
Biblical World, 104
Biltmore Conference, 119–120
Bin Laden, Osama, 149
biologism, 64
bishopric, Anglo-Prussian, 45
Bismarck, Otto von, 156
Bitlis, 89
Bliss, Howard S., 70, 72, 103, 108
Blumhardt, Christoph F., 189n50
Bodenheimer, Aron, 195n22
bolshevism, 109, 125
Bosporus, 115
Boston: Female Society of, 26; missionary center, 2, 5, 23, 41, 55, 90; Park Street Church, 39; Prison Discipline Society, 27
Boutmy, Emile, 65
Brandeis, Louis, 111
Bristol, Mark L., 112–114
British Church Missionary Society, 25, 41
British Empire. *See* Great Britain
Büchner, Ludwig, 65–66
Bulgarians, 70, 92
Bulwer, Henry, 52
Bureau of Indian Affairs, 32
Bush, George H. W., 131
Bush, George W., 131, 161, 196n6
Bustani, Butrus al-, 50
Butler, Elizur, 31

Caesarea, 73, 75, 106
Cain, 101
Cairo, 103
caliph, 40, 54. *See also* Sultan-Caliph, Ottoman
Calvinism: Islamic, 4, 162; and the Jews, 26; and piety, 33, 80. *See also* Protestantism
Canning, Stratford, 48, 52
capitalism, 163
capitulations, 36, 112, 128; abrogation of, 88
Castro, Fidel, 127
catastrophism, apocalypticist, 10, 80
catechism, American political, 2
Catholic mission, 57, 75, 91, 135, 142. *See also* church(es); *millet*
Caucasus, 85, 95, 109
Central Asia, 67
Central Intelligence Service (CIA), 114, 127
Central Turkey College, Anteb, 106
Cherokees, 28–32, 124
Chester, Colby, 96, 112
Chicago, 132
chiliasm, 7. *See also* millennialism
China, 73
Chirac, Jacques, 161

Christ. *See* Jesus
Christian (Alliance and Evangelical) Missionary Alliance, 60, 132
Christianity: foundation of, 103; "revived in the East," 5, 44–47, 64; revolution of modern, 141
Christianity Revived in the East; or, A Narrative of the Work of God among the Armenians of Turkey, 44
Christian Right, 138–139, 150, 160
Christians: Oriental, 42; Syriac, 44. *See also* churches
Christie, Thomas D., 181n31
church(es): Armenian Apostolic (Gregorian), 47, 49, 54, 58–59, 75; Baptist, 122; Barth and, 117, 122; Catholic, 15, 21, 142, 175n22; Congregational, 104, 130; destruction of, 58; early, 8, 12, 15, 103; Greek, 75; of humanity, 76; Jewish origins of, 134; millennial end of (*see* millennium); in North America, 19–21, 24, 28, 43–44, 104, 117, 161, 171n28; Oriental, 47; post-1945, 140–143; Presbyterian, 130; Protestant, 21, 25; Southern Baptist, 133; in Turkey, 106; Turks in, 75. *See also* Christians; Jesus; *millet*
Church Missionary Society (CMS), 25, 41
Cilicia, 87
civil law, 144, 162, 196n5
civil religion. *See* millennialism
Cohen, Benjamin, 108
Cohen, Israel, 110
Cohn, Joseph H., 132
Cohn, Leopold, 60, 132
Cold War, 117; end of, 151; in Near East, 139, 159; starting in Greece and Turkey, 125
cold warriors, American, 127–128, 149 (*see also* Cold War)
Committee Union and Progress. *See* CUP
Comte, Auguste, 66
Constantinople, 26, 36, 46–48, 65–66, 79, 86, 94, 110, 126
constitution, Ottoman, 47–49, 64, 67–70, 157. See also *millet:* constitution (*nizamname*)
Constitutional Foundations of the New Zion
containment, anti-Soviet, 121, 123, 125, 127
Conversion: appeal to, 9, 131; dramaturgy of, 103, 134; of Israel, 117; of Muslims and Jews, 44–47; a nation's, 77; Pauline, 77, 103; question of whether it had to take place before or after return to Palestine, 26; as reconversion, 103; secularist, 76; as spiritual restoration, 23
Coolidge, Calvin, 99
counterrevolution of April 1909, 69
coup(s): CUP (1913), 80; in Iran (1953), 114, 127; in Turkey, 128
covenant, 19, 23, 103, 118, 145, 148, 181n33
Creeks, 29, 32
CUP (Committee Union and Progress), 58, 63–70, 85, 105; going to war in 1914, 83; one-party régime, 69. *See also* ABCFM; ARF
Cyrus (Persian king), 18, 23, 100, 123, 159–160

Damad Ferid, 93
Daniel, Book of, 8
Dardanelles, 69, 85
Darwinism, Social, 64–65, 68, 74, 84, 90, 118
David, King, 39
Davison, Roderic, 82
Daybreak in Turkey, 69
dede, 53–54
Deir ez-Zor, 86
Deir Yassin, 141
demographic engineering in Asia Minor, 81, 90
DeNovo, John, 112
Depression, Great, 117, 131
Dersim (Tunceli), 52, 86–87, 105; campaign of 1937–1938, 96
destiny. *See* manifest destiny
dialogue: of confrontation, 162; *muhabbet,* 53; religious, 96, 102, 142–143, 150
Dink, Hrant, 128
din ü devlet, 3
disinterested benevolence, 27, 99, 154
Disraeli, Benjamin, 45
Diyarbekir, 88–90
Dodge, Cleveland H., 108
dönme, 110
Dulles, Allan, 127
Dulles, John F., 127
Dwight, Henry O., 44, 46, 49
Dwight, Timothy, 40
Dyke, Henry van, 61

eastern provinces. *See* Anatolia
Eastern Question. *See* Oriental Question
eastern Turkey. *See* Anatolia
Eban, Abba, 123, 137
economy: millennialist, 98; spiritual, 154; of symbols, 2, 123, 159
ecumenical movement, 151
Eddy, W. K., 104
Edelman, Samuel, 89
Eden, garden of, 46
Edinburgh, 68, 71, 73–74, 78, 87
Edirne, 81, 86
Edwards, Jonathan, 20, 26–27

Egypt, 12, 36, 41, 138, 192n81; British invasion of, 37; French invasion of, 17; as a metaphor, 120; pre-islamic, 18, 21
Egyptian invasion of Syria, 36, 44
Egyptology, 118
Ehman, Johannes, 88
Eichmann, Adolf, 134–135, 145–146
Eisenhower, Dwight, 124, 131, 158–159
Elbistan, 52
England: early modern, 11; as protector of Armenians, 55, 60. *See also* Great Britain
Enlightenment: European versus American, 17–20, 26; and the Jews, 11; and millennialism, 9, 26, 116, 153, 155
Entente, 83
Enver Pasha, 85–88, 91–92, 156
equality, 48, 64
Eretz Israel, 99, 147
Erivan, 87
Erzincan, 86
Erzurum, 52, 86
eschatology: American, 132, 166n5; evangelical, 160; individualistic, 131; misuse of, 161; Muslim, 50, 150, 166–167n5; in the Ottoman world, 10–11; Protestant, 110; term, 8. *See also* apocalypse; millennialism
ethnonationalism. *See* nationalism
Ethridge, Mark, 124
Euphrates College, Harput, 89
Europe, "Christian," 15, 70
European Union: and apocalypticism, 151; Turkey's accession to, 4, 129
evangelicals, 6, 132–134, 145, 158. *See also* Jews
Evarts, Jeremiah, and ABCFM, 28–31, 104, 154
evil: in American society, 10; force of, 1, 13, 78, 151; question of, 135; in religion, 121, 130, 148
exceptionalism, American, 8, 53, 121, 152
Exodus (film), 122
Ezekiel, Book of, 161

Fahreddin (*müfti*), 81
Faik Bey, 75
Fall and Rise of Israel: The Story of the Jewish People during the Time of Their Dispersal and Regathering, The, 4
Fanon, Frantz, 12
Farhat-Nasr, Sumaya, 193n6
fascism, 109, 140; "clericofascism," 148; "islamofascism," 195n22
Fasel, Pierre, 141
Female Society of Boston, 26
Ferid Pasha, Grand Vizir Damad, 93
Finch, Henry, 12
Fisk, Pliny, 38–42, 44, 129
fitna, 11
Fitzmaurice, G. H., 59
Flesseman–van Leer, Ellen, 193n8
Florida, 28
Flusser, David, 134
Forty Days of Musa Dagh, The, 146
Fowle, James L., and ABCFM, 75
Foyers turcs, 65–67
France, 36–37, 115; defeated, 125; as a model, 36; Protestants in, 25, 27; revolutionary, 17, 23
Frankfurter, Felix, 108
French Revolution. *See* France: revolutionary
Fundamentalism: Muslim, 113, 143; Protestant, 6, 66, 131, 134, 158

Garabedian, Nishan (alias Rupen Khan-Azat), 58
Gates, Caleb, and ABCFM, 93
gavur, 58
Gaza, 144
Geneva, 57, 66
Geneva Convention, Fourth, 144
genocide: Armenian, 86, 90, 126, 155, 186n15; Jewish, 134, 159. *See also* Shoah
Georgia, 28–32, 44
geotheology and geostrategy, 3, 151, 158
Germany, 21–22, 64, 75, 84, 124–125, 157; of interwar, 114, 148; Nazi, 99, 116, 118–119, 148 (*see also* National Socialism); post-1914, 134; Weimar Republic, 118; and "Whitsun event of 1914," 118
Gezmiş, Deniz, 128
Girls' College in Marash, 106
globalism: American missionary, 2, 13; secular, 6, 13, 158. *See also* millennialism; Wilsonianism
Gobat, Samuel, 45
Gog and Magog, 151, 161
Goiran, Roger, 127
Gölcük, Lake, 88
Golden Rule, 99, 108, 111, 124
Goldmann, Nahum, 111
Gold Rush, 32
Goodell, Abigail, and ABCFM, 46
Goodell, William, and ABCFM, 24, 44, 46, 48
Gospel, 2, 7, 25, 30, 38, 81, 98, 106, 109, 134; and culture, 73; of Mammon, 126; as old Israel's legacy, 39; Social Gospel, 71; synergy of, with Israel, 116; universal, 80
Graffam, Mary L., and ABCFM, 88
Graham, Billy, 131, 133

Grand National Assembly, Ankara, 96
Great Britain, 22, 34, 36–37, 64, 115, 125, 155; aporia of, in Palestine, 123; imperial, 20, 21, 109, 123; and native Americans, 29; philosemitism in, 45; as protector of the Ottoman Empire, 36–37; and role of a Cyrus, 18, 23, 25; threat to, 118. *See also* England
Great Depression, 117, 131
Great Works of Christ in America (Magnalia Christi Americana), The, 19
Greece, 41, 115, 125, 127; war of independence of, 36, 47
green belt, policy of the, 149
Greene, Joseph, and ABCFM, 79
Gregor, St., 49
Grew, Joseph, 112, 114
Grosssteinbeck, Friedrich, 175n42
Güven, Fethullah, 196n5

Haeckel, Ernst, 65
Haifa, 135
Hajin, 76–77
Halide Edib (Adıvar), 67
Halil (Kut), 87
Halil (Menteşe), 69
Hamidiye Alayları, 56, 82
Hamlin, Cyrus, and ABCFM, 58
Harbord Report, 95
Harnack, Adolf, 118
Harput, 52, 54, 68, 89, 93, 96
Harvard College, 19, 38
Haskell, Edward B., and ABCFM, 72–73
Hatch, Nathan, 21
Hatt-ı Şerîf of Gülhane. *See* Reform Edict
Hausner, Gideon, 135
Hebrew Christian. *See* Jewish Christian
Heman, Johannes, 109
Herrick, George F., and ABCFM, 103
Heydrich, Reinhard, 134
Hijaz railway, 56
Hilfsbund für christliches Liebeswerk im Orient, 60, 90
Himmler, Heinrich, 134
Histadruth, 111
History of the Jews, The, 25
Hitler, Adolf, 13, 45, 119, 121, 129, 134, 145, 147, 149; as a metaphor, 146–147, 158; post-Hitler order, 119, 137, 149
Hnchag, 57, 109–110
Holocaust. *See* Shoah
Holocaust memory, 138, 144–146
Holocaust Museum, Washington, 146
holocaust(s), 58; "final holocaust," 146, 149; new, 158
Holy Land, 17, 38, 43; Holy Land mania, 45; making of the, 19
Holy Law. *See* Shariah; Torah
"home-feeling," American, 46
Hopkins, Samuel, 20, 26–27
Hull, William L., 134–135, 138
Humann, Hans, 91
human rights, 27, 55, 62, 95–96, 113, 126–127, 129, 138; movement after 1895, 60
Hüseyin Cahit (Yalçın), 83

Ibn Saud, 113
ideals, American, 138
imaginaire, 2, 18, 21–22, 150
imperialism, 4, 18, 23; British, 23; and liberalism, 78; messianic, 109; versus millennialism, 5; Napoleon's, 18; Ottoman, 4, 103; plot theories, 81; Western, 62, 65, 72–73, 154; U.S., 61, 128, 139, 158
İnan, Hüseyin, 128
India, 73
Indianophobia, Jackson's, 29
Indian removal, 28–32, 53, 102, 104, 114, 154; Indian Removal Act, 28, 32
Indians (native Americans): evangelization of, 32–33; Five Civilized Tribes, 29; as Orientals, 28; treatment of, 111. *See also* ABCFM; Bureau of Indian Affairs; Indian removal
Inönü, Ismet, 114
insan-i kâmil, 53, 177n71
Interessenpolitik, 114. *See also* realpolitik
International College, Izmir, 106
Iran, 21, 113–114, 127, 138, 149, 162. *See also* Persia
Iraq: mandated, 99, 112–113; U.S. invasion of, 4, 7, 151, 161–162, 166n5
Irgun, 141, 147
Irony of American History, 122
Isaiah, 133; chapter 53, 135
Islam: American idea of, 156 (*see also* ABCFM); dialogue with (*see* dialogue); as ethnicity, 65; "fall of," 16; foundation of, 103; and the Jews, 25; "Judeo-Christian sect," 108; Muslim decadence, 77; and nationalism (*see* nationalism); "question of," 143; reform of, 103; and representative government, 48; revolutionary, 149. *See also* Shiite; Sunni
Islamic "Calvinists," 4, 162
Islamic Renaissance, 150
Islamic revolution in Iran. *See under* revolution

Islamism, 56, 128, 138, 156; as a Muslim nationalism, 56
Ismail, Shah, 52
Israel: Americans' identification with, 30, 122; armies of, 38; fall of Mosaic, 8; Great, 144–145; Law of Return, 135; lost tribes of, 38; messianic subculture in, 138; modern state of, 124, 130, 147, 162; project of, 124, 137, 141, 144–147, 152; restoration of, 2, 16–17, 18, 22, 45, 97, 108, 116, 133, 142, 155; settler movement in, 138; world against, 157
Israelis, 122, 133, 141, 159
Istanbul, 26, 36, 46–48, 65–66, 79, 86, 94, 110, 126
İtilâf party, 69
Izmir (Smyrna), 16, 23, 26, 41–42, 79, 106

Jabotinsky, Wladimir, 147
Jackson, Andrew, 10, 28–32, 154
Jaffa, 42
Janissaries, 36
Japan, 73, 118, 125
Javid, Mehmed, 110
jem, 53
Jemal Pasha, 76, 82, 86, 90
Jernazian, Ephraim K., 125
Jerusalem: Armenians in, 42; British consul in, 45; destruction of, 8; global court in, 133; Istanbul instead of, 46; mission in, 44–45, 132; New Jerusalem, 46, 132; Protestant bishopric in, 45; reempowered, 2; Roman conquest of, 120, 147
Jerusalem school of synoptic research, 134
Jesus, 7–21, 22–26, 32–34, 42–43, 97, 108, 152; church of, 25, 84 (*see also* churches); crucifixion of, 135; as global king, 130, 133; as a "Jewish tale," 134; Jews restored to, 5, 8, 10, 21, 40, 155; as judge, 80, 117, 160; as last caliph, 40; Muslims' expectation of, 10, 150; nonrecognition of, 26, 121; second coming (*parousia*) of, 38, 42, 131, 151–152, 162–163; as slain lamb, 39–40, 142, 144, 162; as Son of Man, 8; Turks' belief in, 106; ultimate role of, 121; uniqueness of, 117
Jevdet, 85, 88
Jewish Agency, 119
Jewish Christians, 109, 135–136
Jewish diaspora, 11, 120, 132, 143, 187n31
Jewish homesickness, 21
Jewish lobby, 120
Jewish Question, 17, 143, 147, 155
Jewish World Congress, 111
Jews: American, 20, 26–27, 111, 120–123, 145; Ashkenazi, 45; dereliction of, 39; distinctiveness of, 26, 39; Eastern European (*Ostjuden*), 19, 36, 60, 99, 108–109, 122, 130–131, 135; evangelical, 150; mission to, 25–26, 129; *Muskeljude,* 145–146; nonassimilation of, 26; restoration of (*see* restoration); Sephardic, 45; as target of Nazis, 118–119; unique role of, 121. *See also* ABCFM; *millet;* Palestine
jihad: fighters, 128; Ottoman, on Germany's side, 84; spiritual, 72
John, author of Revelation, 8
Josephus, Flavius, 148
Judaism, 22, 143–144, 148. *See also* anti-Judaism
Judea, 38, 42, 46
Judenfrage. See Jewish Question
Judeo-Christian heritage, 148
Judeo-Christian post-1945 fundament, 122, 142
judgment, 135; America's, 60, 130; of this eon, 121. *See also* Jesus

Kaaba, 149
Kadın Dünyası, 79
Kaiserswerther Diakonissen, 45
Karmelmission, 60, 132
Kashani, Ayatollah, 127
Kayseri, 73, 75, 106
Kemalism/Kemalists, 94–96, 102, 106–107, 114, 126, 128–129
Kennan, George, 117
Kennedy, John F., 127
Kerbela, 52, 54
khedive (viceroy), 36
Khomeini, Ayatollah, 127, 150, 162
King-Crane Commission, 95, 97, 108, 111
Kingdom of God, 9, 17–18, 34, 39–40, 43, 53, 80, 103–104, 116, 122, 141, 145; America and the, 2; Jewish yoke of, 141, 145; new justice of, 160; Sayyid Qutb's, 12. *See also* millennium
Kızılbaş. See Alevi
Kızıl Elma, 4, 35
Klappert, Bertold, 142
Klausner, Joseph, 148
Kleiss, Martha, 89
Konya, 86
Kook, Avraham Y. H., 194n12
Korea, 127; war, 124
Küçük Kaynarca, Peace of, 16
Kulturprotestantismus, 109, 117, 156
Kulturzionisten, 110
Künzler, Jakob, 88, 103, 126

Kurds, 51, 56–58; and Kemalists, 94; as losers of Tanzimat, 56; mission to (*see* ABCFM); and post-Ottoman order, 161; rise of sheikhs among, 57; Sunni, 56. *See also Hamidiye*
Kurz, Gertrud, 142, 193n6

Labor Party, Israeli. *See* Zionism
Laska, Helene, 89
Lausanne Conference: of 1922–1923, 101–102, 112, 114; of 1949, 124
Lavon affair, 135, 192n81
Law on Abandoned Property, 90
League of Nations, 95–96, 100, 115
League of Private Initiative and Decentralization, 74
Lebanon, 50, 62
Le Bon, Gustave, 65
Leibowitz, Yeshayahu, 148
Lemkin, Raphael, 86
Lenin, Vladimir, 189n50
Lepsius, Johannes, 88, 103, 108–109
Leslie, Francis H., and ABCFM, 89
liberal consensus, 117, 122, 130–131; end of, 138–139, 149–150
liberalism and Protestantism, 50, 73
Likud party, 147, 151. *See also* Zionism
Lindsey, Robert, 133–134, 137
Littell, Franklin, 117
London Jews' Society (London Society for Promoting Christianity amongst the Jews), 26, 44–45
London Missionary Society, 24, 41
Luftmenschen, 109, 130
Lütfi Fikri Bey, 79

Macedonia, 69
mahdi, 4, 10–11, 149
Mahmud II (sultan), 36–37
Makdisi, Ussama, 32, 50
Malatya, 128
Malta, missionary center in, 41
Mamuretülaziz, 49, 69, 87, 89, 96
mandate: American, 93, 95; British (*see* Iraq); Palestine (*see* Palestine); French (*see* Syria)
Mandelstam, André, 82
manifest destiny, 32; Jewish, 144; missionary millennialist, 2, 6, 20–21, 153
Marash, 105; Theological Seminary, 125
Mardin, 84
Marshall, George, 125
Marshall, John, 31
Marsivan. *See* Merzifon
Mart, Michelle, 122
Masada, 147
massacres of Armenians: in 1895, 37, 58–61; in 1909, 69, 86–87. *See also* genocide; violence
Mather, Cotton, 29–30
Maybaum, Ignaz, 135, 143, 194n9
McGhee, George, 125–128, 139
McNamara, Robert, 193n1
Mecca, 105, 113, 149
Medina, 113
Memoir of Levi Parsons, First Missionary to Palestine from the United States, 43
Menderes, Adnan, 128
Merzifon, 75, 88
Mesopotamia, 69
messiah, 7–8, 11, 42, 130, 133, 141
messianism, 7–8, 11, 133, 143–145. *See also* imperialism; millennialism; Zionism
Metzger, Max J., 118
mihraj, 53
Military Medical School (*Mekteb-i Tıbbiye-i Askeriye*), 65
millennial dawn, 13
millennial end of churches, 2, 5
millennialism: America-centered, 20, 37; American, 4, 8–11, 26, 32, 129–131, 147, 152, 157, 160; and civil religion, 20, 22, 71; critical potential of, 129; English mentoring for, 24; and exceptionalism, 8; millennialist economy, 97; and mission, 28; and modernity, 17; postmillennialism, 5, 9, 60, 71, 75, 98, 130–131; as term, 7–11. *See also* messianism, premillennialism
millennium: in the Bible lands, 64; evolutionary coming of the, 160; hastening toward the, 23–25, 38; leading the way to the, 116, 124; looking like the, 67–68; move toward, 38, 151; and state of Israel, 143; talk, 28; as term, 7–11; unreached, 153; virtual, 9. *See also* Kingdom of God; parousia
millet: Armenian, 49–51; Catholic, 47–48; constitution (*nizamname*), 47–51, 57, 86; Jewish, 49; *millet-i hâkime,* 35, 56, 58–59, 67, 157; *millet-i mahkûme,* 56, 58; *millet-i sadike,* 57; Protestant, 35, 47–54
missionary archives, 3, 81, 102
missionary community, 2, 23, 26, 28, 32, 40, 71, 84, 94, 100; and Islam, 100. *See also* ABCFM; America: missionary; Protestant International
Missionary Conference on behalf of the Mohammedan World, Cairo (1906), 103, 107
Missionary Herald, 5, 67, 70–71

Mississippi, 28
modernity and millennialism. *See* millennialism
Moody Bible Institute, 132
Mooney, James, 29
Morgenthau, Henry, 111
Moses, 42
Mossadegh, Mohammad, 127
Mosul, 112
muhabbet, 53
muhacir, 79
Muhammad (prophet), 52–54, 103, 105
Muhammed (Mehmed) Ali, 36
Munich, 146–147; new, 158
Muskeljude. See Jews
Muslim. *See* Islam
Mussolini, Benito, 129
Mustafa Kemal. *See* Atatürk, Mustafa Kemal
myth: of imperial Rome (and Egypt), 18, 23; Kemalist, 107, 115; of power, 8, 131; Puritan, 38; restorative, 18, 21

Napoleon Bonaparte, 8, 17–18, 24, 36
Nasser, 138
nationalism: apocalyptic, 68; during Cold War, 127–129; ethnic, 4, 19, 97, 108–110, 144, 157–158; ethnonationalism of interwar, 114, 118–119; jingoist, 73; messianic, 11; Muslim, 56, 65, 156–157; and old history, 21; religious, 20, 81, 138, 144; secular European, 26. *See also* Turkism; Zionism
National Socialism, 117–119, 140, 146. *See also* Germany
NATO (North Atlantic Treaty Organization), 125; in Turkey, 128
Navarino, battle of, 47
Nazım, Dr., 65
Near East: as term, 2–3; U.S. peacemaking in, 138; why "Nearest East?" 116, 153. *See also names of specific countries*
Near East Relief (NER), 90, 98, 101, 111
neoconservatives, 117, 139, 150–151, 161; and Israel, 140; and "realism," 151
New Echota Treaty, 31
New England, 19–21, 30, 34, 38
New Testament. *See* Bible
Newton, Isaac, 17
New Turkey, 70, 76
New York, 24, 60, 119
Niebuhr, Reinhold, 116–117, 120–122, 131, 139, 143, 158, 189n52; as "Christian realist," 117; as "father of us all," 117; ironic stance of, 117, 139, 159
Niebuhr, Richard, 2, 20, 117
Nixon, Richard, 131
Nizamname. See millet constitution
Noradounghian, Gabriel, 69
Nostra Aetate, 142
Novick, Peter, 146
Novo, John de, 112
Nutting, George, 54, 176n70

Occidentalism (*Batıcılık*), 79
Ohsson, Ignatius Muradja d', 40
oil companies, 99, 112; Arabian-American, 113; Standard Oil Company of California, 113. *See also* Petroleum Company
Old Testament. *See* Hebrew Bible
Old World, 4, 9, 34, 60, 68, 84, 115 117, 129, 157–158, 161, 171
Olney, Richard, 60
open door policy, 98, 112
Orient, weekly, 78–80, 82, 84, 110–111
Oriental Question, 16–17, 70, 116, 154; cutting the Gordian knot of, 155
Ostjuden. See Jews
Ottoman-American commerce, 35–37
Ottoman Constitution. *See* constitution
Ottoman Empire: and American missionaries (*see* ABCFM); and reform, 32, 35–37, 46–51, 55–59; and the United States, 16–19; and World War I (*see* CUP). *See also* reforms; Tanzimat
Ottomanism, 57, 68, 71, 74, 76, 108, 146
Ottoman nation, 68, 71, 85; wretched (*biçare millet-i Osmaniye*), 64
Ottoman Protestant community. *See millet*
Ottoman-Russian wars: of 1828, 47; of 1877–1888, 55

Paine, Thomas, 22
Pakistan, 149
Palestine, 18–19, 23–24, 37–44, 99, 108, 110–111; Arab complaints, 110; Arab neighborhood, 124, 136, 138; Arab uprising, 119; Jewish home in, 111; Jewish state in, 119–120; mandated, 119, 122, 129, 132; millennialist starting point, 27; mission to, 60, 132–135 (*see also* ABCFM); Occupied Territories, 149; Palestinian Arabs, 45, 60, 139, 142; partition of, 122–123; pilgrimage to, 19. *See also* Holy Land
Palestinians. *See* Palestine
pan-Turkism, 67, 83
Parchanj, 49
Paris Peace Conference, 93–95, 108
parousia. *See* Jesus

Parsons, Levi, and ABCFM, 23, 27, 38–44, 46, 64, 70, 104, 129
Parvus-Helphand, Alexander, 180n9
Patrick, Mary, and ABCFM, 79
patriotism, American, 151
Paul, Apostle, 67, 75, 109, 126, 133, 145, 148
Pearl Harbor, 118
Peet, William, and ABCFM, 76, 84, 88, 90, 96
Penn, William. *See* Evarts, Jeremiah
Pentecostal Zion Apostolic Mission, Jerusalem, 134
Persia, 44, 52, 160; northern, 85. *See also* Iran
Persian Gulf, 113
Petit-Lancy, Turkist congress in, 66–67
Petroleum Company: Anglo-French Iraqi, 112; Turkish, 112. *See also* oil companies
philo-Semitism, 45, 110
pietism/pietists, 25, 45
pilgrim fathers, 2
Plonsk, 120
plurality, egalitarian, versus hierarchical plurality, 48
pogroms: anti-Armenian (*see* massacres); anti-Jewish, 34
Pomiankowski, Joseph, 86
pope, 16–17, 57
Porter, David, 36
Porter, Noah, 24
Portugal, 125
Posen, 45
positivism, 63–64, 66, 81
postmillennialism. *See* millennialism
premillennialism, 6, 9, 59–60, 98, 130–132, 158; and Cold War, 151; and post–World War II mission, 99, 129; misuse of, 161. *See also* millennialism; Zionism
Price, Clair, 96
Priestley, Joseph, 18
Progressive Era, 63, 67, 104, 116, 131
property tax (*varlık vergisi*), 126
Prophetic Light in the Present Darkness, 132
Protestant diplomacy, 93, 96, 100; International, 25, 57, 62, 74, 108–110, 155
Protestantism: cultural (*see Kulturprotestantismus*); liberal, 109; social force of, 55; subversive, 45, 49, 57, 82, 156
Prussia, 37
Puritans, 9, 11, 16, 21; and defiance of power, 18, 54; first encounter between Muslims and, 37–38
pursuit of happiness, 154, 163

Qu'ran, 12, 149
Qutb, Sayyid, 12, 148, 150

racism, 29, 147, 154
Ras Tanura, 113
realpolitik, 5–6, 13, 98, 116, 146, 158; mix with symbolic economy, 159. See also *Interessenpolitik*
Red Apple, 4, 35
Red Crescent, 87
Red Cross, 79, 141
Reformation, 22
Reform Edicts: of 1839 (*Hatt-ı Şerîf*), 37; of 1856 (*Islahat Fermanı, Hatt-ı Hümayun*), 48–49, 54–55, 57, 156. *See also* Tanzimat
reforms of the Ottoman eastern provinces: obstructing the, 57; of 1895, 59; of 1914, 82–83
Religious Right, 138–139, 150, 160
Reshid, Mehmed, 89–90
restorationism, 22–23, 108, 110, 113, 120, 139, 140, 160
restoration of the Jews, 5, 8–10, 16–17, 21, 24–27, 34, 37–40, 44, 60, 100, 107–108, 138; United States as midwife of, 27. *See also* Israel
Revelation (Book of), 7, 10, 40–41, 160–161; dark side of, 80
Revolution: French (*see* France: revolutionary); Islamic, of 1979, 149; of 1968, 150, 159; Russian (*see* Russian Revolution); Young Turk (*see* Young Turk Revolution)
Reynier, Jacques de, 141
Reza Pahlavi, Shah, 113
Riggs, Charles T., 70, 78, 80, 84
Riggs, Edward, 75
Riggs, Henry, 53, 89, 100–101, 106–107
Robert College, 58, 93, 106
Rohner, Beatrice, 89–90
Rome, 17, 18, 23, 133, 147
Roosevelt, Franklin, 114, 117, 122
Roosevelt, Kim, 127
Roosevelt, Theodore, 70
Rosenzweig, Franz, 117, 142; doctrine of two roads, 143
Rufeisen, Daniel (alias Oswald), 135–136
Rûm, 47, 49, 57, 69
Russia, 16, 19, 37, 82, 180n9; communist, 121; Embassy in Istanbul, 82; Muslims from, 65–66; pilgrimage from, 22; pogroms in, 34. *See also* Soviet Union
Russian Revolution: of 1905, 180n9; of 1917, 87, 118
Russo-Ottoman wars. *See* Ottoman-Russian wars

Sabahaddin, Prince, 74, 79
Sabbatai Zwi, 11

Sabit Bey (governor), 88
Sacramento Valley, 32
Saddam Hussein, 151
şâh-i mardân, 53
sahip-kıran, 4, 10, 94
Said Nursi, 196n5
Saimbeyli. *See* Hajin
Şakir. *See* Bahaeddin Şakir
Salih Zeki (governor), 86
Salonica, 69, 74, 106, 110–111
Samsun, 77
San Francisco, 115
Sanjak of Alexandrette, 115
Sarıkamış, Ottoman defeat of, 85
Sasun, 58
Saudi Arabia, 21, 99, 112–114, 127, 138, 149, 158
Saul. *See* Paul, Apostle
Schauffler, William, and ABCFM, 26
Schellendorf, Bronsard von, 91
School for the Blind, Urfa, 62
School of Religion, Istanbul, 96
Second Coming of Christ. *See* parousia
Second Ecumenical Council of the Vatican, 142
Selim I (sultan), 52
Şerif. *See* Ahmed Şerif
Sermon on the Mount, 118, 149, 163; moratorium on, 124, 141
Seyid Abdülkadir. *See* Abdülkadir, Seyid
Sharia, 148, 162
Shattuck, Corinna, 58–59, 62
Sherwood, Samuel, 20
Sheykh-al Islam, 52
Shiite version of Islam, 52. *See also* Islam
Shoah, 109, 115, 120–121, 130, 135, 137, 144, 160; business, 145; in American culture, 145–147; Israeli response to, 145–147; lessons of, 138; uniqueness of, 142
Silberg, Moshe, 135
Silver, Rabbi Hillel, 120
Simpson, Albert B., 60
Sivas, 52–55
Six-Day War, 138, 143, 150
slavery. *See* ABCFM
Smilansky, Yizhar, 193n4
Smith, Eli, and ABCFM, 44
Smith, Floyd P., and ABCFM, 89–90
Smyrna. *See* Izmir
Social Darwinism. *See* Darwinism, Social
socialism, 17, 117; as a language of solidarity and democracy, 127. *See also* America: and socialism
Society for the Rise of Kurdistan, 93
Society Switzerland-Israel, 142
Solomon and Sheba, 122
Son of Man. *See* Jesus
sopalı seçim, 80
soul of America, 116; struggle for, 30, 155; Israel and, 129
South Carolina, 28
Soviet communism. *See* bolshevism
Soviet Union, 124, 133, 151
Special Organization (*Teşkilat-i Mahsûsa*), 69, 85–86
Stalin, 129
Stern, Avraham, 147, 194n17; Stern gang, 142, 147
Struggle for a Soul, The, 134
Sufi, 52–53, 72, 105; heritage of medieval Anatolia, 80; spiritual *jihad* (see *jihad*)
Suleiman I (sultan), 52
Sultan-Caliph, Ottoman, 54, 56, 58, 62, 65, 112
Sunnis: questioned, 1–2, 51–52, 81; identity, 65; messianist, 149; ruling group, 3, 6, 35, 59, 155–156; versus Shiites, 178n79. *See also* Islam
Sunnitization, Ottoman imperial, 4, 36, 56; missionary Hanafi, 56, 62
Sutter, Johann A., 32
Swiss Socialist Party, 84, 189n50
Switzerland, 22, 75
symbolic economy. *See* economy
Syria, 1, 16, 41, 44, 46, 60, 108; Armenian camps in, 86, 90–91; Christians of, 92; under Egypt, 36; independent, 138; mandated, 115; repressions in, 138
Syriac Christians, 35, 44, 56
Syrian Protestant College, 1, 4, 66, 70–72
Syrisches Waisenhaus, 132

Tableau général de l'empire othoman, 40
Tahir Bey, 75
Tahir Jevdet. *See* Jevdet
Talat (Pasha), 66, 82, 86, 110
Talitha Kumi, 45, 132
Tanîn, newspaper, 76, 78
Tankut, Hasan R., 178n79
Tanzimat, 32, 36–37, 55–56, 59. *See also* Reform Edict
Tarsus, 106
Tashnag. *See* ARF
Tchemishgezek, 54
Teheran, 127
Tekin Alp, Moïz Kohen, 66
theology: Calvin's, 171n33 (*see also* Calvinism); natural, 121; of occupation, 144; of substitution,

theology (*continued*)
142; post-Shoah, 121, 140, 142; pre-Shoah, 142
Thom, Daniel, and ABCFM, 84–85, 140
Torah, 148
torture, 12, 86, 89, 127, 130
tragic mind, 147, 149, 194n17
Trail of Tears, 28–31
treaties: with the Cherokees, 39–41; with Saudi Arabia, 113
Treatise on the Millennium, 24
Treaty, American-Ottoman (American-Turkish): commercial and naval, 36–37; commercial and naval 1929, 114; establishment and sojourn, 114; agreement on extradition, 114; claims settlement, 114
Treaty, Balkan (1934), 115
Treaty, Montreux, 115
Treaty of Berlin, 55; art, 61, 55, 57, 82
Treaty of Lausanne (*see* Lausanne Conference); Turko-American, 113–114
Treaty of Sèvres, 87
trialogue. *See* dialogue
Trialogue, 143
tribulation, biblical, 131
Trotsky, Leon, 180n9
Truman, Harry, 122, 124, 139, 159; containment (*see* containment, anti-Soviet); and disgust over Israeli treatment of Palestinian refugees, 123; village in Israel named for, 123
Tucholsky, Kurt, 118
Tunceli. *See* Dersim
Turkey: New Turkey, 70, 76; Young Turkey, 63, 67; Republic of Turkey, 102, 105–107; and the European Union, 129; and the United States, 112–115, 126, 128; deep state (*derin devlet*), 129; multiparty system, 129. *See also* Ottoman Empire
Turkification, 115, 126
Turkism, 65–67, 102, 157
Türk ocağı, 65. See also *Foyer turcs*
Türk yurdu, 65. See also *Foyer turcs*

Ulema, 52, 127
ummah, 52, 56
United Nations, 122; foundation, 125; in apocalypticist literature, 151
United States: embassy in Istanbul, 37, 114–115; imperialism (*see* imperialism); Israel-centrism, 100, 159; master of war, 124; modern dynamics in, 153; Senate, 36; State Department, 102, 112, 122. *See also* America; Ottoman Empire; Turkey
Urfa, 58–59, 69, 89, 126
Ussher, Clarence, and ABCFM, 61, 93–94, 104
USSR. *See* Soviet Union

Valley of the Wolves—Iraq, Turkish film, 4
Van, 61, 93
Vienna, Ottoman attack on, 4
Vietnam War, 7, 139, 150, 163
violence: anti-Armenian, 76, 81–83, 156; governmental, 83, 87; mass, 59, 83, 93, 139; "necessary," 109; in the United States, 73; political, 84, 182n48; salutary, 12; and settler theology, 144; revolutionary, 12, 58, 60–61, 63
Vogt, Carl, 65
völkisch, 111, 188n37
Voltaire, 17, 26

Wahhabi/Wahhabism, 21, 112–113
Waldmeier, Theophilus, 62
Washington, D.C., 30–31, 117
Washington, George, 114
Weimar Republic. *See* Germany
Weizmann, Chaim, 119, 123
Werfel, Frank, 146
Westbank, 144
White, George P., and ABCFM, 88, 178n79
Wiesel, Elie, 146
Wilentz, Sean, 30
Wilhelminian Kaiserreich. *See* Germany
Wilson, Woodrow, 4, 108, 115, 131, 159; entering war, 140; Near Eastern policy of, 93–97, 99–100
Wilsonianism, 13, 93, 99; after World War II, 115, 128. *See also* globalism
Wise, Stephen, 108, 111, 120
women: education of, 79; emancipation, 27; equality of, 64; and the Gospel, 81; movement of, 79; rights, 79, 113; unveiled, 79. *See also* Bible
Woodworth, William Sage, and ABCFM, 106–107
Worcester, Samuel, 31
World Missionary Conference in Edinburgh, 68, 71, 78, 87. *See also* Edinburgh

Yale, William, and ABCFM, 111
Yezid (Yazîd I. ibn Mu'âwiya), 54
Yezidis, 56
Yishuv, 99, 111, 119
Young Men's and Young Women's Christian Associations, 72
Young Ottomans, 48
Young Turk Revolution, 47, 67–71
Young Turks, 3, 51, 63–67, 76. *See also* CUP

zealots, 148
Zertal, Idith, 146
Zeytun, 86
Zion, 97; as understood by missionaries, 2, 5, 13, 16, 21, 38, 42; cradle of, 153; hill of, 39; question of, 140, 145; triumphant, 41; walls of, 42; zeal for, 100
Zionism: Jewish, 10, 13, 19–20, 93, 97, 108–111; activist, 144; American, 99, 111, 119; apocalypticist, 150; Christian, 100, 107, 120, 122, 131, 139, 144, 166; compared to Kemalism, 114, 132; compared to Armenian nationalism, 109–110; Labor Zionism, 110, 138, 147; messianist, 143–145; premillennialist, 131, 138, 151, 161, 166; revisionist, 148; in the United States, 14
Zionist Central Office, 110
Zivilisationsbruch, 160
Zohrab, Krikor, 69, 81
Zwi. *See* Sabbatai Zwi

Hans-Lukas Kieser is Professor of Modern History at the University of Zurich. He is editor of *Turkey beyond Nationalism*, coeditor (with Dominik J. Schaller) of *The Armenian Genocide and the Shoah,* and author of *Der verpasste Friede* (The Squandered Peace) and of *A Quest for Belonging.*